About the Author

Liz Evans has contributed to *The Guardian,* *Independent on Sunday*, *New Statesman*, *NME*, *Melody Maker*, *Vox*, *Select* and *Kerrang!* In 1994, Pandora published her first book, *Women, Sex And Rock 'n' Roll*. She lives in north London with a mad scientist, her two cats, Beavis and Mr Tooty, and ridiculous amounts of books and CDs, and is currently harbouring an ambition to be quite good at snowboarding.

Girls Will Be Boys

Girls Will Be Boys

Women Report on Rock

Liz Evans

An Imprint of HarperCollins*Publishers*

Pandora
An Imprint of HarperCollins*Publishers*
77–85 Fulham Palace Road,
Hammersmith, London W6 8JB

Published by Pandora 1997

10 9 8 7 6 5 4 3 2 1

Compilation and Introduction
© Liz Evans 1997

Liz Evans asserts the moral right to
be identified as the author of this work

A catalogue record for this book
is available from the British Library

ISBN 0 04 440950 8

Printed and bound in Great Britain by
Caledonian Book Manufacturing Ltd, Glasgow

This book is dedicated to the memories of Chris Ackland and Sandra Cotter, to all those who knew and loved them, and to two new lives – Frankie Williams and Georgia Claire Balch.

Contents

Acknowledgements

Thanks to all my friends and family, especially: Joan Evans, Ted and Maria, Katy and Johnny, Dawn Thiselton, John Wills, Pinkie Maclure, Lou Simpson, Kutty, Rachel Bovill, Dominic Wills, Angela Knight, Claire Dowse, Emma Lyne, Billy Chainsaw, Miki Berenyi, Julie Whittle, Hilary Dyer.

'A' – for helping me to start snowboarding.

Phil Alexander, Paul Rees, Scarlett Page & everyone at Kerrang!

Belinda Budge and everyone at Pandora.

My agent, Carol Heaton.

Amanda at RMP, Rob Jefferson at Mushroom, Chris Sharpe at XL, Tone at Creation, Melissa Thompson at Savage and Best, Craig McClean at *Blah Blah Blah*, Chloe at Heavenly, Ruth at Virgin, Lindsay Baker, the British Newspaper Library, Emma Georgiou at *Select*, Karen at the *NME*.

And especially to all the contributors.

Introduction

n June 1995, an article appeared in *The Sunday Times* declaring that gender was no longer relevant to rock culture. According to the article, there was now an 'increasing number of fans for whom gender has ceased to be an engrossing, central issue', and an emerging batch of female musicians, like (the 'asexual'!) Björk, Justine Frischmann of Elastica and Polly Harvey, who couldn't give a stuff about their sexuality. On top of that, a handful of books dealing with the subject had been published (five to be precise, beginning with my collection of interviews, *Women, Sex and Rock 'n' Roll* in 1994). According to *The Times* journalist, 'the point at which the publishers muscle in on the act marks the end, rather than the beginning of the battle'.

Needless to say, this article was written by a man. A man who didn't seem to understand that all five of these books were on the marketplace, not because publishers had decided it was a good idea to flog women-in-rock missives to Courtney Love fans, but because six authors (*The Sex Revolts* was written by husband and wife team, Simon Reynolds and Joy Press) had noticed a radical shift in female roles within rock culture, and felt moved enough to analyse what was happening, examine the minds involved, or simply to trace the history behind it. To suggest the initiative came from the publishers was not only ignorant and naive, but also vaguely insulting to the mostly female writers who'd produced the books. To suggest that the subject was now thoroughly documented and therefore effectively redundant because of these books (remember, there were only five) was absurd, but typical of the way in which gender issues, in relation to rock music, have been repeatedly stigmatised and derided ever since guitars were first plugged into amplifiers.

Understanding Harvey and Frischmann's reluctance to discuss gender issues to mean a complete disinterest in them was also incredibly short-sighted. Abstaining from debate is simply another way of making a point – and more likely a point about the way in which the subject is handled rather than the subject itself. Ask any female musician or singer about her experience as a woman in the music industry, and, provided you do so intelligently and sensitively, you'll be met with anything but indifference and complacency. But ask her banal, pointless, patronising questions about being a girl in a band, or a woman-in-rock, and of course you'll induce rolling eyes, sighs and impatient silences. Women are sick of being typecast, stereotyped and pigeonholed. They are not sick of being women.

Undoubtedly, the 90s has seen a change in the gender balance within rock and pop. Women have integrated themselves and girls with guitars don't get gasped at anymore. But you can't argue with 30 years worth of male dominated rock culture, and you can't pretend that five or six years is all it's taken for women to catch up. And you certainly can't kid yourself that sex and sexuality aren't important. Sex is absolutely intrinsic to rock culture. Furthermore, male and female sexual expressions have never been the same. So while say, Björk, has never 'struck conventionally feminine or feminist postures in any of her songs or videos', as *The Sunday Times* article pointed out, her 'achievement' has been anything but 'asexual'. Unless that is, you happen to think only conventional feminine and feminist postures are sexual.

In recent years, artists like Björk, Garbage's Shirley Manson, Courtney Love and Skunk Anansie's Skin have all proved that real sexuality lies as far away from convention as the North

Pole does from the South. All of them are very aware of
what they're doing as women, rather than just as people,
they know the power of their own sexuality, and they're not
scared to use it or to talk about it, as the pieces in this anthology demonstrate. In her interview with Garbage, Sharon
O'Connell delves into Shirley Manson's sexual persona, and is
met with a friendly, honest response; Lucy O'Brien discovers
just how tired Skin is of being typecast as the angry, bald,
black lesbian; and during a five-hour long conversation with
me in her Los Angeles home, Courtney Love discusses the
importance of image for women, in terms of obvious sexual
imagery in relation to her life as a stripper, the effect losing
weight had on her career and her quarrel with best friend Kat
Bjelland over clothes. Far from being over, the gender debate
is as alive and as relevant in the 90s as it has ever been.

Male journalists, who are undoubtedly in the majority when it
comes to rock journalism, are quite simply sick to the back teeth
with women banging on about something men really don't prior-
itise. Effectively (in conjunction with the managing editors and
publishers of the music press – most of whom are male) they
control which topics are covered, which bands are featured and
how a magazine's overall journalistic style is determined. Most
editorial positions are taken up by men, as are most freelance
positions, and despite half-hearted claims by certain editors
about redressing the balance on their papers and magazines,
women continue to find themselves marginalised.

No doubt this is why male journalists feel they can afford to
declare the gender issue dead and buried. For them, it isn't really
an issue. It merely challenges their authority in a world where they
know what's what and who's calling the shots. Even in this supposedly enlightened, post-feminist age, men still feel profoundly
threatened by women.

A tightly woven old-boy network still exists throughout music
journalism, especially at the roots of supposedly more liberal,
right-on and cutting edge papers. Tabloid methods and principles

are used in the running of these papers, who demand an almost militant loyalty from their journalists (I was once castigated by a male editor for remaining too loyal to my interviewees – apparently I was supposed to be prepared to betray their trust and stitch them up, like some front-line scoop-sniffing newshound), and a typically boysie, almost trainspotter-like knowledge of music is highly respected, regardless of the type of personality involved. Consequently, more than a few male journalists have about as much character as a piece of cardboard.

The attitude of some of these charmless specimens towards their female colleagues is, at times, quite alarming. One male journalist who worked for a best-selling weekly music paper once informed me that a 'special effort' was being made by the (all male) editorial team for a female freelancer. Never mind that the woman in question had been employed as features editor on two top British style magazines, as well as having written a book. On another occasion a female journalist was treated like a silly child by the same weekly, because, although she'd contributed to the biggest selling Sunday broadsheet in the country on a regular basis, she was only 17. In my eight years as a journalist, I've suffered serious abuse from a male colleague who refused to speak to me for the full 14 months I worked on a magazine with him (in an office of six, that's not much fun), I've been reprimanded by an editor for having a relationship with someone who worked with a band I once interviewed (as though it were his business), and been lectured (by the same editor) for walking out on an interview with an ageing male rock star who not only tried to make me sit on his knee, but then declared I must be having my period when I objected to his attitude.

Of course it's not all bad. The editorial team on *Kerrang!*, Britain's top rock magazine – which many people assume, ironically, to be produced by sexist numbskulls – is absolutely brilliant, utterly respectful and completely on the level. And there are many, many male journalists who don't behave like arrogant pigs or social retards when it comes to their female colleagues. But the reality for female journalists in the music industry can be very tough. And it's not just the close-knit boy-writers' club you have to contend with – it's the boy-bands as well.

When I started out in rock journalism, I was 22 years old, and comparatively naive. In on-the-road situations, surrounded by musicians and roadcrew, where the only other females were actively, shamelessly seeking sex, I felt distinctly uncomfortable. Stranded in some foreign town, backstage at a party, no longer able to rely on my role as professional music journalist once the interviews were in the bag, I'd end up feeling alienated and vulnerable. One way of coping with this was to turn defensive, but it wasn't particularly effective. Another way of coping was simply to retreat to my hotel room, but that was lonely and boring. Since then of course, I've learnt how to establish the boundaries, and in more recent years have thought nothing of sitting up all night in many a musician's hotel room guzzling vodka and smoking 3,000 cigarettes. When you know how, it's not hard to lay down your terms, but before you've gained experience, and with it, confidence, it's easy to feel isolated.

During her attempt to secure an interview with Keanu Reeves while he was visiting Britain with his band, Dogstar, Kate Spicer ran straight into all these problems, as the piece she's contributed to this collection shows. Although Kate *is* an experienced, confident journalist with a respectable CV to boot, this particular assignment brought her into confrontation with all the awkwardnesses which usually affect the novice. She literally had to run around town after Reeves like some lovesick teenager, her self respect suffered a beating, and the whole grey area of groupie and girl reporter, which still persists in the minds of some of the more sexist (and usually American) male musicians, raised its ugly head. In the end, Kate got her interview, but the difficulties she faced as a female journalist are far more illuminating than anything the movie star had to say.

Despite the sticky moments music journalism holds for most women, it would be dishonest and self-defeating to dwell on them alone. Hanging out with rock stars, drinking free beer, travelling across America and watching your favourite bands play for nothing is by no means a bad way to earn a living, and anyone, be they male or female, who moans incessantly about such an occupation deserves to be placed at a Woolworth's checkout for at least 10 years, and see how that compares. Of course it's important to acknowledge the problems women have had to deal with as journalists (as it is in any occupation), because until this is done the headway women have made, especially in this last decade, cannot be truly appreciated. But it's just as important to realise how effectively women can interact with rock bands, no matter how laddish or lairy, that they're not easily intimidated or necessarily smitten, and that, if needs be, they can stay up all night drinking the mini-bars dry, and still ask incisive questions the next day.

The onset of 90s' Lad culture has done nothing to deter the female rock journalist. Sylvie Simmons' gutsy contributions to American magazine *Creem*, exemplified in these pages by her visit to the Motörhead household, and Mary Anne Hobbs' rock reportage for first *Sounds* and then the *NME*, for whom she nearly came to blows with Jon Bon Jovi in Paris, provide ample proof that women could more than cope with the hedonistic, egotistical, occasionally predatory habits of rock musicians during the decadent 80s. And since the lager lout has been revalidated by men's lifestyle magazines lauding the joys of Club 18–30 holidays, semi-naked soap opera actresses, provincial beer festivals and fat footballers, with rock music welcoming, if not heroicising, stout and skinny boys in bulky anoraks with pudding basin hairdos, brandishing anthemic tunes which could easily be belted out from the terraces, women have responded by laughing, leching and laughing, or completely out-ladding the lads – and laughing.

As Miranda Sawyer once declared on a television documentary about laddism, lads are the kind of boys who live with their mothers and think it's rebellious to leave their beds unmade. Although her trip to America with Happy Mondays (Shaun Ryder being the forerunner of all things laddish) evidently left her in no doubt of the difference between a beered up boy with a big gob and a little knob, and a wise musician with a seriously chequered past, insatiable appetites for anything illegal, and an irrepressible urge to veer towards self-destruction in the pursuit of pleasure. Ryder is more lad blueprint than lad-by-numbers, and Gina Morris's profile of Black Grape, Ryder's current band, provides further proof of his unpredictability and refusal to comply to anyone's law but his own. Did this faze Gina? Frankly, yes. But it didn't stop her from diving in with both feet.

Ryder may be the Real Deal, but it's Oasis who've come to epitomise the essence of British lad culture. Narky Mancs with fuck-off attitudes, the Gallaghers' brotherly feuds, excessive lifestyles and outrageous comments have fuelled both the music and tabloid press ever since they exploded into 1995 with their debut album, "Definitely Maybe". Working class heroes who escaped the drudgery of life in a northern town by sheer gall and a clutch of brilliant songs, all blatantly nicked from the past, Oasis have risen to world domination, and have fired a million dreams on the way. Daniela Soave spent a week with the band in Japan before they'd hit mega-star status, and defied all of their preconceptions concerning her (quietly spoken single mother, writing for a sensible bloke's magazine) by drinking them all under the table, consistently, for seven days. 'You're fookin' mad,' Noel told her, in no uncertain terms.

Oasis' biggest rivals are, of course, Blur. Releasing singles and scheduling gigs simultaneously, purely in the name of competition, slagging each other off in public, even trying to pull each other's birds, the two bands have acted as a focal point for the whole North/South divide. Blur, fronted by the ex-drama student Damon Albarn, whose dad was a leading light on the 60s' London art scene, and who cites Martin Amis as an influence, and public school educated fop Alex James, who frequents the Soho House drinking club with the likes of Keith Allen and Damien Hirst, represent the artsy, middle class end of the spectrum. Oasis, on the other hand, sprung from Manchester's backstreets where they had run-ins with the law, single-handedly revived the art of hotel-trashing the second they became famous, make no secret of their excessive drug consumption, and idolise The Beatles, the original working class heroes. In her interview with Alex James, Barbara Ellen takes the opportunity to compare and contrast Britain's two most popular bands, citing the case for Oasis while allowing James to let himself look rather foolish. When he asks her for a shag, it's pretty clear who probably ended up feeling embarrassed.

As the features by Barbara, Daniela, Gina and Miranda all show, women are neither intimidated nor offended by the lad. Whether he's necking back the Red Stripe, snorting coke in the loo, or trying to get into your knickers, he's fairly harmless at the end of the day. And while bands like Oasis may signify a return to white boy rock, this time women, having established themselves as an equal force within rock culture, are getting their hands dirty with the best of them.

As well as the hardcore lads and the sad media invention lads, designed to boost the morales and rob the wallets of prematurely balding Mr Byrites, there are the lads who are just, well, lads, in the old fashioned sense of the word. Young fellows, as the *Oxford Paperback Dictionary* calls them. Like Tim Burgess of The Charlatans, who gets so drunk with Sylvia Patterson during her interview that he can't remember where he lives, The Prodigy who hail from Essex, and treat life like a big boys club, but who don't mind at all when Lisa Verrico joins them on a snowboarding trip for the first issue of *Blah Blah Blah*, and the Manic Street Preachers, one of Britain's most intelligent and talented bands, who go awry in Bangkok's red light district and find themselves being reprimanded by Barbara Ellen as a result. Not only do these features bring a female perspective to the regular blokes-in-rock experience, they also reveal a relatively unsouped-up version of the lad as male human being, as opposed to seasoned thug or celebrity bad-boy – pure and simple humanity being something which 90s' lad culture has more or less managed to eclipse with its over-excited attitude towards birds, booze and blow.

While it's important to acknowledge the impact of lad culture on men and women, and the significance of female achievement in rock culture, such as the ground gained by Riot Grrls, who exploded into being at the beginning of the decade (hence the inclusion of my Grrl piece, first printed in the *NME*), it's also worth noting the female *sexual* response to man-made rock music. The sheer uncultured force of rock music, despite what certain tight-lipped feminist theorists would have you believe, has always elicited a celebratory sexual reaction in women. Rock music is incredibly sexy, it makes women feel sexy, it makes women want to *dance*, and dancing can be very empowering, whether as a physical release, a method of seduction or simply a means of communication. Of course there are women who want to fuck musicians, and sometimes that entails being part of a very unhealthy power imbalance (although not always, it depends on the woman), but fucking musicians has nothing to do with getting off on their music – at least, not necessarily. There are no pieces in this anthology which deal with this sexual element. Even Emma Forrest's fantasy about moving in with Liam Gallagher is playful rather than lustful. As a rule, women don't write lecherous pieces because they've already had to fight against the groupie/journalist syndrome in the first place, but if someone has a response to rock music, there's likely to be a sexual element.

The main problem with the female response to rock music, whether sexual or not, is its lack of life in print. The numerous anthologies of rock writing which have appeared over the years contain a pathetically low amount of contributions from female journalists, and while there are admittedly few women working in the music field compared to men, even they haven't been fairly represented. Aside from *Rock She Wrote*, Evelyn McDonnell and Ann Powers' valuable collection of (mainly American) women's music reportage, there has been no acknowledgement of the female perspective on rock culture, other than female-authored books and the marginal amount of journalism which appears in the rock weeklies and monthlies. It's a catch–22 of course. While I was searching for pieces for this anthology, I became increasingly aware of how few women there are working as music journalists, and how few of them have written, for whatever reasons, about certain bands. For example, only two women have ever interviewed The Prodigy at length and hardly any women have spoken to Oasis, or even Garbage. Women have not, as a rule, interviewed hardcore rap acts like Ice T and Ice Cube, nor have they written a significant amount about dance, although Sheryl Garratt's informative feature on house music was one of the first ever to appear in this country. My interview with Screaming Trees disproves the rule that hard rock is a men-only preserve, although grunge, the now much maligned term for the Seattle-based guitar rock which exploded at the beginning of the 90s, was mainly covered by male writers, despite the change in attitude brought about by liberal-minded bands like Nirvana and Soundgarden. And Charlotte Raven's article on drum and bass marks a departure from the male monopoly of the genre.

The choice of material for this anthology was undeniably a limited one, but it was enough to warrant a collection, and a good one at that. Projects like these always run the risk of appearing to be gratuitous gestures, but while women continue to suffer for their sex, there's no excuse for using gender alone as a reason to stand up and be counted. However, there is a balance which needs redressing, a history which needs to be told, and a tradition which needs to be established. Hopefully this anthology will go some way towards inaugurating a long overdue change.

Liz Evans
London, November 1996.

Chicago House

■ **Sheryl Garratt**

The Face September 1986

heryl Garratt was one of the first journalists ever to report on house music, the Chicago sound which rejuvenated British club culture. Although this piece was written more than a decade ago, the effect house has had on the whole dance scene has been hugely significant, and holds as much relevance today as it did back in 1986.

"Sue the bastards!"

We've been in Chicago for two hours now, and for reasons too ridiculous to explain we are sitting in an Armenian restaurant talking to Jay B. Ross, attorney at law for DJ International. Ross, a respectable if portly-looking citizen, suddenly reveals that he too has a deal with the label and launches into a performance as The Rapping Lawyer. Events have taken a distinctly surreal turn. Only in America could an attorney sell himself via 'Sue The Bastards' T-shirts with his name and number on the back; only in Chicago would a label sign its own lawyer to work on a song with Farley Funk, Arthur Baker and two 15-year old hip hop hardliners. Even more confusingly, the label has also signed William 'Refrigerator' Perry of the Chicago Bears, Indiana soul lady Loleatta Holloway, a Greek pop group, several hip hop crews, NY punkette Screaming Rachel and other oddities too bewildering to mention. Which makes the question we're here to answer seem all the more difficult: what is this 'house' music they're hyping so heavily back home?

A day later and I'm in Paragon Studios to hear a re-recording of Marshall Jefferson's song "The House Music Anthem" for London Records upcoming house compilation. Chicago studios, I've found, are unlike any other; when one person cuts a House track, everyone else comes down to watch. There's a party going on in the control room; Harri, vocalist on the classic house track "Donnie" by The It, is dancing with a dog's choke chain and lead around his neck '76 style, and Marshall is doubled up on the sofa in a fit of anguish, envy and admiration. "Aw God, I wish I could look weird like that!" he wails, fishing out a nappy pigtail from behind his standard Afro for my inspection. "My girlfriend made me grow this so I'd look more like a recording artist, but I wish I could deal with people staring at me like that."

Backing singers Rudei Forbes, Prof T. C. Roper and Curtis McClay are here, while Lewis Pitzele, DJ International's Vice President in charge of Promotion is – as always – on the phone. Chip E, the label's 20-year-old Vice President in charge of A&R (living proof that in Chicago, every boy can grow up to be vice president) sits quietly in the corner; DJ Ron Hardy revolves on a chair and Frankie Knuckles is busy working on the mix. John Stoddart is taking photos, Marshall is videoing his first ever interview with a British journalist, and in the background the vocals float through the monitors: *"This is house music."* It seems as good a time as any to pop the question, so I do. What *is* house music? Suddenly all hell breaks loose.

"House music? I couldn't even *begin* to tell you what house music is. You have to go to the clubs and see how people react when they hear it. It's more like a feeling that runs through, like old time religion in the way that people jus' get happy and screamin'. It's happening! It's ... house!"

"Let me see if I can put it better. It's more like eighties disco songs in eighties style."

"It's Chicago's own sound."

"'Cept it comes from New York, and they don't know it."

"It's rock 'till you drop, that's what it is!"

"It's a status symbol to party all night at the Muzic Box. Everybody goes there – all the hippest kids in the city!"

"You'll leave there a changed person. You might go and seek religion afterwards! You'll love it. It's gonna be hot, it's gonna be sweaty and it's gonna be great. What you'll experience is honest-to-goodness, get down, low down, *grutsy*, grabbin' type music. Boom boom boom!"

Long a centre for gospel, jazz, blues and advertising jingles (really), the Windy City is revelling in its new-found status as a dance music centre. There's a new (and beautiful) city for the UK hacks to fly to *en masse*, and the man from the *Chicago Sun Times* is calling my room to ask how seriously *The Face* is taking all this. "It hasn't crossed over to the Yuppie crowd here," he tells me with satisfaction, citing a commission to write about Chicago rock bands for *Creem* as one of the best things to emerge from the affair.

Local radio, meanwhile, only started introducing house records to their regular playlist after DJ International took their crew to the New Music Seminar in July, held a party in NY's Better Days Club, and began attracting media interest. Larry Levan had been playing the music at the Paradise Garage for some time along with a few other NY clubs. Arthur Baker has recorded his own homage, "Chicago", but Lewis is adamant that "it took the English media to make the radio play its own local talent". Yet, Farley "Jackmaster" Funk claims a crowd of 2,000 at La Mirage on Friday and Saturday nights, while Ron Hardy at The Muzic Box on Thursday and Saturday and Frankie Knuckles at COD's on Friday both attract capacity crowds. Maybe it's because the faces are mainly black that they don't count.

BUT LET's begin at the beginning. In 1977, New York DJ Frankie
Knuckles was asked to come to Chicago to establish a new gay
club called The Warehouse. At the time, he recalls, DJs were a
rarity in the city, and all except two bars – Le Pub and The Bistro –
used jukeboxes instead. Things didn't look promising, but the
club had the advantage of being the only after-hours venue,
opening at midnight and closing when the last dancers left on
Sunday afternoon. A small three-storey building with a seating
area upstairs, free juice, water and munchies in the basement
and a dimly-lit dancefloor in between, Frankie told the owners
to give him five years to create an impact. It took him two.

"It was absolutely the only club in the city to go to," he recalls
with little visible self-congratulation. "It wasn't a polished atmosphere – the lighting was real simplistic, but the sound system was
intense and it was about what you heard as opposed to what you
saw. Comfortably, the place held about 600, but coming and going
all night I'd say we did about 2,000–2,500 people. The crowds
came in shifts – those who were always outside at 11.45, they'd
'jack' until about 3–4am when the bar people would arrive. Then
there'd be a whole different crowd that would come about 9am
which is how the parties carried on until the afternoon.

"Most of the music I played was inspirational – all the dance
things that were popular in '77/'78, but the voice had to have
a nice sound and a message that was more than just '*I met
this chick*'. Most of the time it was either really heavy instru-
mentals or vocals talking about doing something for oneself.
Like D-Train's 'Keep On': '*I can't let nobody keep me from
reaching the top*'. That type of stuff."

Frankie's seamless mixing and his combination of obscure US
oldies with Euro-imports meant that while hip hop swept across
America, disco never died in the windy city. It wasn't long before

the straight kids too were crowding through the club's door, and when they began walking into record stores demanding Frankie Knuckles music or "that sound they play down the house", house music was born.

———

SOME STILL maintain the name comes from the house parties held in the mainly black South Side of the city or in the Bronx-like projects called Cabrini Green, but most of those with suss say the term came from The Warehouse. Such was the infatuation with the club that younger artists such as Chip E and producer Jessie Saunders' brother Dr Derelict clearly remembers a time in the early eighties when all the youths were dressing gay, acting gay, trying their hardest to *be* gay. The scene is still a remarkably amiable mix of sexual tastes largely free of macho and misogyny, though mention should be made here of Farley Funk's mildly amusing nasty (as in rude) romp "SMMFD" (Suck My Mother Fucking Dick). It appears on the flip of "Jack The Bass" under the alias Jackmaster Dick, and comes complete with Dickappella mix, fetish fans. Besides, when the radio stepped into the scene, most gave up the idea of being gay and decided to be a DJ instead.

The mix shows started on WGCI, but things really took off when rival R&B station WBMX responded by gathering together a group of street DJs under the title the Hot Mix Five. Led by Kenny Jason, the team also included a young DJ popular on the South Side: Farley Keith Williams, aka Farley Jackmaster Funk.

The Hot Mix Five have since defected to WGCI, leaving Frankie Knuckles to head the WBMX side, and the mixes are now an integral part of Chicago city life. Thirty minute mixes are aired at regular intervals throughout the day – around 18 records per session, mixed together as one continuous medley without repeats. The serious event, though, is on Saturday night when the stations air five-hour shows with each DJ offering an hour-long mix. From 250,000 to a million of the city's inhabitants tune in at some point – about a fifth of the population.

"In my neighbourhood there seem like a million kids all on the streets with radios blasting," laughs Shawn Christopher, backing singer for Chaka Khan and the voice on the DJ International single "People Of All Nations."

———————

FARLEY IS reputedly the wealthiest and definitely the best-known of the house DJ/producers, and although he owes much of his success to the radio, he is as dismissive of it as the rest. The stations' alleged refusal to acknowledge their records outside of the mixes and to play anything more energetic than 117bpm has earned them almost universal contempt among the house fraternity, although Farley admits it was the Hot Mixes that spread the scene.

"Chicago is a DJ city," he insists. "If there's a hot record out, in Chicago they'll all buy two copies so they can mix it. We have a talent for mixing. When we first started on the radio there weren't many, but then every kid wanted two turntables and a mixer for Christmas. We've been on air for six years now, so a kid who was 11 then is 17 and a DJ or at least a fan of the mixes. And if a DJ can't mix, they'll boo him in a minute because half of them probably know how to do it themselves."

The frequent exposure also meant that they soon ran out of what Farley calls "Bootsy Collins/SOS Band type-tracks" to mix, and so they turned to Paul Weisburg of Imports Etc for ideas. Now selling an odd mix of the house tracks and dusty $13 LPs by the likes of Wire, even the mighty Farley bows in homage to the shop and to its owner's inventiveness. "He was the only person in the city selling those imports. Italian records like Trilogy's 'Not Love',

'I Need Love' by Capricorn, 'Brainwashed' by Telex. There was one called 'Don't Forget To Buy This Record' – a tripped out name for a record! That was really big here, but we couldn't get no more imports so somebody bootlegged it – that happens a lot."

Another variation was digging out old Philly songs and adding a faster, boosted rhythm track. Farley started taking his drum machine to play along with records at his club The Playhouse, and there was a booming trade in records consisting solely of a bassline and drum patterns, often recorded by a local DJ.

From this to complete records was a short step, and Farley finally made his debut with "Aw Shucks" on his own house label. Showcasing the distinctive thumping bass drum – "Farley's foot" – it was overlaid with computer samples of a dog barking, James Brown grunting and lots of silly voices. Like all house records, it comes in a choice of mixes, was made cheaply and somehow sounds even cheaper.

But that, everyone tells me, is part of the appeal. It's the reason why Frankie Knuckles hasn't yet indulged his fantasy of lush, layered productions a la Trevor Horn ("Frankie Goes To Hollywood were *sooo* big here!") and as Farley explains, "Our sound is so different because we can make just a bassline and a rhythm track and we can sell 10,000 copies of that just in the city. All you need is a feel for music. There are people who've been to college to study music and they can't make a simple rhythm track let alone a hit record. It's weird. And it seems like a waste of time to learn all that because now a little kid can pick up a computer, get lucky with it and write a hit. It's no use working with ancient sounds."

For aspiring artists, then, this is the house that Jack built.

"Basically, it's a good vocalist with a nice bass drum pattern that really thumps. I love the foot, because that's what gets people moving. The foot establishes the beat, the snare sustains it and from there the hi-hat picks it up and gives it energy. There's a lot of funk in house, which people don't realise – they say it's hi-NRG but it's not because it has a lot of soul in it, it's real funky."

Now making his own records (14 at last count), producing other house artists, re-mixing outsiders such as the Dazz Band and branching out into rap, Farley finds less time for the clubs, but still says they are central to his work. "I love playing for the crowd – it's unbelievable when 2,000 people really get going. I can make a record on my four-track recorder at home, take it into the club and play it on the reel-to-reel. If they like it I'll copyright it then play it in the Hot Mix about two weeks later, then I'll call round the record stores. If you play a record in the mix, kids will go into stores with the tape and ask for it, and if there's a demand, right away I'll try to get it out.

"I was looking for a deal with a major label but it's kinda hard because I'm the type of person who would put out five records in two months and they'd make me wait."

VINCE LAWRENCE of The Bang Orchestra has just released his debut LP and a single, "Sample This" on megabucks label Geffen and Jessie Saunders of Jes Say Yes Records is in the process of signing to a major too, but on the whole house still works on the level of ducking and diving. Chip Edhardt became DJ Chip E while still at High School, but in spite of guest spots at Muzic Box, The Playground and The Candy Store, he didn't get big enough quick enough. A spell behind the counter at Imports Etc convinced him he could make records as good as some of the DJ product he was selling, so he sold his turntables and spent the money in the studio laying down some rhythm tracks. There was enough cash left to make a single test pressing: "I already knew the Hot Mix Five so I gave it to Kenny Jason and he played it immediately. Then Farley took it and it got passed around and gained a lot of popularity from that. So by the time I had my first 1,000 pressed – I borrowed my mother's income tax cheque – we sold 500 in the first day out of one store, and the rest within a week. I ordered another 3,000 and we sold them in about a week. That was the 'Jacktracks' EP."

Meanwhile, Rocky Jones of the record pool Audio Talent had decided to help one of his DJs, Steve "Silk" Hurley, release a track called "Music Is The Key" by J.M. Silk. When the first pressing sold out, he swapped his hot-rod Corvette in exchange for 10,000 more copies: DJ International was born. Chip was amongst the early signings, producing the stuttering, stripped-down dance track "Like This" and the upcoming "Godfather Of House" under his own name, working with Harri and friends on "Donnie" as The It, and producing/mixing other artists for the label and its subsidiaries.

For Chip, the formula is much the same as for Farley: "A lot of bottom, real heavy kick drum, snappy snare, bright hi-hat and a real driving bassline to keep the groove. Not a lot of lyrics – just a sample of some sort, a melody to remind you of the name of the record so you go out and buy it."

How long can you keep doing this, I ask, before people get bored? Chip looks thoughtful for a while, then turns back to face me with a grin.

"I'd say about the next 20 years."

AND SO far, the outlook seems good for DJ International. Having just signed a distribution deal for release via London Records in the UK, the bigger names are busy packing their cases and checking out addresses for the best London warehouse parties. Songs are being recorded in Spanish for the city's large Hispanic community, and the version of "Love Can't Turn Around" sung by Darryl Pandy and recorded by Farley and Jessie Saunders has been played in uptown clubs like The Limelight as well as the house parties and dance dives.

"I'm glad to see our creation's out now, after all this time," states Farley with satisfaction, but others aren't so sure. Everyone is keen to stress that Chicago is brimming with talent, that there is an endless stream of hungry young DJs and gospel-trained voices to keep the house burning, but DJ International has signed over 100 artists now, and you can't help but feel that many will have their hopes disappointed. Lewis Pitzele hands me a sheaf of press shots telling me he can't remember the artists' names, but at least I can see what they look like.

There's Kahlid, a pretty, dreadlocked 14-year-old with a silver sequinned jacket who's being hyped as the next Michael Jackson. At the New Music Seminar, Lewis had him in a hotel room at the Marriott singing along to tapes of "Ben" and Whitney Houston's "Saving All My Love For You" to any and every journalist who came in the door. Kahlid was discovered while busking to earn extra money; Lewis happened to be in the same street selling balloons and decided he'd found a star. Kahlid smiles when I say he must learn to say no – he says he knows what he's getting into and he's learnt the word already.

Then there's MCO, a rap duo plus DJ who have been told to write a tune celebrating house but are really resentful that hip hop hasn't made it big here: "Even Alabama made a rap record! Everyone thinks Chicago is a soft sucker city. We don't understand house music – we only know how to write bad about it cos they're always putting hip hop down." They suggest putting their feelings onto vinyl then getting another group to rap a pro-house reply, setting up a Roxanne-style battle. They could have a point.

But then so could Professor T.C. Roper, self-styled king of Ropeology, which he claims is rhyme with reason, a Chicago style of advanced rap designed especially for roping in the girls. Or the boys, if you prefer. Like much I've seen, I get the feeling he's making it up as he goes along, but he claims to know nine other ropers in the city and to be teaching advanced classes to a crop more. Who knows, it could sell...

"Whatever you do, you can't sway away from why people were interested in the first place," says Chip calmly amidst all this. "We have to keep that house music feel to it. Otherwise it would be suicide." Chip is thinking of recording a tune called "I Can't Live Without My Beatbox" to emphasise the point: hardly an original title, but then originality isn't that high on the house list of priorities.

Stealing, as several people explain, is when someone hears your idea and gets it out on disc locally before you do. It's nothing to do with borrowing or adapting riffs from old records. These are DJs, after all. And so, Chip quite openly admits that "Like This" was inspired by ESG's "Moody". Anyone you ask will tell you how "Love Can't Turn Around" is a reworking of the Isaac Hayes tune " I Can't Turn Around", and there's a thousand more if you care to look. Me, I prefer to dance.

WHICH BRINGS us back to the question we started with: what is house? The answer finally came after a late-night studio session with Frankie, Chip and Joe Smooth. Joe Smooth is the house Doctor. He irons out the problems at DJ International's frantic office, plays a role in most of the label's productions, and is known as a perfectionist. Chip has been sampling my voice all night for use on future records, and it's Joe who complains that I breathe too much and asks me to say parts again. He asks me to intone "Life is strange" through the sampler and when I ask why he smiles inscrutably behind dark shades, "Trust me," he says. I feel I may regret it.

By 4am, Frankie has finally come up with a mix that satisfies Joe's requirements, and at 5am we are outside the Muzic Box, a run-down warehouse-type building under the railway tracks in Lower Michigan Ave.

"Hey Frankie!" yells a voice from a parked car. "I heard you on the radio last night. You sounded good!"

Everyone knows Frankie, and it seems like it takes us 30 minutes to edge from the entrance to Ron Hardy's DJ booth because
they all want to say hello and shake his hand. Frankie has a theory that dancing is the poor man's luxury, but the rich like it too
so they have to go where the poor people hang out because
that's where it's happening. But just as white Washington has
never gone to the Go Go, no Yuppie will ever enter this dingy,
dimly-lit drive.

People stumble out of the main room dripping with sweat to
drink the water provided in a tea urn, the only liquid available in
the venue. Open the door and it's like stepping into a furnace:
5am on a Thursday morning, and the place is still full of bodies
jacking up and down, hands in the air, and all at a pace that
makes the pogo feel like a slow waltz. *"House fever!"* declares a
flyer on the wall. *"It's for real – let's see the animal in U!"* Others
remind people of special Sunday night holiday events: *"No
school on Monday!"*

Ron mixes "Go Bang" by Dinosaur L into a treated tape of Aretha
singing "Respect", then Willie Colon and Denise Lasalle *acapella*
leads – unbelievably – into Sade singing "Maureen" without the
advanced aerobics on the dancefloor ever slackening. Just over
an hour after it was finished, Frankie's mix of "You Can't Hide
(From Yourself)" is on the reel-to-reel making its club debut,
and the crowd like it well enough. The excitement in the air is
as palpable as the heat.

Frankie smiles. "So now you know about house."

Motörhead

■ **Sylvie Simmons**
Creem February 1987

Motörhead are one of rock's institutions. Mainman Lemmy has carved his own legend, and provided a role model for many a budding rock star. His frank, down to earth attitude, die-hard rock 'n' roll philosophy, occasionally dubious and always uncompromising take on life and inexhaustible party-animal behaviour has earned him respect and affection from most in the music industry.

Here, Sylvie Simmons visits Lemmy's house, enjoys a nice cup of tea with one of Britain's most enduring rock traditionalists, and employs the more-ballsy-than-the-lads style she honed at *Creem* to paint a picture of Motörhead – with teeth.

It's old, it's dark, it hides a thousand evils behind a facade of normality and drapes drawn against the sun. On a dull west London street it could be any old house, but it isn't – it's *Motörhouse*! Home of Lemmy, legendary Lemmy, the Lone Ranger of metal and his Tonto, Wurzel! A nasty little boy watches me walk up the front path, picking his nose. Lemmy once said if he moved in next to you the lawn would die, and it looks like the neighbour has too.

As I'm thinking of the possibilities – install him in Number Eight Downing Street and watch Maggie wither away – he appears at the door in a haze of smoke and Carlsberg. The little boy makes a perfect scale model of the World Cup football with the contents of his nose. Lemmy leads me inside...

Cosy, smoky and dark. Two downstairs rooms knocked into one with an arch in the middle where Lemmy's model aeroplanes (crafted with love, painted with precision) dingle-dangle on little wires. A fireplace crowded with Motörabilia and scary masks and World War Two stuff. A far wall plastered with a collage of Samantha Fox pictures, the top-less D-cupped model and, loosely, singer, that Lemmy was going to work with until she got a hit on her own (there's a photo of the spaghetti-eating contest where they met; Sam's dad, recognising Lemmy as a music industry great, asked him to "help" his daughter). Out back there's a garden with more weeds and concrete than the Smiths. By the sofa, various props of civilised life, whisky, beer, ciga-rettes, videos, TV set, and a nice cup of tea Lemmy just made. And in the corner there's a parking meter. Why's there a parking meter in the front room Lemmy?

"Well" says Lemmy. He says "well" just like he'd sing "well", Lauren-Bacall-to-the-nth-degree, soaked in Jack Daniels and strained through a filter-tip. "I was coming out of the Embassy Club one night with this bird and it was just *there*, you know?"

I know.

"I thought: 'That would look good in the garden', so I picked it up and hailed a taxi. And she's going 'No! You'll get arrested!' and I said, 'Well, I'm not going to fucking *walk* home with it!' So I hailed a taxi and I said, 'Do you mind if I bring this in?' and he said 'No mate, I don't give a fuck.'"

This being one of those jovial and rightly world-famous London Black Cab drivers who mow down old ladies, small cars and bi-cycles with a smile. So here it is, in the front room. Should be out front making them some money, I suggest.

"We've tried it but you can't get the money out," shrugs Lemmy.

Wurzel comes in, plonks himself down on the sofa, lights up a cigarette.

Which of them's the domesticated one I ask, complimenting Lemmy on the nice cup of tea.

"Thank you. It was a teabag. You just put it in a cup of water. *He* usually makes it. I wouldn't say he was domesticated though."

Wurzel has just discovered that his cup of tea is full of washing-up liquid; Lemmy recommends milk.

Do they do their own laundry?

"No," says Lemmy. "We used to have a machine but it broke down. It's difficult when you're bachelors."

But this is a man who's learnt to rise above difficulties in the past three years. It was that long ago that two-thirds of his band – Philthy Phil Taylor and clean-behind-the-ears Brian 'Robbo' Robertson – disappeared, and a legal battle with Bronze Records began that prevented the new line-up of Lemmy, Wurzel, Pete Gill and Phil Campbell from putting out a record. While the label was releasing compilations and the press was writing obituaries, Motörhead was out on the road – Australia! Hungary! Scandinavia! The United States! Tromso! Tromso! ("Even the people who *live* there have never heard of Tromso. It's past the fucking Arctic Circle!") – honing itself into the tightest pack of metal animals this side of *Metalzoic*, and climaxing in a 10th anniversary show at London's Hammersmith Odeon where the Motörheadmen past and present joined onstage in a rousing chorus of the song that started it all: "Motörhead".

Lemmy wrote the song for Hawkwind before they kicked him out after five albums in 1975, and sang it with Pink Fairies, Larry Wallis and Lucas Fox, when he put together his new band, "the worst band" as critics called it, "in the world". Soon came Fast Eddie Clarke and Philthy Animal and the line-up we scholars call Classic Motörhead, and two of the best metal albums to ever scream though speakers: "Overkill" and "Ace Of Spades".

And then Eddie left in disgust over Wendy O'Williams, ex-Thin Lizzy Robbo came in for one album, "Another Perfect Day". Only it wasn't – and what with poor sales and poorer record company backing, it looked like Motörhead was done for, over, flat on its back and deader than the neighbour's lawn.

Except to Lemmy Kilmister. "Motörhead is my livelihood. It's what I enjoy doing. If I gave it up what would I have left? Fuck all."

So he didn't, and as soon as he could he put out an album. "Orgas-matron" is it and it's damn near brilliant. Lemmy thinks so too.

"The best one so far, don't you think?"

"I'm rather partial to 'Ace Of Spades'," I say.

"It's certainly the best thing we've done since 'Ace Of Spades," says Lemmy. "And this is definitely the best Motörhead."

Other than the obvious difference to all but the innumerate, how's this Motörhead different?

"Enthusiasm," says Lemmy. "That's the main difference. It's such a relief to be with three geezers who want to be in the band, in Motörhead as a *thing*, all together, us against the world. The others got really *jaded* about the whole thing. You had to put a pistol up their arse to get them to play any of the old songs – even 'Motör-head' for fuck's sake! If I went to see Little Richard and he didn't play 'Long Tall Sally' I'd be round the fucking dressing room banging on his door! This lot really want to do it, and I've never had that sort of thing in a band since Eddie left, really, and it wasn't there for quite a while before he left either."

The dispute between Lem and Ed over sticky nipples is public domain by now. But why did Phil leave? He seemed as permanent as a wart.

"I don't know really," says Lemmy. "I don't think *he* knows. It's just that it wasn't going that well with Brian Robertson, so we fired him and got these other two guys in, and on the day we got them Phil announced he was leaving.

"He was just fed up and he didn't think it was going to get any better. I think he was just depressed about being in a heavy metal band and never getting any honour from his fellow musicians – do you know what I mean? Because you never get the *respect* side of it. You might be a fantastic player, but nobody expects you to know how to play. A lot of HM bands have got musicians that are a damn sight better than what you'd get in a *jazz-fusion* band, but you don't get any fucking Emmy awards, no accolades."

Does that bother him?

"No, it doesn't bother me because I'm a cobbled-together bass player anyway. I'm not supposed to be playing bass, I play rhythm guitar, so I'd never be in a poll for bass players, and I'm not exactly Maria Callas either," a wicked chuckle, "so I get voted in because I'm a *character*."

Certainly is. Even trendy *Sounds* and *NME* writers wear Motörhead T-shirts.

"It's because," says wise Lemmy, "they get them for nothing."

But not Brian Robertson, uh-uh. You always got the impression, seeing him with Motörhead, that the band was a bad smell under his (daintily freckled) nose.

"I know what you mean," says Lemmy. "The fans felt the same way. He was always more like I'm-Brian-Robertson-Guest-Guitarist instead of one of the band. But he was a good player. I think 'Another Perfect Day' was a good album."

Wurzel nods, so I ask him, was he a Motörhead fan before joining? Lemmy looks up from his whisky.

"I had two albums," beams Wurzel like a schoolboy who knows the right answer. "'Ace Of Spades' and 'No Sleep', and then I heard 'Another Perfect Day' – a friend brought it round and said 'Have you heard the new Motörhead?' and put it on and I really liked it. But it didn't do very well did it?"

"Certainly didn't," growls Lemmy.

So much so that a lot of people – actually let's be honest, it was just a couple of people in the press – rang the death-knell for Motörhead.

"I don't even listen to them," says Lemmy. "I've always been determined that *they* don't tell me when it's finished. I do. They all thought I was going to have a new name for it too, lay Motörhead to rest, cross its arms over its chest, shut its eyes and leave it. Well, I invented Motörhead, it's Motörhead as long as I'm in it. And I'm not going to start again, going round the boozers – I'm too old for all that shit," he cackles. "Can you imagine? The Red Lion in Brentford again? A fucking nightmare!" he chokes.

Lemmy's 47, Wurzel's 37. Where did he find him?

"Under a rock," grins Lemmy. It's a wicked grin. "I was looking for a toad and I had to make do with him."

Did he kiss him and turn him into a prince?

"More likely to turn into a lay-by," says Lemmy, making one of many references to Wurzel's manly prowess. ("Don't mention the measurements or that'll be it," whispers Lemmy. "The rest of us will never get a bird in America next time. Just say, when he gets undressed people *throw buns* at it...")

What were you doing before Motörhead I ask Wurzel.

"What? Musically?"

Unless there's something else you want to tell us. Feel free. *Creem* is a mightier organ than yours.

"Well I was on the roof killing moss, spraying chemicals on it," he demonstrates, "and in the evenings I was playing with this band called Bastard."

"Which is a coincidence," says Lemmy, "because that was what I was going to call Motörhead originally."

"The reason I called it Bastard was because I was sick of it up to here with all these wallies," Wurzel goes on, "so I thought I'll call it what I want and just get on with it. Which is what Lemmy wanted to do."

Describe the new band in sentences of two syllables, I demand of Lemmy as Wurzel goes to make more tea.

"Wurzel's sneaky and cheerful, Phil Campbell's young and horny and Pete Gill is old and flash, like me," says Lemmy, "but in a different way."

Does he feel his age?

"You find you have a reserve of energy that clicks in, that goes into overdrive when you need it," says Lemmy.

Does he eat salads?

"No."

Has he ever eaten a salad?

"Yes."

And that's why he doesn't eat salads?

"Yes."

"Who wants to eat rabbit food all the time?" asks Wurzel, who's come back with the tea.

"Rabbits," say Lemmy and I in two-part harmony.

There's harmonies on the new album – on one track anyway, "Ain't My Crime", only not dippy metal harmonies; Lemmy it's a love song. Personal experience?

"Of course. If you get through life and you don't get married or don't die it's going to happen."

Is Lemmy a confirmed bachelor?

"Well, you get set in your ways," Lemmy shifts onto the floor. "Because if somebody says to you, 'Don't do this, don't do that, don't live like that' you say 'Fuck you!' and that's another one gone isn't it? So I'm not expecting to live with anybody really seriously again. Except Wurzel, and that really *is* serious. I find him walking back-wards and forwards in the kitchen singing to himself at all hours, or telling himself jokes under his breath and laughing at them."

Tell me about first love, I ask, whimsically.

"Tender, romantic and hopeless," Lemmy answers, whimsically. "Actually on the first one you're so shit-scared that nothing hap-pens, ever, and all these macho stories you get in the locker room, it's bullshit. It never happens!"

"Mine," Wurzel's gone all misty-eyed, "was called Ethel Taylor..."

"Ethel?" perks up Lemmy. "Mine was Kathleen Sweeny. A little slip of a Catholic girl..."

And he's got a lot to say about religion. Always has had – the evil and hypocrisy of the whole damned thing's been as permanent a fixture with Motörhead as the fetching horned death's-head. Lemmy's favourite song on the album's the title track, "Orgas-matron" – "the lyrics really, they're very personal; maybe people will hear them and not think I'm just a gorilla in a leather jacket."

Two thousand years of misery, of torture in my name

Hypocrisy made paramount, paranoia the law

My name is religion, sadistic sacred whore – That's some of them.

"That's how I feel about the whole fucking thing," steams Lemmy, detailing wars, inquisitions, poverty, the Vatican, the Pope's withered balls and Catholic girls in the club for God. His mother was a Protestant, his father left them – and he was a Protestant *vicar* for Christ's sake, the Reverend Sydney Kilmister – and she had to write to the Pope to get permission to remarry Lemmy's Catholic stepfather! His father, he says, is a hypocrite. No love lost, they didn't contact each other until Lemmy was grown up and already starting a band. They met up. Dad asked forgiveness, said he'd do anything to make it up to Lem, who asked for some money, not much, just enough to get the band off the ground. Dad said no, he didn't think it was right for his son, he'd send him to school to be an accountant instead. Lemmy said fuck off, and the rest is metal history.

So that's where the doom and gloom interest came from?

"I think that's my star sign," says Lemmy, who's a Capricorn – who are all (except for Jesus) miserable sods. But "I'm on the cusp of Sagittarius so that's what my outgoing bit is. I've got the depression and the doom and the pessimism of a Capricorn but I laugh at it because of the Sagittarius bit. I think it's funny! The oncoming death of the universe as practiced by the human race is inevitable, and I just think it's fucking hilarious! They put a new war on the telly every night and I just fall all over the floor – here they go again!"

"It's true what you say about cusps," pipes up Wurzel, who's a Libra and Scorpio mix.

But do they mix a good cocktail?

"Yes I do actually," says Lemmy. "I invented a cocktail called the Motörheadbanger. I made it out of the entire band and crew's duty frees on the French tour last year. It's really quite interesting, and quite expensive to get it mixed up, but you only need two and the world ceases to exist."

Do they throw many parties at the Motörhouse?

"No. I just go to everybody else's. It's a much more sensible idea. Why have a dog and bark yourself?"

Why indeed. Are they kind to animals?

"Yes actually, but we don't have any."

What's the best party Lemmy's ever ligged at?

"You've got me there – I've got a lot of parties to go back through, because I *do* like a good lig. Couldn't have been one of ours because I avoid ours like the plague. I always tend to grab the girl and leg it out the side door before the party starts. I'd sooner be in the crowd than at the fucking party. But the Stones one was a good one – at the Roof Gardens, after they did the 100 Club."

That was where Eric Clapton came up to him, patted him on the shoulder and said "Are you Lemmy? I've always wanted to meet you." And Eric Clapton was one of his fucking *heroes*, even if it *was* Hank B Marvin he impersonated (complete with all the moves; he did it during Hawkwind and they weren't amused) in front of the mirror! That was also the party where Wurzel, seeing a ravishing blonde across the room, confided to Ron Wood, "Cor, I wouldn't mind having a shot at that after the party," and Ron pointed out it was *Mrs Wood*...

Lemmy says he goes to these ligs for the beer and the girls, not the music. If AC/DC or ZZ Top were in town, that'd be a different matter; he'd be there every night. Contrary to popular belief, he doesn't just listen to metal

"I'm just as likely to listen to Mike Oldfield or Joni Mitchell; people think when we go home we listen to fucking Judas Priest albums. They must think you're a moron! I listen to a lot of rock'n'roll, Chuck Berry, Little Richard."

He just *plays* metal because it's exciting.

Which musician would Lemmy least like to spend the night with?

"Divine," he says.

"I thought you were going to say Paul Weller," says Wurzel.

"Easier to stand than Divine," says Lemmy.

If he could be a spot on anyone's face, who would he choose?

"Jimi of Bronski Beat," chuckles Lemmy, "and then I'd have lots of friends!"

And talk turns to Raquel Welch for some reason, Lemmy's Ideal Woman, and we're going to *watch videos*, so I've only got one more thing to ask: is there anything about the Real Lemmy that would shock and surprise *Creem* readers?

"Yes," says Lemmy. "I'm a woman."

The French Connection

■ **Mary Anne Hobbs**
Sounds December 16 1989

J on Bon Jovi and his band have always enjoyed the attentions, not to mention the disposable income, of a huge female following. But as Mary Anne Hobbs discovered in Paris, there is more to the singer than a fluffy mane and a sugary sweet grin. During the following interview, she narrowly avoids the thick end of his fist, thanks to her delightfully tenacious interview technique. Who said girls just wanna have fun?

"This country sucks dick" hisses Jon Bon Jovi.

The rock star is not feeling very well. He's got a touch of the flu – *and* he's in Paris.

"Everyone here should speak English for starters..."

Strong words indeed for Jon, who has accessed the households of millions with an impossibly respectable public image.

We are hurtling between a spot of abortive video making at the Eiffel Tower and the soundcheck, in a heaving mini bus.

Up front, the colossal cellulite bulk and motionless expressions of The Haystacks Division of The Jersey Syndicate (tour manager Paul and bodyguard Reggie) are really quite oppressive.

The two men rarely stray from within a couple of feet of the singer. They are gracious but firm, alloting Jon's time in the interests of his maximum convenience. Their scheduling is not open to question.

On the back seat of the bus, the band send-up the Dalai Lama (currently resident in the same hotel as Bon Jovi) and merrily discuss their multi-thousand dollar credit limits.

Jon sulks, at a pitch midway between the two parties.

We drive past a dead person, the victim of a motorcycle accident. He's lying in the road, his boots still sticking out of a polythene shroud. Everybody groans and, for one disturbing moment, I fear I may vomit over the beautiful sheepskin jacket that wraps the singer.

But I don't.

———

BON JOVI are the All-American triumph of the '80s. Damn it, their keyboard player even changed his surname from Rashbaum to Bryan because it was "too ethnic", following the singer's lead sometime after Bongiovi had become Bon Jovi.

The band's first two albums, a self-titled debut in 1984 and its successor "7800 Degrees Fahrenheit" floundered.

Then came "Slippery When Wet".

Songwriter Desmond Child (now the veritable SAW of American rock), was drafted in to co-write both of the smash hit singles "Livin' On A Prayer" and "You Give Love A Bad Name".

In 1986 – *following* the release of the singles – "Slippery" became the fastest selling album of all time. A commercial monster that kicked the crutches from under Bon Jovi and jettisoned the band into the rock hyper-bowl, rubbing sales figures with the likes of Def Leppard.

Just how much of his success is Jon prepared to attribute to the alchemy of Desmond Child?

"Nothin'," he snaps. "What the fuck do I owe him anything for?

"Basically, he didn't achieve success until he wrote with *us*. He'd written a few songs with Kiss and Bonnie Tyler, and none of them were hits. We get together, the chemistry works and we write some great songs."

If Desmond Child hadn't come in with you at that point, there's a chance Bon Jovi would have stiffed. The singles are the strongest tracks on "Slippery" after all.

"That goes right along with what I think of France – Suck my dick" he spits.

Bon Jovi retained the services of Child and he pomped up "Bad Medicine", "Born To Be My Baby" and "Blood On Blood" on their fourth album "New Jersey", released last year.

There are no songwriting credits on the album sleeve.

Theoretically, then, with Child's midas touch and the cunning man-agement of convicted drug-smuggler Doc McGhee, any band with a fundamental knowledge of rock guitar could've been Bon Jovi.

"Boy, you're really looking for some shit. If you were a guy I woulda hit you by now.

"Doc McGhee didn't even have a gold record when I started with him. He didn't have anybody returning his phone calls.

"He had two club bands. One from LA (Mötley Crüe) and one from New Jersey (Jovi).

"Both bands got pretty successful. But Doc wasn't a big-time manager seven years ago. I'm telling you, he was the *lowest* guy I talked to."

IN 1982, Doc McGhee was arrested for smuggling an estimated 18 tons of marijuana into the US. Last summer, he received a five year suspended sentence, on condition that he serve 3,000 hours community service.

McGhee is a shrewd geezer, not likely to appease the judges delivering meals-on-wheels to deprived addicts.

He fulfilled the sentence on a grand scale, organising the Make A Difference Foundation, a charity concern designed to raise money to help victims of drug addiction and alcoholism.

Bon Jovi themselves pressed the 'SAY NO TO DRUGS' slogan on the peel-off backing of their tour passes and launched Doc's campaign – headlining the Make A Difference festival, an anti-drugs and alcohol abuse benefit in Russia, just prior to the last UK appearance at Milton Keynes Bowl in August.

Farcical really, that any mogul busted for handling such an astounding quantity of dope, would seriously stage an anti-narcotics benefit.

"I thought it was a great idea," counters Jon. "It was a Godsend, because it turned around something that was bad and hit millions of people with a message."

Ah, but the joy of making history (especially out of a suspended sentence). This was the first event of its kind ever to be staged in the USSR, and naturally the media swarmed over to shoot up a little pseudo-perestroika. Handily, four other bands managed by McGhee – Skid Row, Gorky Park, The Scorpions and Mötley Crüe were on site to reflect the glory.

But the festival was turbulent. There were squabbles about billing and Mötley Crüe accused Bon Jovi of turning what should have been a charitable affair into their own private promo-circus.

At home, the salivating tabloids alleged that a bloody fist fight between the Jovi singer and Mötley drummer Tommy Lee had taken place at the festival.

Who won then Jon?

"It's bullshit. Believe me, it's not true," he groans.

Mötley dispensed with McGhee's services, left the country with Doc's former partner Doug Thaler, and are now in litigation.

"Bon Jovi are like a bunch of babies. It was meant to be equal billing over there, and no one was meant to be headlining, Bon Jovi ended up trying to undermine things with pyrotechnics and lazers. We were very disheartened that there wasn't, like, this 'brotherly' thing. We felt we were getting second rate treatment from our manager, so we sacked him," Mötley's Nikki Sixx was quoted recently.

"I don't know anything about Mötley Crüe to tell you the truth," says Jon. "Mötley have an album out, so they're talking.

"They sit around and bad mouth people like us or Doc McGhee because it makes good press. Picking on a band like us gets them into anything, because we're big enough to throw stones at."

Aerosmith pulled out of the event near curtain call didn't they?

"Aerosmith were never really in."

It was suggested that the band were sceptical about where the proceeds would actually be going, wasn't it?

"It's nothing that I have any control over, but the money that was made is gonna go to clinics they're opening in Russia and the States. They're gonna send doctors from Russia to America to show them how to deal with the problem."

Bon Jovi have just contributed a sorry rendition of Thin Lizzy's "The Boys Are Back In Town" to the "Make A Difference" album which has just been released.

The LP features queasy cover versions of songs synonymous with rock stars who died by drug or alcohol abuse. Almost a concept album and equally appalling.

"It's not a Bon Jovi album, so I'm not responsible," shrugs Jon.

"New Jersey" however is. Consumed by nine million popcorn eaters, the album that Bon Jovi will work long into the '90s is proof indeed that you don't need a classic to clean up.

"I don't know if 'Slippery' or any of our albums are classic. It was the best I could do. I couldn't have written any better songs than the ones that are on 'Jersey' at that time. Nothing else was coming out – so that was it."

———————

GUITARIST RICHIE Sambora might be having a bit of a knees-up with Cher at the moment, but Jon Bon – the "Boy Springsteen" – has just married his high school sweetheart Dorothea.

The wedding was a small "secret" affair, another paragraph which runs alongside wholesome tales about (for example), The Pizza Parlour Jury, a bunch of "kids" invited into the studio to help select tracks for both "Slippery" and "Jersey".

Recently, at the climax of an all-day MTV Bon Jovi special, Jon actually gave away the house he grew up in in New Jersey!

Bon Jovi have just lifted their fifth single, "Living In Sin", from "New Jersey" and the Syndicate play out their decade in the UK, with dates between December 27 1989 and January 7 1990.

Can Bon Jovi maintain their billion dollar Y-front allowance?

Will they be giving away their *State* on satellite TV in 1999?

"This band is more and more like a *Rocky* movie every day. If we're not up, we're down, but we're struggling to get up again," says Jon.

"There's always a Jagger. There's always a new kid who wants your spot. But I'll be damned if I'm going down without a fight."

The Man Whose Head Exploded

■ **Miranda Sawyer**
Select September 1992

P resent day rock culture owes a lot to Happy Mondays. They put Manchester on the map, sparked off a trail of hedonism, and fired a whole generation of bands into being. They also took it to the limit with their completely uncontrollable habits, as Miranda Sawyer found out when she chronicled the making of their "Yes Please" album in Barbados and New York. Car accidents, crack habits, trashed hotels, break-ins, punch-ups and shattered bones litter Miranda's exhaustive, award-winning tale, leaving no one in any doubt about either her investigative skills, or the Mondays' talent for trouble.

January 17 1992

Thirty five thousand feet above the Atlantic Ocean, cruising at 570 miles an hour, the British Airways Boeing 747 laps up the nine hour flight from Gatwick to Barbados. It's due in at 7pm. An hour and a half to go. Sitting stiffly in his seat, Shaun Ryder jerks his head to look around at the rest of the Happy Mondays, seated in different parts of the budget class section. Didn't one of them just say...? But no, they're all absorbed in the film. Voices... He wipes the sweat from his brow and gives his head a shake. But the voices won't go away, they're getting louder, screaming round his head now, ripping up his nerves by the roots, giving him the horrors. He tries to smile at his baby daughter Jael, but his body gives an involuntary twitch as he does so, nearly sending his drink into the aisle. Jesus. He can feel himself getting angry. He makes a concentrated effort to calm down, controlling his shuddering, breathing carefully, slowly... *God it's like fucking Norway in here man why don't they turn the heating up why don' t they stop shouting when it's hot it's cold can' t you hear man stop it stop it...*

Shaun's shoulders shake and he begins to laugh. He's thinking of the cleaner back at Manchester Airport, the poor bastard who had to mop up 1,500 mls of methadone, Shaun's supply, broken in the departure lounge, bottle smashed and precious liquid seeping over the rubber floor.

7.30pm

"He says we've got to have a return ticket back out in order to enter Barbados." Nathan "McDog" McGough is getting annoyed. First the customs had wanted their work permits, and Nathan, knowing that they weren't necessary, sorted it out pretty easily. But now they're making things really awkward, saying no one can come in without an exit ticket. Nathan has a return flight to the UK, but no one else has. "But we don't know exactly when we're going to leave Barbados," McGough repeats impatiently to the customs official. "We're recording and staying at Blue Wave studios. We're going to Miami in a couple of months to do the mixing and we'll be leaving then."

It's to no avail. An hour and a half later, £3,000 lighter, Nathan holds 12 air tickets to Miami in his hand and the Happy Mondays are free to go. The band, Nathan, his girlfriend Lara, Shaun's girlfriend Trish and baby daughter Jael, Bez's girlfriend Debs and their baby Arlo, and Simon Machan the Mondays' programmer and live sound engineer pile into the waiting passenger vans. Their luggage and equipment are loaded on and they set off for the studio. Night has fallen, it's dark, the narrow, unlit roads are littered with frighteningly huge craters and there's hardly any traffic. And all you can see around you is sugar cane. It feels primitive, a very weird place...

January 19

First day in Blue Wave studios. Converted from stables by a Mr Edward "Give me HOPE Joanna" Grant, the studios form part of Bayley's plantation, a low 17th century colonial style house, high on a hill, surrounded by sugar cane fields. Inside, Happy Mondays have got their muso heads on. Ignoring a sign reading "No Food No Drink No Smoking Past This Point", they pull on fags, take the occasional swig of beer or the local rum punch, and work. Tina Weymouth and Chris Frantz (former Talking Heads bassist and drummer, and producers of the Mondays' new album) want them to rehearse the six songs they've already got, then get them down rough, mistakes and all, on to the guide tracks. Then, after writing the rest, they'll get each of them in to perform their parts live all the way through.

The band are more than happy with this idea. As Paul says, they've not done that for about five years, just played together in the studio for seven hours a day – and they concentrate hard all day.

January 20

There's a phone call for Nathan at the studio. An irate cleaner demands his presence at Sam Lord's Castle, a hotel on the east of Barbados with villas in its huge grounds ("like a really nice upper-class Pontin's in Barbados," – Gary) where Paul Ryder, Gary and Paul "PD" Davis are staying. Nathan placates her, fearing the worst, and sets off. He knows that Shaun stayed over there as well last night... Did they all have a fight? Have they emptied the house contents out the window? Have they emptied the house contents *through* the window?

The cleaner is practically apopleptic when he arrives. "They have destroyed this house," she announces dramatically and throws open Gary's bedroom door. Nathan wants to laugh.

"What's wrong with it?" he asks, quite sincerely. "I mean it's a tip, but it's no more than you'd expect from four lads having a weekend together."

Gaz has emptied every single item of his clothing on to the floor ("it all needed ironing"). There's cigarette packets, towels, ashtrays, bottles... The cleaner won't be soothed. Gary, PD and Paul move out.

January 23

It's early afternoon and the sun scorches down on Bayley's Plantation. Tina Weymouth, long, fair hair flapping in the constant Barbados wind, stands in the courtyard watching her children Robin (nine) and Egan (five) climb a huge, bearded fig tree of the type that gives Barbados its name – it means The Bearded One in Spanish. She smokes a cigarette, fanning herself with her other hand.

Gradually she becomes aware of a thin figure in the distance, padding slowly up the hill towards the house. It looks like Bez, but it can't be – Bez has driven the jeep into town. Tina shades her eyes, strains to see clearly. It is Bez. And there's something odd about the way he's walking, he seems to be holding his right arm awkwardly...

Nathan: "I went and picked up the jeep that morning. It was a really nice one, open-topped Suzuki, only six months old. By afternoon I discovered Bez doing handbrake-turns in the fields outside the studio. I explained to Bez that Suzuki jeeps turn over really easy, they're only aluminium and they've got a really high centre of gravity, and that Alex Sadkin, Grace Jones' producer, had died in the Bahamas in one of the very same vehicles. I knew all this, so I just said to Bez, Be careful, keep it on the roads.

"And that afternoon, he went off to buy some bottles of rum punch, and on the way back, instead of taking a road, he just drove across the plantation fields, hit a huge rock covered by some weeds, and the thing just somersaulted through the air! It landed on the roof with him inside it. Half a mile from the studio. And I don't know how he got out of there with a bust arm. The distance between the driver's swat and the roof was about nine inches."

Shaun: "I drove to town that way one day and I couldn't do more than 15 miles an hour without getting thrown out of that car. Bez must have been doing 55."

January 26

End of the first week. Casualties: one house, one arm, two cars. To add to Bez's rollercoaster jeep antics, Shaun has written off another vehicle. Numbed by tranquillisers prescribed by the studio doctor as a methadone-substitute, pissed on rum punch, he smashed his car into a wall on Saturday night. And then hit another wall. Blew all four tyres, and then drove on it for two miles. The tyres are shredded down to the metal.

Nathan's been dividing his time between the hospital, the car-hire firm, the estate agent's, and the bank. Despite all this unforeseen hassle, the manager's happy. Each day when he comes back to the studio, he listens to what the group have done and it lifts him. They came to Barbados with six songs and Chris and Tina have had them in the studio every day, playing the grooves, writing, rehearsing, working hard. They work from 11am to about 7pm. And it's paying off. They're sounding brilliant. Nathan decides not to tell the record company about what happens outside the studio.

January 28

Shaun sits on the toilet with his pipe, smoking a rock of crack.
It's his tenth of the day. Each of the white raisin-sized rocks
contains about 25 grammes of cocaine, and as Shaun has
discovered, the island is crawling with the stuff. £1 a rock, he
thinks, as the little pebble heats up to emit the cracking sound
that gives it its name. That's £24 a rock cheaper than at home,
and it looks like he can get the price down even lower. The
Mondays chose Barbados – Shaun too – partly because they
knew there was no heroin there. They'd thought there were no
Class A drugs at all, just weed. Shaun has discovered otherwise. He hides in the toilet from the others, smokes crack,
works on his lyrics.

February 1

The car rental company have insisted that the Mondays return
all the hire cars. After Bez's roll and Shaun's "mishap", Nathan
has put his back window in by reversing into a tree in Tina and
Chris' courtyard. "Mind That Tree" has become a song title,
although, along with "Lady Dickhead", "Naughty Neck" and
"Salford Soca", it will change when the lyrics are added.

February 6

"I've just done 30 rocks," states Shaun, in a matter-of-fact don't-
give-me-any-shit-about-this-one-McDog style.

Nathan gapes: "What?"

"30." Shaun gives him a sidelong grin: "I'm tanning the stuff, man."

Nathan can't believe it. He reasons with Shaun, knowing that he's
never been that bothered with crack in Manchester. *Why? You just
used to smoke the occasional rock at home, you're stupid, you've*

come off smack, you've come off methadone, what's the point *of this, you know you're not doing yourself any good...*

Shaun half-listens, half-agrees.

"I know, I know, man," he says. "But I wanted a different buzz for the record." He's laughing but there's some truth in his excuse. He doesn't want this one to sound like the smack-sodden "Pills'N'Thrills", he wants to hear music the way he hasn't heard it before. There's so much ragga stuff going on down here, he's really getting into it. Still, he promises Nathan he'll cut down. It's not a real problem yet.

February 7

Shaun watches the boy run lightly away from Bayley's Plantation. He knows what he's been doing: the dealers have noticed that Shaun's not been smoking for a day and their boys are putting free rocks in his letterbox. Shaun shrugs. What can he do? He can't pass up free gear.

February 8

Tina and Chris laugh at their older son Robin learning how to do the Happy Mondays wrist-flick. Shaun's teaching him and he's a natural, throwing his hand at right angles to his arm till he gets a click from the fingers.

Playing drums along with someone else is, Gaz has discovered, a pretty good laugh. When he and Bruce started working together, listening to each other on earphones while drumming, it was dirty looks through the glass between them. But now it's mega.

"This could be a Dire Straits album if we're not careful," he tells Chris as a joke, "playing with a proper drumhead like him."

Chris tells them it sounds great, nearly perfect enough to be laid down properly.

In another room, Tina helps Shaun with his lyrics. "This is brilliant," she bubbles, "make these two lines the chorus." Shaun likes working with Tina, she's really good at editing things down right, but he can't be bothered much at the moment. It's too nice out. He's still writing his lyrics in the toilet, even though everyone knows he's smoking there, because he's got used to it now, it's easier for him to get his head together there. But he really can't be arsed today. The studio's got no windows and he's losing his patience.

"I'm off out for a bit, Tina," he says suddenly, and leaves.

February 10

First Gary's apartment is burgled, now the old couple in the apartment next to PD have been robbed at gunpoint. PD is getting nervous. They're getting too close, they're moving in. Still, he and Belinda can move soon. After three weeks of searching, Nathan has sorted out new accommodation: a £1,000 a week house on the western beach of the island ("an *It Ain' t Half Hot Mum* house", as Gaz calls it) and "Kinky Afro" (pure '70s kitsch with semi-circular leather couches and paintings of half-naked girls) owned by a model and renting at £200 a week. PD is moving to the beach house in four days. He can't wait.

February 18

Coming out of hospital after another operation on his right arm, Bez decides to go down to the beach where PD and Mark are staying. And there's PD, in the middle of the bluest blue ocean, being pulled along in a rubber tyre by a speedboat. It looks like a brilliant laugh and Bez wants a go.

"You've got to really hold on, Bez," explains PD. "Honest, I could hardly breathe cos of the vibration. Don't you think you should watch your arm a bit?"

But Bez doesn't care. He's going on it, he can just use his other arm a bit more, take the weight off...

Within two hours, Bez is re-admitted to hospital, his bad arm snapped once more.

February 24

Five weeks gone, and things have settled down to some sort of routine. PD, Mark and Gary don't go out much, just eat at the studio in the evenings with Tina and Chris, watch the children playing with the toads and the cats (Eddy Grant's wife has 150 cats in the plantation grounds). Every evening the sunset streams across the sea, straight through their beach villa. With Jane coming to stay with Mark, all the Mondays' girlfriends are here now. Tina teases that they've become "sex-machines", cleaning up their acts, giving up drinking, playing a lot of tennis, staying in at nights playing Trivial Pursuit. Gaz has even given up smoking. When he'd arrived, he'd been coughing so much you could hear it on the guide tracks. But since he's finished his work, he's been getting healthy, going swimming, going to bed early – "eaten me first bit of fruit," he jokes.

But Shaun and now Paul too are smoking a lot of crack. Paul keeps it quiet, doesn't go out much, but Shaun goes smoking in the cockroach-infested mud huts with the locals. "Listening to hardcore ragga, rock 'n' rolling it up," he grins.

The kids on Barbados play their reggae at the wrong speed, 78 instead of 45. Shaun's really into it – "heavy as fuck" he says. He drove past a shooting in Bridgetown the other day. Saw some cop get blasted, shot about 12 times. The police control all the weed in Barbados – they'd had to score off a bad cop when they'd first got there – and he reckons all the cops are on rocks too.

February 26

After a beach barbeque on Chandos, the beautiful western beach house where PD, Mark, Simon and Gaz are staying, Shaun rolls his car. Driving at 60 miles an hour down a road designed for no more than 20, he misses a corner, rolls "a proper bouncing rolling-over car crash" and walks out of it with a tiny vertical cut on his forehead between his eyes. When the rest of the band drive past the remnants the next day, they can't believe it.

March 8

Tina's on the phone to Nathan in England. She can't keep Shaun away from crack.

"He's stopped writing, he's off out all of the time and when he is there, his vocals are just no good. And Paul's bad too. Gary and Mark and PD are getting a problem with them. They've stayed straight and done their bit and they feel Shaun and Paul aren't doing theirs."

Nathan promises to talk to them. The situation's getting out of control. He feels helpless in England, but he can't leave – he's still fighting his ex-girlfriend for custody of their child.

Nathan manages to get hold of Shaun. He's horrified when Shaun admits he's up to 50 rocks a day. 50. How does he have the time, McGough wonders. Each one lasts 15 minutes. 50 rocks of crack is over 12 grammes of cocaine each, affecting the brain within ten minutes of smoking it. It acts quicker than if he'd injected it. He's seen Shaun go over the edge before, but he's always pulled through. Now it looks like he's lost it. He tries Paul, but Paul won't even admit he's got a habit. He denies it flatly. There's no way either of them can go to Miami for the mixing, thinks Nathan. The crack epidemic is out of control there and he isn't going to risk someone being blown away.

March 10

The album's finished now, except for the vocals. Tina and Chris have kept things to schedule, only taking Sundays off. 11 to 7 every day, building the ten tracks up with live performances from each musician, no loops.

Everyone is over the moon about the music... but Shaun is out of control, writing rubbish, sounding terrible. Nathan tries once more, asks Shaun to come back to Britain and get sorted out. He won't. So Nathan cancels the rest of the Barbados session, stops Tony Wilson from going out there, and eight car crashes, ten songs and two crack addictions after they first stepped on to Barbados soil, the Happy Mondays are forced to return to Manchester.

When he arrives at Manchester airport, Shaun leaves Trish with two trolleys, all the suitcases, the presents and the baby, gets into a taxi and drives off into the night.

England

March 11 to May 3

Nathan: "Everyone was really pissed off. There was a lot of bad feeling, it went all over the place – among the band, towards each other, some towards Shaun, less towards Paul, ill-feeling towards me because I'd come home back to England and I'd cancelled the session and I wasn't even there. But until I'd been given full custodial rights over my child I wasn't leaving the country.

"Everyone came back to Manchester, but people weren't speaking for a couple of weeks. A lot of people had done a really good job out there – they'd just done what they had to do and done it brilliantly. But they were let down by Shaun, let down by me in some ways, and some probably felt Paul had let them down too.

"I really didn't give a shit about people not talking to me. I had my priorities. Get Shaun clean, and get custody of my baby. Paul stayed on in Barbados for an extra week and he seemed to be straightening himself out with Tina and Chris' help. He wasn't even two-thirds of the way along to where Shaun was. Shaun was just like unstoppable. Just completely on a mission, and when you're on crack you just can't be reasoned with. You might be in the same room as other people, but you're in a different space. You just become hollow, like a little hollow walnut. Just void and empty.

"I went to see Shaun when he got back, and the next day I drove him down to London to see a consultant. He said that Shaun had to go for treatment and Shaun was not into it. I don't think he was annoyed with himself, he was just really exhausted by this stage.

"He went to a clinic just off the King's Road in Chelsea. It cost £10,000 a week. I was down there every week for at least a couple of days and on the phone to him every day. From the moment he came back I was his guardian, because he needed someone to see it through with him."

Since the Mondays have been back there have been a series of half-truths appearing in the music press. On April 4, a news story reveals that the sessions have ended in "disarray" and that Shaun has been admitted to a London clinic "allegedly only able to record vocals for one song due to his worsening physical condition, believed to be drug-related".

Later reports indicate that Shaun has come off methadone and that the previous stories are untrue, but rumours still abound. On May 20, Nathan issues a typically bullish statement: "*When this LP debuts at number one in September, I hope the snide critics will choke... Happy Mondays always were and always will be the greatest, most important band in Britain.*"

Shaun: "Going to rehab was like being in a hospital drama group. I've been trying to come off smack for two years, but this time I done it proper. Played the game, not be an arsehole. You know they're brainwashing you, but you just have to go for it, you have to get into that way of thinking, man. I thought, this time I'm doing it for moi. For me. I'm 29, I've been on heroin for 12 years and I don't want to be a junkie at 30.

"I did an interview with Radio One and all the while I was in there – with Simon Mayo or somebody – and I did it from the hospital bed and said I was in the Lake District! I was saying, God, you know there's no truth in these drug rumours...

"When I came out it was weird. I felt brilliant, but it's like taking the stabilisers off. All your emotions come back. After 12 years of not giving a fuck about anything, I was banging me head against the wall trying to stop meself crying over eating meat."

Nathan: "After he came out, I just wanted to keep Shaun out of Manchester because the environment's too drug-orientated. He needed to be kept away from heroin. I'd booked us an apart-ment in Newquay and we went down there for two weeks. Shaun did a bit of writing, got a bit of space. He went home for a week and then went to Comfort's Place in Surrey to do the vocals."

Comfort's Place, a recording studio owned by Bucks Fizz pro-ducer/songwriter Andy Hill, is secluded and hard to find. Tina and Chris, having recovered from Barbados in their holiday home in the Bahamas, have done a bit of mixing in Miami and then flown to Britain for Shaun's vocals. There are three songs still to write, as well as all the recording of both Shaun's and Rowetta's vocals, and so Chris bans from the studio anyone not completely necessary for work.

"Hot-housing is important for an artist to create," says Tina later, "Shaun is sociable and gregarious, he loves company and he loves to spin a tale. We had to keep him from getting distracted."

Paul has come back from Barbados and spends five days in bed at his mum's, coming off crack "while big brother gets pampered in hospital". Once he's up again, he decides to go and see Donovan play. Backstage, he meets one of Donovan's daughters, Astrella, and the next day the two of them set off on a tour of Britain, following the Donovan tour by car, going to places Paul's never been to before.

Gaz joins a gym to work off his beer belly and build up his chest. Mark's girlfriend Jane has become pregnant in Barbados. It's their first child. Mark spends his time researching his family tree and finds that his ancestors drifted over from Europe and ended up in Ireland. He messes around with a weird instrument he bought in Egypt last year and gets SEGA finger from playing too many computer games.

PD moves into his first house. He gets a beagle and calls it Chops. He walks it in the fields around his new home, relishing in the fact that no one assumes he's a mugger in this new area.

Bez is miserable. His arm isn't healing properly. Since he snapped it the second time it's been oozing pus and he thinks he's got gangrene. He's going to have to have a skin graft from his leg, and a metal brace put into his arm for six weeks. The doctor insists that he's going to have to sort it out with the operation in a week's time, so Bez goes on a bender, partying in Leeds and Manchester for seven days solid. Then he goes into hospital.

New York

June 1 to June 24 1992

In Axis Studios on 54th Street, between 8th and Broadway, Steven Stanley slices his wheely chair between mixing consule and tall stack computer bank. The round-headeded Jamaican, mixer for Talking Heads and the Tom Tom Club since "Once In A Lifetime", presses and releases buttons labelled things like "Prime Time" and "Prime Slime"; he does so with a flourish, as though playing the final chord of a piano concerto. He gazes constantly at the computer screen above him. Shaun Ryder's voice booms snarling off the sound-room walls. "*SLIMEY BOG-EYED MONG WORM AT THE BOTTOM OF THE BOTTLE*" – it sounds like he's about to rip its head off. With his teeth, Chris Frantz laughs at this. "And it started off as a ballad," he smiles.

The door opens and the balladeer himself sticks his head into the room. "Stevie, me li-on," he rasps, and the Jamaican bursts out laughing. "Looking good today, Stevie," adds Shaun, "Top shirt."

It is a most remarkable fashion item: crisp white sleeves and back, set off by a purple streaky front which portrays – in fetching Hallmark greeting card style – two large cats and three cockerels.

"Cocks and pussies," notes Shaun.

Stevie roars. "You the only one who got it man!"

Shaun grins his lop-sided grin and exits, protesting at the noise at such a delicately early stage in the day. It's 4.15pm. He looks terrible. Tina and Chris celebrated their anniversary yesterday and he's got a banging head to remember it by.

"That bitch bargirl might as well have given me the whole bottle of vodka," he grumbles. "I kept saying I didn't want it too strong but she wasn't having it."

He perks up at the sight of Cindy Crawford on MTV. "Ah Cindy, baby," he sighs and sinks into the leather sofa with Paul and Simon, who are both obviously suffering hangovers to rival his own.

In the kitchen, Tina is talking about art, about Shaun and his talent. "You see," she says in her gentle New York drawl, "Shaun didn't end up as a postman. He bit the dog. Creativity and art sometimes require the artist to, like, slum out in the gutter. But it also means that he should mix with high society too. Artists should be allowed to cross all social barriers and classes, because they must be allowed to experience in order to create."

It's refreshing to hear someone talk about the Happy Mondays in the same way that they'd talk about Van Gogh. How did Tina find working with the artist?

"Shaun's very self-critical – a lot of it is to tell him, yes, you're allowed to change this line and you can change the way you sing this because you could do it better. And making him believe that he could do it better. But you mustn't change this line because it was good and you didn't recognise it. We're helping them all to do their art and if they need an idea, we have to be ready with one, so we keep it rolling, keep everyone pushing up that level of consciousness…"

Shaun and Paul's consciousness doesn't seem much above ground-floor level today. But, as the day progresses, they become more lively and demand a visit to their local. Two blocks east of the studio, the Irish bar is where the Mondays always drink when they're in New York. We stride out in the muggy air. Shaun is edgy. He wheels around menacingly when someone taps him on the shoulder. A huge, awkward youth in the long shorts and long socks uniform of an American summer blurts, "Are you Shaun Rydurr? Can I shake yurr hand? I'm rilly lookin' furrward to the next albuhm." Shaun relaxes and shakes his hand. He'd known we were being followed, but he hadn't been sure what it was about. You just always have to be double-sharp in New York.

Mick, the barman, greets Nathan, Shaun and Paul as they enter the long, dim, wooden-floored bar. "He's thrown us out of here loads of times," confesses Nathan. "But he always lets us back in."

All three suck hungrily at their Guinness. Paul introduces his new girlfriend Astrella (he split up with his wife last year). He's obviously very in love and confides later that he'd seen her picture in a Sunday supplement two years before they'd met and fancied her even then. "And she can sing, she's got a really good voice you know. And she's a ballet dancer."

Shaun is regaining his form in direct relation to his Guinness intake, regaling us with tales of The Wanker over from the studio. Apparently, if you go out on to the studio balcony at about 9.30pm, focus the house binoculars (kept specially for the purpose) on to the apartment block on the other side of Eighth Avenue, you can see him at work, stopping and starting his porn videos while conscientiously giving his tackle a good going over. "Four along, four down's a good window as well," grins Shaun. "Always plenty of action there..."

"They want you to watch I reckon," says Paul. "They always keep the curtains open."

"They get off on it," Shaun agrees. "John the studio technician says he's seen the lot there. Bestiality, the lot, man."

Shaun's at home with a Guinness and an audience. He takes over the conversation. He's funny and devastatingly honest, accompanying his more shocking revelations with a sly grin and a wicked wrist-flick, so that you sometimes find yourself laughing at horrible atrocities. He switches easily from stories about waterskiing in Barbados to tales of stomach-curdling, off-the-record illegalities to a direct confession of his rehabilitation experiences.

"When you're on heroin, you don't give a fuck about anything," he's saying now. "Twelve years and I didn't care about a thing. Apart from meself. I said terrible things... like about Sinéad. I said that awful thing about her... (*Shaun's remarks were to the effect that she'd only done one song and that was a Prince one, and that 'a good shagging' would probably sort her out*) And I just wouldn't say that now. I really regret that. She's lovely.

"But you just don't care when you're on smack. You're a deadhead. Then I came out of rehab, went out for a meal with Nathan and I asked him what veal was. He said, baby cow – and I just couldn't eat it."

"Yeah, and a few months before you'd have not cared if it was a baby baby," says Nathan.

June 20

Shaun sits quietly in the bar across from the studio. He doesn't want to talk to the three American journalists who are presently being treated to a play-back of the eight songs mixed thus far.

He's bored to tears. No one told him what to do with all the extra hours he'd have *compos mentis* when he gave up smack and rocks. There's too much time to kill when you're straight.

Up in Axis, the journalists are enthusiastic. The tracks are excellent, the loose swagger of the Happy Mondays as cocky as it's ever been, but played taut and sharp, sparkling. Each song is different. There are no album fillers, and the lyrics still make Chris Frantz chuckle as he tries to translate for his compatriots.

"'Theme From Netto'", he explains. "Netto is Mancunian for nothing."

"Like nish," chimes in Tina sweetly.

The journalists look more enlightened. "And in 'Angel'," ventures one, "does that line really say '*when The Simpsons begin*'?"

"It's '*when the symptoms begin*'," says Nathan.

Shaun wants to go out tonight. He's on the door for Arrested Development and then Sasha and Graeme Park from Manchester are DJing at The Limelight. But he can't. He can't go out in New York without smoking a rock at least, he can't enjoy himself in a city like this without doing some gear. Ecstasy's no substitute, and he's a monster on E. He puts his head in his hands, waits for the urge to go – it usually passes in a few minutes. But not tonight. He wanders painfully back to his hotel and goes to bed.

June 21

Sitting on a rocky outcrop overlooking Central Park's boating lake, basking in the Sunday sun, Shaun Ryder is wondering whether to go on the record about drugs.

"It just sounds dead corny, man, you know what I mean? That's why I've denied it for so long. I don't really mind saying it, but it looks dead corny in print. Even though if I was reading it about somebody else I'd think great... It always seems a bit *toy* somehow." There's a pause. He recovers his sense of humour, talks in a self-mocking voice straight into the tape recorder.

"But it was all for the sake of the music. (*Laughing*) It was. I dunno. Everything that's ever been wrote about us is drugs, man. But then (*laughing again*) the thing is, everything we've ever *done* is drugs. That's the only reason we got into the music business... But I'm not promoting it – we've been lucky enough to be able to go in clinics, lucky enough not to become real sad cases.

"I mean I was an arsehole in Barbados. Can't even remember much about it. I got it down to 25p a rock in the end. And it starts off as a laugh, it really does. But you can't stop it. You can't stop it. Don't ever be thinking rocks are a good time. (*Viciously*) It's *bad* man. You're dead, you really don't give a fuck about anything. It's worse than heroin for killing the emotions. You just can't be told."

We talk about his baby for a bit. He'd wanted a girl. "And she's beautiful, man. I don't know where she gets it from. Blonde hair, big blue eyes. Double smart."

Her birth made a difference to Shaun's coming off smack. "I didn't want her growing up with a junkie for a father."

Did you write "Monkey In The Family" and "Angel" – the LP's two drug songs – after you'd been in rehabilitation?

"Yeah, well, they're not drug songs. I know that's what people are gonna think they are, they're gonna think that a lot of the songs are autobiographical and they're not. I mean, 'Monkey In The Family' right, Chris just got loads of words, like he wrote down loads of dances and he'd write words like monkey and lion and shit. And then he said, Try and use as many words as you can there. When you start doing interviews things start getting turned into something – oh this is about your love for this and this is about your relationship with that, and I fucking hate that, man. Cos it ain't. Everyone will say it's about drugs. And it's not.

"Like 'Angel', we was just talking one day and Mark Roul, the recording engineer, came out with it then – when you've got to meet somebody new, like this, it's like going to a new doctor and he says, When did the pain start? What have the symptoms been? And I just said, Right, Mark I'm having that. And then I open the paper and Marlene Dietrich is saying, It took more than one man to change my name to Shanghai Lily. So I thought, Well that's a ridiculous line, I'll have that one. *'Good steady job in a small town'* from 'Stinking Thinking', that came from us watching Eno being interviewed by Paul Morley. And Morley was saying, Steady job in a small town ... and Eno says, Well that's a real David Byrne line that – steady job in a small town. And me, Tina and Chris were all sat there laughing and I said, Well I'm having it then! "

We walk through the park. Shaun is saying that the LP was going to be called "Rubber Lover", because of the picture of "Our Lady and baby Jesus" on the sleeve, but Deee-Lite got there first. So now it's "Yes Please", from the way Dawn the studio cook answered the phone at Blue Wave.

Wandering through the liberally-sweaty roller-skaters he tells me something disgusting about two of England's most well-loved cabaret stars. He emits a filthy cackle and flicks his wrists, clicking his fingers.

Rock 'n' Roll Rebel With Too Many Causes

■ **Suzanne Moore**

The Guardian November 6 1992

Sinéad O'Connor has, at times, represented something deeply disturbing within popular culture. Her refusal to keep quiet on subjects she feels passionately about has led her into serious trouble. She has spoken out wildly against patriarchal religion, the distorted history of Ireland, and child abuse among other controversial topics, and this aggression, combined with her obvious vulnerability has both endeared her to and alienated her from her audiences.

Here Suzanne Moore responds to the trouble Sinéad caused in America at the beginning of the decade, considers just why she is so unsettling, and ultimately rejoices in her incredibly human (ie. flawed) attempts to make the world sit up and notice her plight.

The cab driver is a Democrat. But then I haven't met anyone in New York who isn't. "We gotta get a better looking First Lady in the White House. And he's a real man – I mean what kind of man would turn down Gennifer Flowers?" It's only 11 o'clock but Bush has already thrown in the towel. Clinton is doing his sexy croak on the radio. And then comes Hillary, the woman they say will bring lesbian creches to the White House.

Later on, I watch it all again on TV, feeling that Marilyn Monroe should be there to sing for the President. But she's not. Unfortunately Madonna is too busy doing Sex, but it is not Madonna who has grabbed the headlines here this week. In fact, Madonna fatigue has clearly set in.

No, the woman people are talking about is Sinéad O'Connor, or Shine Head as the press so disparagingly refer to her. America may have voted for change but no one is ready for the kind of changes that O'Connor has been increasingly vocal about demanding. With an instinct for disrespecting the finest of American institutions, such as Bob Dylan and *Saturday Night Live*, she has become an object of vilification here.

A couple of weeks ago, she was booed off stage at the tribute to Bob Dylan. She got the wrong Bob: she chose to sing a Marley song instead of a Dylan one. She was already unpopular because prior to that she had ripped up a photo of the Pope on *Saturday Night Live*, declaring, "Fight the real enemy." As my taxi driver said, "She's lucky the Catholics are not Muslims. Otherwise she would be like Salman Rushdie."

A rock 'n' roll fatwah? Is that possible? Surely rock stars are supposed to be uppity, shoot their mouths off, kick ass occasionally. OK, so she may be a rebel with too many causes for her own good but why has she caused such a stir? Unlike that other Catholic girl, Madonna, who manufactures provocativeness, O'Connor's gestural politics, however misunderstood, have a certain rawness that is genuinely shocking. Her outbursts are about sex as well, but this is not sex as some stylised hedonism; for Sinéad O'Connor, sex means child abuse, rape and abortion. With her cropped hair and Bambi eyes, she has always had an image that depends on the tension between toughness and vulnerability. Sometimes she roars like a lion, other times she sings like the terrorised child she once was. The most striking image we have of her is in the video for "Nothing Compares 2 U", when a single tear runs down her cheek.

Now, apparently, she is so disillusioned with the whole music industry, she has decided to give it up. The medium cannot take her message. This stance is in some ways remarkably petulant. Loosen up woman, one wants to say, you're only a pop singer, not a politician or a philosopher. The expectation that she should be able to change the world – or that we would want her to – with 12 inch records seems incredibly naive. Yet it is an illusion under which many male stars continue to labour. Likewise, it is acceptable if not obligatory for male "rock 'n' rollers" to misbehave.

Sinéad O'Connor's problem, apart from the obvious one of being female, is that she misbehaves in all the wrong ways. Instead of smashing up hotel rooms and checking into rehab centres, she will keep making statements about imperialism or boycotting award ceremonies and refusing to let the "Star Spangled Banner" be played at her concert.

Much of what she does is spectacularly misguided. Putting a photo of a murdered Guatemalan child on the cover of her last single – an image that has nothing to do with the song – in the end furthers no identifiable cause but her own. Her current press statement links all kinds of suffering, from the genocide of Native Americans to the religious oppression of Irish people to child abuse, and is stunning in its inadequacy at any kind of coherent political analysis. O'Connor simply wants to claim all oppression as her own. But her comments on the Tyson rape case are as embarrassing as they are offensive.

However, there is something in her confused vision, a refusal to maintain the boundaries between the personal and the political, that makes me glad she's around. Angry women don't always make a pretty sight and O'Connor's anger has clearly not been anaesthetised by years of therapy. Instead it is pulsing, explosive and often fairly arbitrary. In American eyes, she has an "attitude problem", yet the outrage she generates is a precious thing. Her egotistic naivety, her downright nuttiness, her inability to do what is expected of her seem like a much-needed antidote to the endlessly manufactured controversy dreamed up by PR men. Her persona is ultimately far less able to be assimilated than that of a bad boy like Guns'N' Roses' Axl Rose. Name me another woman who can generate this kind of publicity without taking her clothes off.

And, as my taxi driver rants on about how Sinéad O'Connor isn't even good looking, I must admit that there is something about her sheer bloody awkwardness that stirred the most dormant feelings in me. I actually felt quite patriotic.

Fatal Attraction

■ **Liz Evans**

Unedited, unpublished version
of *Select* feature December 1992

C ourtney Love has caused more trouble than any other rock star, male or female. Enchanting, brilliant and talented, but highly unpredictable, difficult and, some say, twisted, Love has touched nerves in places most performers aren't even aware of. Although her tabloid-friendly antics of recent times have done much to eclipse her true power as an artist, the effect her music and her personality has had on female rock culture is profound.

I spent an exhausting five hours in Love's company for this interview but when it was published, editorial changes caused a great deal of upset all round. Here, therefore, the piece appears in its original form.

It's nearly midnight in the Hollywood Hills and the air is still and warm. This year's baddest girl is waiting for her superstar husband to unlock the gates to an elevator which rises up to their ridiculously decadent home overlooking the city of Los Angeles. Cautiously picking his way down the steps towards his wife, the slight blond figure of the world's most reluctant rock hero soon appears from behind the gates, cradling a tiny bundle in his arms. "You stink!" greets the bad girl, kissing him through the bars, taking her month old daughter from him as he lets her through. The elevator sails upwards before crashing to a halt, and opens onto a winding pathway lined with flowers. Just around the corner lies the house, perched above a breathtaking view of tall shocks of palm trees, snakes of urban orange and a clear blue-black canopy. The door opens onto a kitchen where Polaroids of dad giving baby a bath are stuck up over the sink and a luxurious circular leather lounge seat occupies the dining area. Adjoining the kitchen is a large room with a mirrored wall where a huge canvas awaits the painted inhabitants of the rock hero's imagination and beyond is the main living space, buzzing with the noise of MTV. Here childcare books with titles like "Fatherhood" lay scattered across a side table, a flowing white fairytale crib provides the centrepiece and a Buddhist style shrine rests against a wall.

"Isn't it rock starry?" enthuses the bad girl, "I decided if we were going to have a place up here it had to be really rock starry, with a pool and everything. I thought we really had to go all the way!"

Welcome to the domestic bliss of Courtney Love and Kurt Cobain, a couple who never go half the distance.

THEY'VE BEEN described as the nineties reincarnation of Sid and Nancy, John and Yoko, even Adam and Eve. They've been romanticised and fantasised over in astonished and gleefully horrified tones. In anticipation of their seemingly inevitable self destruction, the media circus holds its morbid breath and wrings its sweaty hands. He is the victim, pale, frail, passive, easily and tragically led, a shorn Samson, powerless to resist. She is the fatal attraction, a siren from the gutter, deadly as nightshade, dancing like Salome for his head to be served up on a platter. Their mythology is no blueprint, it was etched centuries ago into the psyche of humankind through ancient legends and the religions of the world. Woman is traditionally the downfall of man, and the role fits Courtney Love like a glove.

Certainly Courtney Love is no Maid Marian. Innocence abandoned her at birth, but she has dealt not so much in immorality as am-morality. While this doesn't altogether excuse some of her blacker exploits, it makes her motives more interesting than if they were merely evil. Her life has been a series of explorations into her own limitless horizons. She decries earth's ineffectives as "pussies" and pursues her goals doggedly. Consequently, Courtney usually ends up with what she wants, and this fearlessness of her own per-sonal and sexual ambition, being still a relatively unacceptable female characteristic, frightens the hell out of people. So when she married the world's most talented and successful rock star to emerge since the turn of the decade, her wedding was seen as the culmination of the ultimate gameplan. The new, alternative rock generation was, in a word, spooked.

Perhaps it's not so strange that everybody has absolved their mem-ories of Courtney's initial impressive impact on the rock industry in the light of Nirvana's overwhelming enormity. Memories after all, are easily exhausted. But it does seem alarmingly peculiar on lis-tening to "Pretty On The Inside", her debut album with her band Hole, and on reading over the reviews, most of which awarded her full marks from journalists stunned into a new listening experience. Even more so when you consider that she was actually offered a bigger deal than her husband by Geffen, the same record company which signed Nirvana. More than anything, it strikes one as being horribly unfair, that the woman who screeched and whispered such graphically violent physical imagery into jarring life with a sonic backdrop of roars and murmurs, should have become nothing but Mrs Cobain, parasite extraordinaire.

"I dealt with the graduation of my own career, but I didn't deal with the graduation of Kurt's which is pretty scary." says Court-ney sitting in her "rock starry" splendour. "I do find myself in this stereotype now. I mean what happened to the person I was last year? I wasn't too happy with her, but she was better than this one. I've always provoked a severe reaction and I know it's self caused because I don't believe in victimisation. It's true. I am manipulative – but what the fuck do you want me to do about it? I manipulate my life so I can live it. The thing is, I think everyone wanted Kurt to exercise his rock star image and go out with lots of girls, and I symbolised this separation from that. But it's too fucking easy to be a junkie and marry a rock star. Anybody could do that, any stupid bimbo could do that! Any girl, anywhere in the world could do that! I want to write great songs, and it's not because I want to be famous – wrong again! That's why I gave up all that acting shit. Of course when I was little I absolutely wanted to be a star, but that kind of thing becomes more refined as your priorities fall into place.

"I'm the only one who can do what I want with music and I know it. And it's really arrogant to say that, but arrogance can be so misconstrued. But I've been assimilating and assimilating and assimilating for so long now that I know what I want to say and I'm not afraid to say it. I know what I'm supposed to do and what I'm not supposed to do is go shopping with someone else's fucking money. And break up bands. And induce people to take heroin. That's just bad girl rock."

Despite what Courtney says about shopping, she clearly enjoys it. For what it's worth, she's keeping count of how much she owes Kurt ($6,000 to date), although he insists she doesn't owe him anything. Her argument is that if you've earned success you ought to enjoy it. She feels it's almost criminal not to, while he prefers to ignore it as much as possible. Her glib attitude towards David Geffen's money reduces the seriousness of fortune. She's like a child in a giant candy store buying things which please her eye or taste good, and this offsets her husband's sullen reluctance to indulge. They balance each other perfectly. When she's petulant he smiles, when he sulks she teases, and when they look at each other there's a secret understanding which could be interpreted as conspiratorial. Maybe this is where outsiders sense danger.

"I always thought of it as a hindrance," says Courtney of her intriguing partnership, "When I first started going out with him, Kim Gordon (of Sonic Youth) took me aside and warned me that he was going to take things away from me, and that my band was too important for that to happen. I knew it was dangerous, and had I not been in this relationship ... well, I can't predict the future, but I do know it's going to be a lot harder now. I'm a part of his thing whether I like it or not, but I was a part of this on my own as well. What's so pathetic is that I got signed because of my band. And you know, no one asks him about this relationship. No one asks him how his life would have been if he hadn't met me. They just force him into having to stick up for me. Other people think I'm monstrous, and sometimes I wonder. But I'm really glad we're married because his core is solid, you can't penetrate it. Nobody else is ever going to make him feel any different and I really admire that. I'm not so sure I'd have that strength. If this was the other way round I'd probably resent something like this being brought into my life. I'm weaker than he is in some ways. I aspire to that sense of self that he has, but I don't have it."

What Courtney has brought into Kurt's life is controversy of the finest calibre. Most notably her personality, which can be threateningly loud and unpleasantly attention seeking, her rumoured participation in Nirvana's internal strife, her willingness to discuss the couple's heroin habits and her pregnancy made ugly by her drug use, have fuelled the negative reverberations. She has explanations for each accusation. Claiming to be friends with both Dave Grohl and Chris Novoselic, Nirvana's drummer and bassist respectively, Courtney admits to having had fights with Novoselic's wife, Shelli, who was asked not to attend her wedding to Kurt in Hawaii after a last minute decision concerning who should and who should not be there. According to Courtney, it was as much Kurt's request as hers, her husband having had his own disagreements in the past with Shelli. Nirvana's main pressure however, obviously stems from the level and pace of their currently uncontrollable success, which has distressed all of them, including Kurt whose biggest fight with Courtney occurs two days after this interview, when she tries to make him admit that he loves being a rock star. She believes in the importance of making an impact on popular culture, he just wants to exist in his own peaceful, profoundly creative way. They make it up over blueberry pancakes and French toast in a reassuringly shabby Los Angeles diner. For the time being, he's won.

———————

IT IS the heroin allegations which have stained the couple most deeply though. In their September 1992 issue, *Vanity Fair* magazine ran an interview with Courtney which resulted in her life being drastically and terrifyingly exploded. A number of sources close to Nirvana, as well as Courtney herself have called the feature a "hack job", in which Courtney was misquoted, often way out of context. Such apparently tabloid treatment, reputedly dished out by a good friend of Madonna's, led to Courtney being required to undergo extensive medical and foetal tests. It also attracted the attention of a nurse working at LA's celebrity Cedar Sinai hospital, where Courtney gave birth to her child. After reading the *Vanity Fair* piece, the nurse allegedly photocopied Courtney's medical records and sold them to *LA Weekly*. A lawsuit is currently underway against the hospital, as well as another which Courtney refuses to talk about.

In the state of California, a mother giving birth to an addicted baby is liable for prosecution. A baby will be especially prone to addiction if the mother uses opiates or narcotics during the second trimester of her pregnancy, but if the drug is in her body during the first trimester only, the chances of harming the baby are remote. The risk of miscarriage is also greater, and mothers taking drugs are likely to deliver prematurely, or produce smaller than average babies. Whilst Nirvana were touring in Spain earlier this year, Courtney was admitted to hospital when she experienced minor contractions which may have resulted in her miscarrying, but she had foetal tests to ensure her child's safety and thankfully danger passed. Her efforts to come off heroin during the first three months of carrying luckily paid off. Frances Bean is a small baby but then her father is a small man. Most importantly she was not born addicted to anything.

"Taking drugs when you're pregnant is appalling," admits Courtney. "But when I did drugs I didn't know I was pregnant. I have to take responsibility for how I caused everything, but how liberal do we want to get? Am I supposed to have an abortion because I've been taking narcotics?

"The first time I did drugs I didn't want to, but I did it once and then again a year afterwards, and then again a year after that. Eventually it became one of the things that kept me going back and that happened just after me and Kurt got together. It was good for a while. We just thought, hey, let's get really fucked up! But then it was there in my life and I had to get out of it. I gave in to it because it is kind of romantic, but it's so alienating. It's letting the devil into your life. I absolutely knew it was Satanic, and it had a bad, bad connotation, but you think nothing can touch you. After a while it kills you. It kills love. It stopped me playing guitar. You get to a point where you don't feel anything anymore. Hide, sleep, hibernate, hide, sleep, die. Nothing's too sharp, nothing's too sensitive – I understand the appeal of that. But it's a very dangerous thing, and although for me it was very brief, about two or three months, it was very scarey. I got myself off it. A doctor told me I should get on methadone and I said yeah and sell my soul to the devil! Coming off by yourself is depressing and frightening, but by no means intolerable. I mean it wasn't like I'd been doing heroin for years or anything. But I'd never do it again. It just isn't worth it.

"Now I have my baby, but I don't want to talk about it because she's too much mine. I don't care if people want to decide what kind of mother I'm going to be. They don't have the right to judge.

But I feel like I've accomplished something real. I feel I have a lot of paternal qualities as well as maternal ones. When I had to deal with the consequences of *Vanity Fair*, all that urine testing and shit, I was in such a rage I could have killed someone. It was instinctive, it was a different mother love thing – to actually see myself killing someone."

The naked intensity of emotion exhibited in Courtney's songs no doubt originates from this instinctive source. Her ability to articulate extreme and savage passion using the female body as battleground is part of a new language currently being explored through songwriting by women such as Polly Harvey and Babes In Toy-land's Kat Bjelland. Like these individuals, Courtney inscribes the female experience into the sphere of rock music with uninhibited force and a burning fury, breaking ground with a disturbing, yet essential vision. It comes as no surprise then, to learn of her peculiar background, one which could be termed as dysfunctional if it contained half the history it actually does.

———————

THE ELDEST of five, all of whom had different fathers, Courtney never knew her paternal parent. Hank Harrison was a "crazy, unscrupulous man" who repulsed her mother and lived in San Francisco where he worked with the Grateful Dead. After the arrival of Frances Bean, Courtney's mother paid her new grand-daughter a visit, and chose the moment to inform Courtney that she had been conceived in an act of rape. Courtney doubts this, she doesn't believe anyone could have a baby with someone who violated them. But whatever the truth is, initially she was brought up in Los Angeles by Linda Caroll her mother, a "witchy-poo" woman who hung around with hairy, Gestalt therapy people and was herself a therapist. In response to her mother's friends, who presumably forsook bras and allowed their body hair to sprout, Courtney quickly developed a keen physical awareness and a desire for glamour, something which was to be deepened when she took up stripping years later.

"Those women didn't take care of their bodies," she remembers. "They had no containment of glamour. That word, glamour, it wasn't originally a fifties term at all. It originally meant spell. If someone had a glamour, they had a spell cast on them. It comes up in Chaucer's *Canterbury Tales*.

"Stripping definitely has a glamour to it, but it's a cheap, seedy glamour. You don't need a brain to do it, you can put yourself together by numbers. But it did earn me a lot of money. Actually I think stripping's a really powerful thing. It attracts the lowest common denominator type of man, so it doesn't make you hate men. Those men expect tans, denim shorts and long legs. And big tits. It's all about tits. But if you're a good dancer you can use your charisma and make money. It was how I got a guitar, how I put a band together – how I got a fucking apartment! And you can strip when you're fat. It wasn't until I got thin that I got a normal job. I walked into a vintage clothing store and they gave me the job because I was thin.

"When you're fat you look guilty, although I guess I was too arrogant to actually feel guilty. I wouldn't want to play that fat game anymore though. Frightwig were very important as a band, but they got dismissed because they were fat, and that is one reason why I created myself out of being fat."

When Courtney's mother moved to New Zealand to work on a farm, she took her eldest daughter with her and sent her to boarding school, from which she was duly expelled for drinking gimlets (vodka and lime) with boys from a neighbouring school. Her headmistress, Mrs Vulner, otherwise known as The Vulture, was a "classic butch dominatrix" who had two German Shepherd dogs and once picked up a girl with one arm when she found her sexually engaged with a boy in some bushes.

"She told my mother I was a bad student, but that I'd make a great actress," laughs Courtney.

After her less than graceful dismissal, Courtney attended a Quaker school in Australia before being sent back to the States to live with a therapist friend of her mother's in Eugene, Oregon. She ran away and was caught stealing a Kiss T shirt from a Woolworth's store. Thus began her delinquent phase, during which she was moved from one institution to another, eventually escaping to Portland where she began to strip and where she discovered the attraction of boys in bands.

"That's when I decided to marry a rock star, and then I got my first guitar and it was like NOOO! The thing about being a groupie is where do you draw the line? Because I've always, always gone out with guys in bands. It's what the guys do in those scenes. The ones that don't are, I guess, either not motivated or too gutless to charge the expression."

Nevertheless, Courtney describes this time as her heavy metal groupie phase. It lasted for three months until drag queens taught her to be bitchy and punk rock saved her. Finally Courtney felt liberated and spent two months dancing in Japan to earn enough money to fly to Ireland to visit her father, and then England with her best friend Robin. There the two girls hounded Julian Cope and spent a couple of months in his Liverpool house "doing acid and making trouble", apparently at Cope's request. Eventually they were driven out of town and returned to Portland with Liverpudlian Chrissie, to form the Italian Whore Nuns, the first of many "lame" girl bands. They struggled until Robin discovered Spandau Ballet, Courtney discovered Joy Division, and the two parted company. Aged 17, Courtney moved to San Francisco where she spent six months singing with Faith No More, and began a long and shaky relationship with keyboard player Roddy Bottum.

"I lived the whole Ophelia thing, that whole Daisy Chainsaw thing," she remembers, "I had torn dresses and dreadlocks and *real* dirt on my knees. But I never knew what to do with my hands, I hated it. I lived with the bassist, Billy Gould, and Roddy for months, they had a real wifey relationship. Roddy was all frail and delicate and beautiful, you just wanted to give him soup. And every time I broke up with a boyfriend I'd crawl back to him."

When fronting Faith No More dissolved for her, Courtney headed back up to Portland where she met Kat Bjelland, now vocalist and guitarist with Babes In Toyland. Forming a close friendship, the pair moved into Susan Silver's house in Seattle (Silver now manages Alice In Chains and Soundgarden, and is married to Soundgarden's vocalist, Chris Cornell) where Courtney started seeing a reformed junkie who also lived there. Allegedly, she reintroduced him to drugs, so Susan kicked the pair out.

"We were these really evil, drug rock sex girls, and we were going to take over the town," reminisces Courtney.

Following their attempt to dominate Seattle, Kat and Courtney moved back down to San Francisco where they were joined by Jennifer Finch, who currently plays bass with L7, and started a band called Sugar Baby Doll. Jennifer and Courtney had met through the penpals section of American underground rock paper *Flipside*, but musically they conflicted and after just two shows, Sugar Baby Doll disbanded. But not before Jennifer had alerted Courtney to the open calls for parts in Alex Cox's movie *Sid And Nancy*. Courtney auditioned and landed the small part of Nancy's drug dealer friend, only just missing the main part of Nancy herself.

"I tried out with Gary Oldman, but I didn't get it. Christ, imagine if I had done now! I had a little part in it though, and I got really involved in casting extras and doing wardrobe stuff and it was really fun. A month later Alex wrote *Straight To Hell* in a hotel room on pot, and he called me and asked if I wanted to go to Spain and star in his movie. What am I going to do – am I going to say no? I mean yeah, like San Francisco was really thriving! So I went and I was in this really horrible movie. I was so out of touch with those people. The Pogues and Elvis Costello – they were of another generation."

By this time, Courtney and Kat had formed Babes In Toyland with drummer Lori Barbero. Kat and Lori flew down to see the premiere of *Straight To Hell* and were disgusted with the entire movie world. Courtney found herself living in a bungalow two blocks away from her present Hollywood home, with an agent who described her over the telephone to prospective employers as a cross between Bette Midler and Madonna.

"I was like – no, I'm James Dean! She sat down and told me, Courtney, you've got to remember you are what you are. And I said, but I'm not what you think I am."

Terminally bored, Courtney moved up to Minneapolis where the Babes were now based, following Kat's attempt to run away from her overbearing friend and regain control over her own life. The pair linked up again briefly, but musical and personal differences reared their ugly heads and eventually Kat kicked Courtney out. Describing her relationship with Kat as "almost romantic", Courtney still expresses regret at their failure to produce music together.

"I think we could have been The Beatles. She knows it, she absolutely knows that I feel this way. I totally believed in her. But then this whole violation with the clothes happened. I know to a guy it wouldn't be a big deal, but when you're a girl you have to work it out more. It's like with this white hair thing. Something happens when you have white hair. I can't explain it but it's the thing for me. When I was in hospital having Frances I dyed my hair brown, but I felt like clay that hadn't been moulded, I didn't have any power. Now my image has been depicted as being contrived though. I can't even get dressed up and go out without feeling like a cartoon!

"But anyway, Kat had her own thing. It was sort of Victorian with little boots and dresses, and then she started moving into this whole little girl thing. I don't even care about that image thing too much, except that it was her who did that to me. But the whole thing with ripping off and ripping off and ripping off is that it's petty and the mad press wants it to be the ruin of both of us. We're both capable of transcending it though."

Apparently what really finished this intense friendship was Kat's pursuit of Kurt. In ten years the pair had never fought over a man, and this symbolised the ultimate betrayal for Courtney. Without hearing Kat's version of the tale, or Kurt's, it's difficult to piece together an unbiased picture of this, although a source close to Hole has unwittingly confirmed it.

Courtney still hasn't found peace musically. According to her, Hole's original bass player, Jill Emery, never showed any creative initiative, and drummer Caroline Rue couldn't play fast enough. Guitarist Eric Erlandson, whom Courtney once dated and whose playing she has likened to that of a girl's, remains a valuable colleague, and it was also he who managed to find drummer Patty Schemel in Seattle. Patty's musical history reads a little like Courtney's, which explains their mutual excitement about working together. Having spent the eighties in unsatisfactory girl bands such as Doll Parts and Sybil, she shares something of Courtney's frustration. Her most incriminating biographical fact is that she once dated Sub Pop co director Bruce Pavitt, but it was many years ago, and she hastens to point out that it was she who dumped him. At the time of writing, the search for a bassist continues, although rehearsals are underway, three new songs have been written, and everyone's feeling positive.

———

WHILE COURTNEY Love will never be on the straight and narrow, she seems more focused and more determined in the wake of this year's traumas. Her husband has proved his loyalty, her baby is healthy, and her band is coming back to life.

"I thought if I had to stand up in front of people who were going to watch me out of morbid curiosity, I'd rather kill myself. Then I thought no, this is what I do, this is why I got attention in the first place, through playing. I'm a hard worker, and if you work hard you can get anything you want. Without a work ethic your life spins out of control, you don't achieve anything for anybody. When I got into drugs I stopped chanting and I stopped swimming, and both of those things give me a certain discipline. And I stopped playing guitar. I believe in discipline which is why I chant, but I don't believe chanting can make you change people's wills, and you definitely can't chant for other people. I consider religion to be personal, and the chanting gave me real discipline, a real balance in my life. But love, hate, people, a career – that's all down to hard work and talent and stamina and power. Discipline is the key."

Bet you never expected to hear that from Courtney Love.

Touch Me, I'm Sick

■ **Liz Evans**
NME January 23 1993

W hen grunge broke, a misguided general consensus amongst certain factions of the music press deemed it to be just another permutation of long-haired macho rock 'n' roll. How wrong could anyone have been? Most of the bands who tumbled out of America's northwest, like Nirvana, Alice In Chains, Mudhoney, Tad, Soundgarden and Pearl Jam held no truck with any of rock's traditions (except, tragically, heroin). In fact, collectively, they altered the face of rock culture for good, dispensing with the crass superficiality of the Hollywood eighties scene, and replacing it with an authenticity and a calibre of musicianship not seen for years.

Screaming Trees are veterans of the Seattle scene. Having struggled through all kinds of storms, they've finally earned themselves respect and success. The following interview shows up just some of their personal idiosyncrasies, proving beyond doubt why no one has a case for labelling them macho rock dudes.

"LAST NIGHT, everyone wanted to kick our drummer, Barrett's ass. He didn't really do anything, he was just very drunk and running around with this straight razor.

"All the stuff that had been confiscated from the show was given to Alice In Chains and their singer Layne got this razor, so Barrett got it off him on the tour bus and I thought he was going to kill us. He was cutting himself and running around with blood all over his face. It was kind of crazy."

In a bar across the road from Chicago's Riviera Theatre, where he is due to appear on stage in roughly four hours. Mark Lanegan takes another hefty slurp of his Bloody Mary.

Since his band, Screaming Trees, joined fellow Seattleites Alice In Chains on their American tour, he's rarely been without a drink. A four-day spell in a Montreal hospital has probably been the longest time Lanegan has spent away from alcohol, although the reason for his admission seems to be tenuously linked to his recreational habit.

"I slipped on some steps. Cut my leg. It got infected. I had red lines running up and down it and they told me if I didn't rest I might end up losing it, so even though everyone else had left, I decided to stay behind for a while. Basically I had blood poisoning."

Meanwhile, the tour was merely carrying on in the haphazard manner in which it had started.

"The very first day of this tour, Ben from Gruntruck (the opening band on the bill) and I got left behind in some bar, so we rode on Alice's bus where we made an incredible mess. We snuck off when we reached the next town and we only had ten bucks between us, so we slept underneath the freeway. I didn't know where the hell we were, but it turned out we were in Orlando, Florida, so the next day we found our hotels and played the show. Apart from that, this tour's been great. I just wish I could remember some of it!

"Er, can I get another one of these please?"

AFTER SEVEN years of conflict and hardship, Lanegan can now afford to yell for a bartender whenever his raging thirst needs soothing. For, despite a paranoid bassist, a musically inept guitarist, a dangerously lunatic drummer and a near-pickled vocalist, Screaming Trees' rich brand of country-punk flavoured hard rock is finally earning them the bittersweetness of success.

With the eventual release of "Uncle Anesthesia" this year (it was recorded in 1990) closely followed by the even more glorious "Sweet Oblivion" soon after, the Ellensburg boys' major label career was stitched onto the map, alongside numerous other northwest luminaries. A deal with Epic delivered the budget demanded by worthwhile producers, and the difference between these and earlier, scruffier Trees recordings is delightfully obvious.

An appearance at last year's Reading Festival, plus several headline dates of their own, allowed Screaming Trees the chance to fortify their audio efforts in the flesh. Live, Screaming Trees possess a furious energy which belies their more unassuming individual personalities.

With the cuddly figures of brothers Van and Gary Lee Connor flanking the imposing, albeit inebriated, Lanegan, banging their hairy heads to Barrett Martin's muppet-like activities, the Trees breathe a curiously authentic log-town spirit into the grand scheme of rock 'n' roll. They are, without doubt, the most unlikely guitar heroes, to the point where they almost don't exactly know what it is they're doing, let alone why. Which probably explains why they're so darned good.

"I write songs because I'm in a band. That's what you do," shrugs Lanegan. "I write the lyrics and Lee writes the songs. Actually he writes songs all the time. The other day I was trying to sleep in a hotel somewhere and he was in the next room. I could hear him through the wall playing his guitar and I was like, 'Will you shut up! I'm trying to fucking sleep!'

"He has a tendency to talk about songs too. I don't mind it as long as I don't have to listen to him. He's a reasonable guy and a very funny guy sometimes, but we're not the best of friends. We're total opposites. I mean, I don't like to talk about lyrics. It just seems pointless. I'm not ashamed of them, I just think it's obvious, it's a feeling, it's a song. Songs are songs. The reason I like a song is because it changes the way I feel."

Dismissing all connections between drinking and self-expression, and exploding the myth of seedy bars and the lone romantic with the writerly soul, Lanegan confesses he cannot write when under the influence; a Bukowskiesque lowlife holds no appeal for him. If anything, he visibly cringes at the suggestion of his being an artistic type. His solo career (one album, "The Winding Sheet", released on Sub Pop in 1989, and one still in its gestation) makes him blush.

"Originally it was supposed to be an EP of blues covers and I was going to do it with Kurt and Chris of Nirvana. Kurt and I wrote a couple of songs, but we never taped them so we couldn't remember them. I recorded three songs, but the guys weren't happy with them, although one ended up on the record. Sub Pop suggested I do a solo record and I ended up doing it, although I didn't really want to. It seemed really stupid and pretentious to me, which was furthered by the cover art they picked while I was away in Europe. The whole thing embarrasses me."

The offending artwork is simply a moodily lit close-up of Lanegan's scowling visage. And the album is a truly evocative and haunting collection of poignant emotion. It's nothing to be embarrassed about. Guesting on its follow-up are J Mascis, Tad Doyle, Mudhoney's Dan Peters, the Massachusetts-based Gob-blehoof's Kurt Fedora and Dinosaur's Mike Johnson. Not bad for a contractual obligation, which is, Lanegan swears, his only reason for doing it. His cynicism is quite impressive.

"I wouldn't write unless I had a reason to. Unless someone was paying me. What else would I do? Wash dishes? Serve pizza? I just turned 28 and I've been doing this since I was 19. Thank God for Pearl Jam, that's all I can say. I've never been successful with this OK? I have no idea what success means anymore.

"My dream is to make enough money some day, one big score like a bank robbery or something, so I could live like Ronnie Biggs in Brazil with a Brazilian wife. If I hadn't been in a band I'd have been a prisoner anyway. I always hated working. I was never any good at it. I was constantly getting fired – mainly agricultural jobs, because Ellensburg is an agricultural town. It's also a university town which is why we moved there, my mother was a professor of education.

"My parents divorced when I was 14 and by the time I'd graduated from high school my father had moved to a little log cabin in the woods where he lived for two years before going to Alaska.

"I've visited him a couple of times, I went to be a best man at one of his weddings once – he's been married twice and my mother's been married three times. They were a match made in hell. I've had so many step siblings I can't remember their names, but my real sister's really cool. She's just been arrested for growing marajuana and she's a schoolteacher so I think she's quit her job. She's pregnant too, so I'll be Old Uncle Mark. That's what the guys call me anyway.

"The thing about Ellensburg is that it's so small. I had this girl-friend on and off for about four years. She could rebuild an en gine, which I thought was pretty cool, and she was an artist too.

"One time I went on tour and she had her big opening which I just missed. When I got back I went to see the exhibition and I realised I was in all the pictures. It was really fucking obvious it was me. I came across one – it was amazing, I wonder if she still has it – the front half of me was me, and the back half was like a dog but way scarier, and she had her arm around me and she was reaching underneath and she had these big shears aimed right at my balls! I'm not kidding, it was so mean! Because, like I said, Ellensburg's a pretty small town!"

GROWING UP in a claustrophobically tiny town where the social network is unhealthily incestuous and the main annual event is a rodeo, also caused the Connor brothers the odd spot of bother. Buying beer became virtually impossible and required an exhaustive process of swapping IDs around in case the local vendor spied an under-age Van heading out the door with a sack of refreshments he had no business with.

The boredom became so intolerable that in the end, the only way out was to start a band. At the time Van was torn between his dual existence as a born-again Christian and a born-again punk ("He smoked cigarettes and he was sure he was going to hell for it," recalls the Southern Baptist-raised Lanegan). He was preparing for life as a preacher, until one day he arrived home from school with a drunk. Evidently God was not pleased.

"He came home with this guy Mark. He was really drunk and trying to sing 'Purple Haze' or something." remembers Gary Lee, squashed onto a sofa next to Van, in the tiny backstage area before the show, Barrett, having been swept off in a cab by two women while Lanegan continues sinking Bloody Marys.

"He had to get drunk before he'd sing."

Van consequently fell prey to Satan and his new age church surrendered him to a shaky life of loud guitars and mind-bending substances.

"I went through a transition and I took a lot of acid, but I think I took it one too many times and now I'm paying the price," confesses Van, who is currently suffering from anxiety attacks and looks a little lost.

"I have a hard time smoking pot now too, and drinking's OK, but I'm trying to cut down, although I'm not doing it very successfully. I like doing it too much.

"But I feel really ill all the time, and sometimes I have anxiety attacks. Certain things will trigger it. I'm afraid to go into social situations, like tonight we were supposed to go to dinner with these people but I couldn't, I freaked. I feel like I just want to sit in a small room and hide from everybody. My heart beats real fast and stuff.

"I'm going to get counselling and I'm going to go for the Prozac. It's a drug which helps you when you have a chemical imbalance. The Church of Scientology don't like it because they have something against the pharmaceutical company which makes it, so they spread lies about how it makes you kill your family. But a lot of my friends have come through with Prozac, it just evens out your emotions."

Understandably, Van is having tremendous difficulties with actually being on the road, not to mention getting up on stage. He's missing his wife-to-be (the little sister of Tad's bass player, Kurt Danielson) and he's finding the pressures too easily alleviated by the crates of free beer which keep popping up in dressing rooms.

What he and Gary Lee would most like to do, is to record one live performance and transmit it around the States. Being technologically retarded, by their own admission, this may present one or two problems.

"We're completely technically ignorant," admits a completely unashamed Gary Lee. "I mean, I can hook up stereos and stuff, but when it comes to equipment... It was so embarrassing – I had to do this interview with this magazine called *Guitar For The Practising Musician*. It was a joke! I mean I play all the time, but there's a big difference between playing and practising. Practising is for all those metal guys who read those magazines. I get dizzy looking at that stuff, I actually feel physically sick, I can't even understand what they're saying. The only guy who knows how to play in this band is Barrett. He's actually a musician, which is good I think. It seems like there's definitely a problem when you have a band and no one can play."

SCREAMING TREES may only be able to boast one proficient member, and that member may be a man who stubs cigarettes out on his forehead while in the midst of alcoholic rages, during which he resembles, according to his singer, the boar on the Gordon's Gin bottle (it's quite alarming, believe me), but none of this matters. As a band they're magnificent, and as people, refreshingly human.

That they are so genuinely unaware of who they might become and where they might be going is astonishing, but all the more reason to love them. And you should love them, if only to get that Lanegan cringing.

Rage Against the Man Machine

■ **Liz Evans**
NME March 6 1993

I n 1992, word arrived in Britain of riot grrls. Not a movement as such, not a musical genre, not something which was willing to be categorised or labelled in any way, this wave of female teen activity had been born in America from frustration, anger and disappointment with feminism. Girls created their own media, linked up across the States, and eventually spread their message across the ocean, and riot grrl groups began forming in Britain.

Inevitably the press caught on, and effectively destroyed the fervour by turning it into a fad. Many grrls denounced their affiliation, and moved onto something else, but the ripples continued to spread throughout rock culture, giving rise to female-led bands and debates which lingered for years.

Researching this piece was a long and painful process. I hit trouble from the *NME* editorial team, who were itching for an attack, and the grrls themselves, who were overly suspicious of "the journalist". But after a month I got the full report, even if it did raise a few hackles.

THEY COME from a generation of pissed-off females who've grown up with few valuable role models (thanks to the untold, patriarchally-obscured history of women), without a sense of

ever having been involved in subcultures unless they've been on the peripheries.

Hidden behind brothers and boyfriends, they've been robbed of a strong identity outside of certain approved boundaries. And this time they're not going to take it.

Sick to death of being mauled in the pits at rock shows, these girls are organising themselves into groups which meet up regularly to discuss ideas, provide mutual support and generally have a laugh without the threat of being put down and therefore effectively silenced.

They are producing fanzines, staging gigs, forming bands, running clubs, organising cinema events, handing out flyers – cementing their personal beliefs with action. They are collectively known as Riot Grrls, although they are worried about being labelled and consequently misinterpreted, and the term is now only used tentatively as a convenient means of identification.

Kim Gordon, bass player with Sonic Youth and prime Riot Grrl influence, thinks they shouldn't worry at all. "It's better to label yourself than have someone else label you and in a way that's what they've done. I think the term is really appealing to teenage girls... I mean, it's appealing to me! It would have been nice to have had something like that around when I was a teenager. They're showing girls they can make their own culture and their own identity during those tender teenage years."

Tender teenage years usually involve wild rock 'n' roll behaviour, and although much Riot Grrl activity revolves around bands and music, Riot Grrls stress that these are not absolute priorities.

Unlike punks (although there are some ethical similarities), whose politics got lost in style and the cult of Sid Vicious, or today's slackers, whose dirty guitar rock hinges the scattered fragments of their lives together, Riot Grrls don't treat their gigs or meetings as weekend escape routes, and they don't adhere to any particular dress code. Their experience as females is not part of an attitude. It's a fact of biology and social conditioning, and it affects absolutely everything.

———————

THERE's NO easy ABC to Riot Grrl. But, obviously, it had to start somewhere. Born from a clouded line of artists like Joni Mitchell, The Slits, Poly Styrene, Poison Girls, Lydia Lunch and Teenage Jesus, Jayne Casey and, more recently, L7, Hole, Polly Harvey and Babes In Toyland, and the anger of girls who sensed that things were still wrong in this age of so-called post-feminism, Riot Grrl first erupted in Olympia, Washington and Washington DC, both hives of indie (mainly boy) rock activity.

"I think a lot of the girls who started it had mothers who were radical feminists," says Kim Gordon, "So they grew up with it in the house, it was second nature to them."

Two of those girls were Molly and Allison of Bratmobile, a band from Olympia who also produce a fanzine called *Girl Germs*. During a spring trip to Washington DC two years ago, they met up with Jean Smith of Mecca Normal. It soon became apparent from their conversations that all three shared similar sexual politics, so Molly wrote down the basic ideas. Before long, Bikini Kill's singer Kathleen Hanna became involved and decided it might be worth trying to meet up with other girls.

Intense organisation paid off, Riot Grrl was born and it now has its headquarters at The Embassy building in DC. Further inspiration came from independent Olympian label K Records' International Pop Underground Festival which took place the following summer. Opening with a "Girl Day" featuring Bikini Kill, Bratmobile, Seven Year Bitch, Heavens To Betsy, and the band called Courtney Love amongst others, it was to be a landmark.

Combined with the Riot Grrl meetings already underway in Olympia and Washington, 'zines like *Girl Germs* and Bikini Kill's self-titled text were, and still are, fundamental in providing girls with the impetus to take action. Soon, girls were linking up nationwide, writing their own 'zines, compiling lists of addresses and *communicating*.

Inevitably, the press soon picked up on it, from *USA Today* (where Breeder Kim Deal read about them: "It said they hold meetings in parks, and people get up and they're shaking with fear. It sounds almost like group therapy.") to *Spin* and, most recently, *Village Voice*.

While Riot Grrls are adamant that their network remain firmly underground, it was through the press that British girls got wind of what was happening and were duly inspired to follow suit.

Last October, Karren Ablaze! who has produced her own *Ablaze!* fanzine for a couple of years, pinned up a notice in Leeds Polytechnic which attracted eight girls to a meeting, where they swapped phone numbers and decided to put out a small 'zine of thoughts and feelings. Since then, three of these 'zines have appeared, along with contact sheets full of addresses and phone numbers of rehearsal studios, printing and photographic facilities, promoters and clubs.

Sarah, a Bradford Grrl, has started up Docs & Frocks, a club night at the local 1 in 12 – which has long had an anti-sexist/racist/ homophobic policy – designed to promote women musicians, DJs and sound engineers. She too has formed a band, Witchknot.

———————————

DOWN SOUTH, London Riot Grrls have been meeting since last year, and have issued one 'zine (called *Riot Grrl*) with the second due to appear soon. There's also *Stinkbomb* by Suzie, which is full of girl rants, song lyrics, poems, gig and 'zine reviews and *Her Jazz* by the south London/Brighton based Huggy Bear. *Girlfrenzy*, which has a cartoon of Shonen Knife on its latest cover, is more of a magazine than a 'zine, carrying comic strips, features and interviews on everything from women artists to Valerie Solanas –

founder of SCUM (Society For Cutting Up Men), and the woman who shot Andy Warhol, who has become something of a Riot Grrl heroine.

It also prints manifestos. In issue three there's an early draft of Karren Ablaze's GirlPower International newsletter, *Girlspeak*, which takes inspiration from Washington DC band Nation Of Ulysses' extreme doctrines (they plan to destroy America), as well as the Her Jazz manifesto. ('Abandon and Europhia and Energy = Jazz – Her Jazz') with painter, designer and poet Mina Loy's feminist manifesto of 1914 providing a bit of history.

Two young American sisters, Tam and Jennifer, have been inspired to form a band called Linus and have also compiled fly-ers quoting the likes of Diamanda Galas and Lydia Lunch from the excellent *Re/Search* book, *Angry Women*, vital reading for Riot Grrls everywhere.

And of course there's Huggy Bear, who've already enjoyed more press attention than they appear to like, with their brand of ab-solute disorder, snotty determination, utter lack of inhibition and fresh intelligence manifesting itself in glorious tunes and obnox-ious beats. Maintaining a strong stance on corporate structures, from papers to record companies, they believe in doing things their own way.

———

ON MARCH 8 – coincidentally International Women's Day – former press officer Liz Naylor's Catcall label (named after a '70's anarcho-feminist paper) is releasing Huggy Bear's first long player, "Our Troubled Youth", which shares vinyl space with Bikini Kill's "Yeah, Yeah, Yeah, Yeah". A slab of lawless genius available on tape and shiny black plastic only, this collection of biting blasts smashes down any mystique sur-rounding the making of records. Bikini Kill spent $20 on their side, Huggy Bear marginally more, needing just three days of studio time to record such classics as "Aqua Girl Star". It also breaks new ground for trust, something unheard of in such a greedy business.

"It's a legal minefield," laughs Liz. "There's no contract, no bits of paper involved at all. We talked about it, and the whole idea was to co-operate with people and trust each other. I mean, yeah, OK, one of us might be a crook, but I don't think any of us are. We'll see if we can work it this way.

"Huggy Bear don't have a manager either. Nobody represents them, they're trying to do it their way, which is the most difficult way. It's about pushing forward, going one step ahead and two steps back. We're putting out the record on vinyl in times where people are going 'Oh God no! It's suicide!' And yet they're proving that there are people interested in vinyl. There is something going on. With an indie label it'd be, 'OK, here's $6,000, make some posters, make a video'. Huggy Bear were like, 'Let's go into a studio, bang it out and somebody'll want it!'"

Liz first saw Huggy Bear when they played at Covent Garden's Rough Trade Shop one Saturday lunchtime last summer. People had been telling her for years to start a label, but the prospect of searching for exciting bands amongst the dismal exhibitions on display in London's pub-and-clubland seemed like an invitation to death by boredom. Huggy Bear however, were something of a welcome smack.

"I laughed all the way through, they were just chaotic and wonderful. There were about four A&R people there going 'EEE! Gods! Goodness it's a bit loud! But there's no songs!' They just didn't get it at all, and I got it and I wanted to do something with them. I met up with them and said, 'Do you want to put out a record?' I didn't even have a name for my label at that point.

"With Bikini Kill I'd read an article about them in *Option* magazine (a smallish US publication) and been really inspired. I rang them up and said, 'Look, you don't know me but I want to do this.' So then I wrote them a letter telling them what I'd done before in the music business and they said 'Yes, let's release a record together'."

In the *Option* interview which caught Liz's eye, Bikini's singer, Kathleen established her hard political line. She described the more regular all-girl bands as being "assimilationist ... they just want to be allowed to join the world as it is, whereas I'm into changing the whole structure. What I'm into is making the world different for me to live in."

"I think Kathleen is an entertainer above anything," says Kim Gordon, "she's not some pure ideologist, she wants to entertain and that's why she's playing music, not writing essays."

ON A recent trip to London with Lois (formerly of the band Courtney Love), Molly of Bratmobile explained why she didn't want to talk about Riot Grrl anymore because she felt unable to act as some kind of representative. It was beginning to alienate her from her community, and she felt very uncomfortable with the idea of trying to speak for other girls.

Jenny Toomey, who runs the Simple Machines label in DC with fellow Tsunami member Kristin Thompson, expressed a similar view while she was recording in London recently. It's perfectly understandable stemming, as it does, from a mistrust of the papers which are traditionally loathe to lend real support to feminist interests.

"I hate using the term Riot Grrl, but if it means that these men within the industry have to re-examine their ways, and start realising that they can't get away with it – then good!" declares Liz Naylor, "Riot Grrl is underground and it will have to stay so. I don't think there's any problem with that, there will still be people doing fanzines, communicating and contacting each other. Nothing can stop that."

Equally supportive, although perhaps more realistic, Kim Gordon views it as part of the continuing process of gradual change rather than a specific revolutionary force.

"It's going to dissipate and mutate, it'll get corrupted and lose its potency, but ideologies do serve their purpose for a period of time and then they don't work anymore because they become closed. But that's OK, because something else comes along.

"The most exciting thing I've come across recently is this rock 'n' roll high school which has been going for about three years in Melbourne and 120 girls are enrolled with about eight boys, and all they play is indie rock. They get free lessons and they're encouraged to form bands, and they have all these different rehearsal rooms to go to.

"We just sat there and these bands just got up and played, and it was really amazing. Most of the kids are about 16, and some of them are high school drop-outs and the whole thing's run by this one young woman who doesn't get much funding. It's really bizarre.

"I think if people started schools like that all around the world it would make a difference because it's not just rhetoric, it's activity, which is what Riot Grrls mean when they're talking about empowerment. It's all about confidence."

Not every girl or woman feels the need to affiliate with a group to find that kind of confidence, especially if she's past the isolation of adolescence and enjoying some degree of success. But Riot Grrls provide the option of strength in numbers for those who feel better joining forces. And by taking action they're inspiring each other and obliterating a lot of the "malicious bullshit", as Leeds Grrl Jane Richmond puts it. Especially in relation to making a noise. Of course, you need money and music lessons if you want to be a session musician for Phil Collins, but if you want to be Huggy Bear, you just need the nerve.

"I suppose if they all started to play properly and make nice records, it would be against what they're trying to do," says Emma from Lush. "*Q* readers won't be interested, but more open-minded people will be."

"Whether you can or can't play shouldn't matter in music," says Liz Naylor. "If you use that argument you might as well junk the history of rock music. The thing about music is that you can't define what's good, the whole argument is really redundant. So Genesis can play – so what? I watched Huggy Bear soundcheck at The Powerhaus and they just plug their guitars in and if it works, it works. But there was some asshole at the sound desk going 'Can you turn it up a bit love, it's cracking up in channel six.' It was all designed to intimidate them.

"There'll be the inevitable crop of bands and half of them will be clueless, but more interestingly there'll be more girl labels and sound engineers and women in the industry. Most women in the industry are PRs and there's a lot of good ones, but it's a job where you're one part nanny shepherding witless goons around, and one part sexy rock chick dominatrix. It's social work level again."

"IT WORRIES me, the way everyone's talking about Riot Grrl at the moment," says Emma, "it's beginning to sound like the 'Madchester' scene or something. But we're talking about women, not a city and some dance music, but half the population.

"When the first press piece came out about it, me and Miki were getting drawn into it by people saying we must be manipulated by men because we weren't Riot Grrls! It was like, 'Well hang on, we're women, so you're lumping us all together and then dividing us by saying well they're crap and they're good, and they're not trendy because they're not screaming and shouting!' In the end though, I think it's a good thing. It's much more far-reaching and deeper than any scene. But bands are the easiest way to start, and music is the easiest way to get through to people. And Huggy Bear are big music fans."

"I think it's pretty commendable not wanting to do any press," adds Miki. "If anyone's bothered to witness what's happened to most women in bands, they've basically come out of it totally distorted. There was all that foxcore stuff at one point, and it just seems that whenever any woman tries to use the press as a platform for her politics, she generally ends up being made a mockery of. Just having women journalists isn't enough, you need to have sympathetic women journalists."

"People think you have to be straight and male to play rock 'n' roll and go to clubs," says Come's Thalia Zedek, "but there's all kinds of people who are doing that stuff. Just before I left Boston they had a Riot Grrl night. There's a few bands there like Creamcheese and The Red Hot Vulvas, and I think it's really great, although I don't know that much about it. I'm going to have to get back there and find out what's going on, because I've always been friends with a lot of women musicians there, but there's a whole lot of new bands cropping up."

———————

THE GENERAL mass of assorted and sometimes conflicting opinions and methods surrounding Riot Grrls may have left them open to judgment from those who smugly reckon they've all got it absolutely worked out, but in a world which feels like a battleground too much of the time, Riot Grrls will continue to urge each other on to a better sense of themselves.

"It's a uniquely female thing, for women to consider things, and it's very easy for men to take the piss out of," says Liz Naylor, "but women are bound to feel more sensitive about so-called minority issues, because women are a so-called minority faction. We experience censorship ourselves. The thing about Riot Grrl is that there is no one manifesto. People are expecting some organised front for Riot Grrl, but I think that would detract from it."

Boys can keep their methods of organisation – since when have they been so effective anyway? Riot Grrls don't have to influence anybody but girls. This time, boys can come later.

Siamese Animal Men

■ **Barbara Ellen**
NME May 28 1994

he Manic Street Preachers revived Barbara Ellen's flagging interest in music journalism. Her trip to Bangkok was the funniest and most surreal she has ever been on with a band, and for months afterwards she kept receiving what amounted to politely worded death threats from Thai people, claiming she had "misrepresented" their country.

James, Barbara felt, was irritated by her, Richey couldn't stop talking (she ended up with five hours on tape, most of it coloured by whisky, on her part as well as his), Nicky hid in his hotel room and Sean was, well, enigmatic. Although she was alarmed by Richey's habits (cutting himself etc), she understood that it was none of her business. When he disappeared less than a year later, she was, along with everyone else, very sorry, but still feels proud of the way in which the band have continued their career. It showed guts, she felt, which is something the Manics have never been short of.

> "Bangkok's most serious problems are human ones ...
> Prostitution, crime, narcotics, and the exploitation of child
> labour (being) the chief among them."
>
> – *The Guardian* (1982)

"In Thailand, prostitution is an institution, one that is killing its people. In just nine years, one in 85 will have Aids."

– *The Independent* (1991)

"Look, I didn' t pay for intercourse. I would be too scared ... it was just masturbation, basically."

Do you do this sort of thing back home, do you call up escort agencies in Wales?

"No, of course not."

Then why feel free to do it here?

"I don' t know... Perhaps I did it because I knew that I' d be talking to the press... Perhaps I wanted to make a point about my sexuality."

– Richey Edwards, talking to the *NME*, Bangkok, 1994.

On our first evening in the boiling, stagnant sauna that is Bangkok in its hottest month, we join three of the Manics for a cruise down the River Chopraya.

Having arrived a couple of days earlier to acclimatise, the band were hard at work this afternoon signing CDs, posters and T-shirts for a scrum of over 3,000 Manics hysterics in the blistering heat. Their popularity in Thailand – "Gold Against The Soul" shifted 50,000 units, earning the Manics a platinum disc – is the reason they're here to play two nights at the local 2,000-capacity MBK Hall. A watershed booking: it makes them the first Western band of their kind (ie, below the stadium rocker senility-level) to play in Bangkok.

Nicky Wire is absent tonight, having slickly extricated himself from the excursion with dark references to the Marchioness disaster. The boat is, indeed, a wood, straw and spit shocker straight out of *Apocalypse Now*. On the plus side, once it starts moving, cruising dreamily alongside a riverbank littered with restaurants, bars, pocket-sized temples, and the odd sleeping destitute – it's the coolest we've felt all day. The day-time heat here is enough to send any self-respecting Westerner rabid. Nevertheless, travelling from the airport into the city-centre this morning had been a revelation of sorts. Stripped of the drama of darkness, Bangkok doesn't look like it's got the energy, the get-up-and-go, or even the bikinis to be the torrid meat-market of the world. The Thais we see look downtrodden, world-weary and distant, grumbling to themselves as they shuffle inches at a time through the dusty scenic abbattoir of their environment. Just like home really.

Even the poverty – the sun-bleached tumbledown shacks, the slum apartment buildings, the gorily emaciated cats and dogs – subsides as you near the centre, giving way to gaudy approximations of Western affluence. The sudden rash of luridly painted bars, lavish hotels, bustling stores and half-built office blocks underlining the Manics' belief that Thailand in general, and Bangkok in particular, is a developing economy about to boom. As Richey says, Thailand, with its "ports, cheap labour and resources to grow coffee crops", could well end up being the Japan of the 21st Century.

———————

"RIGHT, ARE we off to Pat-Pong then?"

Having gingerly disembarked from HMS Cat-Basket, we are now jammed inside the silver Manics-mobile, racing towards Bangkok's notorious Jailbait A-Go-Go district.

As party posses go, this is a disparate, half-hearted shower. There's myself, photographer Cummins, the ever-reluctant Sean ("I had some fun a couple of days ago, that's my lot for a while"), Richey, eyelids half-mast, his shoulders obscured by a billowing cloud of Silk Cut fumes, James, silent, save for the obsessive tap of his boots in time to the van stereo, and an entourage that includes a certain Rob Stringer, head of the Epic label. The living embodiment of capitalist evil, Stringer is to threaten me with libel lawyers more than once before the trip is over.

To get to the bars, one first has to navigate the bustling, brightly lit night market, pushing your way through hordes of stony-faced young men brandishing crudely drawn "menus" of sexual positions, shows and prices. Girls hang out of club doorways, bullying, cajoling and, at times, openly intimidating people into entering. For no particular reason we end up in one called The King's Castle; any remaining PC reservations lurking within the group psyche swiftly evaporating in the face of our genuine astonishment at the lameness of it all.

As Sean later remarks: "It just looked like a '70s Miss World competition." Dark and a-throb with dated dance music ("Rhythm Is A Dancer" is practically the national anthem over here), this could be any provincial disco-dive the world over. Except, that is, for the 20 or so pretty young girls in cheap floral swimming costumes dancing vacantly on a central stage.

Scraping their punishingly high stilettoes back and forth across the chipboard platform, the girls – some obviously under sweet 16 – shimmy grimly against the silver poles, their faces zombie-masks, their movements riddled with a laboured suggestiveness that is more *Seaside Special* than *Electric Blue*.

The mainly middle-aged clientele, leering, jelly-bellied Western eyesores to a man, lap it up. It doesn't seem to occur to them that they're sitting in what is probably an HIV-supermarket. Or that, as far as these working girls are concerned, all Westerners are just human fruit machines with the arrow stuck permanently on "jackpot".

The only dilemmas these moral incontinents grapple with are ones of choice: Which girl? Which condom to avoid wearing tonight? Which duty-free perfume to buy for the wife on the plane home? It's all very sordid, very pathetic and, strangely enough, sexless in the extreme.

Isn't it, Manics?

James: "Well, I haven't got a hard-on."

Sean: "I find it very sad that a girl in a swimming costume is all that's required to turn some men on."

Richey: "Very lame, it's male fantasy for an older generation. Just an opportunity for middle-aged businessmen to buy women and feel like studs again."

Sean sits slumped, glumly indifferent, in the corner. James rests back in his seat, eyebrows arched, chuckling every now and then at the torrent of lad's talk spewing from the Cummins/Stringer corner. Richey slides into the seat next to me, and with an awesome articulacy – considering he's drinking as heavily as everyone else – starts talking about what he sees as the misguided liberal snobbery aimed at Thailand.

"All developing economies abuse their young. When Britain was a developing economy we sent our children up chimneys and down coal mines and out into the street to steal. This is just abuse on a wider scale.

"When we ask the Thai people about these girls they say that most of them want to be here. Some get sold here by their families, especially if their parents are drug addicts but a lot are here basically because some kind of flat and sanitation at the heart of the city is better than what they had."

The day before the *NME* arrived, the Manics had been taken to a TV station, passing through areas of extreme destitution described by Sean as "that typical ITN newsreel of total abject poverty".

"It was horrendous," rages Richey. "It's hard for us to imagine what it's like to live in a zinc hut in 125-degree heat with no sanitation and basically no future. Who can blame these people for getting out any way they can?"

We move along to other bars. More wooden-gyrating; more frankfurter waving boneheads drooling down their shell-suits.

By this time, no-one's even pretending to be scandalised. Somewhere along the way (probably ten seconds after entering the first bar), we have become de-sensitised to our surroundings, journalists, musicians and even record company heads all merging into one blurred scrum of loutish Western degeneracy in search of alcohol.

As James points out: "We all used the classic get-out clause. Let's not get moralistic, let's not question any economic factors or anything. We're here just for a drink."

———————

THE FOLLOWING eve, the Manics play the first of two sell-out nights at the MBK Hall. A crushingly hot auditorium located inside a supermarket complex, the venue has the look and feel of half a Wembley Arena crossed with an inner-city school gym. The crowd mill around expectantly, some modelling home-made Manics T-shirts ("Fuck Me And Leave"), others punked up in bondage gear, knee-length kilts and clumpy suede creepers. They look both comical and divine.

So much for Asian reticence. From the first moment the Manics crunch into the set, the fans explode into a churning sea of flagellating chaos, matching their heroes howl for howl, po-go for po-go. This is, after all, a section of the world's youth that has until now been fed a live aural diet of Santana/Bryan Adams/John Denver pop-slop. No wonder they're ready to puke. No wonder they're ready to gorge themselves stupid on a rock band they can actually *taste*.

Instead of bouncers, armed police stand in front of the stage shining torches into the crowd. Others patrol the periphery. It's all a bit off-putting. The ones at the front are even using cattle-prods to keep the front few rows away from the weedy-looking barrier separating the crowd from the front of the stage. For the main part, though, the police keep a low profile, acting as unlikely nursemaids to the casualties being dragged from the thrashing fan-ocean (one of whom breaks a leg).

As Nicky later remarks, "In all honesty, some British bouncers are probably a lot more violent."

To avoid encore hell, the Manics fulfil contractual obligations to play a longer set with a short James Unplugged solo spot (tonight "Democracy Coma", and an achingly cute rendition of "Raindrops Keep Falling On My Head"). Once that's finished the rest of the band return to wail, soar and reel their way through "Motorcycle Emptiness" and "You Love Us".

But, however gloriously Nicky preens, however frenziedly Sean drums and however high James jumps, it becomes increasingly hard to tear your eyes away from Richey. He stands stage left, knees bent, head thrown back, body twitching as he scrapes haphazardly at his guitar. He looks so beautiful, so tortured, so ridiculously rock 'n' roll it takes a while before you notice the blood coursing down his naked torso. He's slashed himself several times across the chest with a set of knives given to him by a Thai fan earlier that day.

A LAD insane or what?

"The only people who are disturbed by Richey cutting himself are those who don't know him," observes Sean witheringly. "They don't understand... We do know him, we do understand."

What's there to understand Richey?

"When I cut myself I feel so much better. All the little things that might have been annoying me suddenly seem so trivial because I'm concentrating on the pain."

He smiles serenely.

"I'm not a person who can scream and shout so this is my only outlet. It's all done very logically."

———

THE NEXT day, the message comes through that the ceiling of the room beneath the hall is on the verge of collapse: could the Manics please play quieter tonight? (HA! No chance).

Watsana – a local radio jock cum fireball rock chick who was instrumental in the Manics playing here in the first place – also gives the band a gentle but firm ticking off for dissing Thai royalty onstage the previous night. Not only did the Manics bloody-mindedly play "Repeat" (opening line: "*Repeat after me: fuck Queen and country*") against Watsana's advice, Nicky topped it off by ill-advisedly shouting immediately afterwards: "Long live the King! May he reign in hell!" Ill-advised in that the Thais take their royalty very seriously. You would too if the alternative involved spending the rest of your life in leg-irons.

When I catch up with Nicky back in his room later he admits to being "completely paranoid, shit scared".

"It's like *The Trial* by Kafka," he quakes, "the way they pick on this fella for no reason and he has to put up with it all. I feel like an arbitrary power can just arrest me and take me away and put me in prison for life and there's nothing I can do about it.

"It makes you realise how free Britain is. For all its supposed oppression, it's not really. It's probably one of the freest democracies in the world." His voice crumbles slightly. "That's the truth, unfortunately."

You really are homesick aren't you?

He sighs.

"I suppose I am. I always get homesick but yeah, ... more so this time."

Nicky Wire may be decadence personified onstage, but off-duty he's so quiet, so loath to leave his room, any forays he does make into society are greeted with the kind of awe usually associated with UFOs or the Second Coming.

There's nothing sinister about it. Not only does Nicky not drink (which rules out going out with us at night), he simply can't be bothered with new cultural experiences, especially ones that have to be taken first hand in a climate that has Satan controlling the thermostat.

"Perhaps I am xenophobic in the sense that I find it very hard to fit in in other countries. Then again," he muses, "I find it equally hard to fit in in Wales sometimes."

In the calm of his room, air-conditioning cranked up colder than Siberia, Nicky ponders on Pat-Pong ("I could never go there. I couldn't even go and see a stripper. Probably because I'm really close to my mother"); Cobain's death ("I find the idea of him taking his own life frighteningly powerful. I've always been a sucker for that."); and his past as a press darling ("The yobbish element comes from my mouth. It's the weakest part of my make-up").

1993 wasn't a great year for the Manics. What with the death of their friend, mentor and PR Phillip Hall, the release of a second gold album "Gold Against The Soul" that Nicky has now reassessed as perhaps too stretched, too ambitious ("We were just looking for that big hit") and their continuing frustration at not even getting gigs in America, never mind cracking it ("It's ridiculous. We're working on our third album and we've only played there five times"), 1994 is, for them, a chance to start over. Not from first punky scratch perhaps (as Nicky points out, "James and Sean are too advanced musically for that"), but at least recovered from the knocks of the recent past. With this in mind, there's an album scheduled for autumn and a sonic-powered double A-sided single ("PCP" / "Faster") out now.

"I had more to do lyrically with 'Faster'," says Nicky. "It's not a post-modern nightmare number, it's more a voyeuristic insight into how our generation has become obliterated with sensations. We could deal with things but we prefer to blank them out so that virtually every atrocity doesn't have that much impact any more. I don't even know if that's a bad thing. I don't know if we're not on some kind of path to a superbeing where all emotions are lost and everyone finally gets on perfectly because of that.

"The world is such a violent place. What we experience from the everyday world, what we read and what we see makes you realise that there's worse and worse things happening all the time. Perhaps," he concludes thoughtfully, "it might reach such a low point of existence something good may come of it."

―――――――

WHEN MYSELF and Cummins arrive down in the hotel lobby to accompany the band to soundcheck, we can feel hot little eyes scrutinising our every move. The Manics' Thai fans are a different breed altogether from the poor wretches in Pat-Pong. Many are affluent student-types who think nothing of waiting around the hotel lobby all day for a snatched glimpse of their quarry. Some even go so far as to shadow the band's van's every move in tuk-tuks (Bangkok's tourist taxi buggies).

The ones who haunt the lobby soon get bored, and suddenly any Westerner who's ever been seen having any conversation, however one-sided and occasional, with a band member is immediately added to their sprawling list of People To Get Photographed With. I lost count of the number of times I spotted some roadie, or some lighting man, or some Head Of Epic grinning into a brace of flashing cameras only to be tossed contemptuously aside when the real McCoy turned up.

The band are carefully polite to these diehards (Sean: "I don't mind so long as they don't keep me talking too long"), quietly accepting that, for now at least, Bangkok's alternative music fan-base is made up of middle-class camera-clickers. As Richey says. "If you're poor in a developing country there's more important things to spend your money on than music. If you've only got enough money to buy food, buying an album isn't high on your list of priorities."

That said, the Manics' second night at the MBK Hall turns out to be about as life-affirming as you can get. They are atomic, from the opening bars of "Motown Junk" to the final, crazed, guitar-trashing moments of "You Love Us". Nicky ripping off the dress he'd sauntered back on in after James' singularly cathartic solo spot (raindrops will keep falling on his "*fucking head*", apparently) and posing on the monitors, a vision of anorexia, anaemia and salaciously brief underpants, until the audience can take no more.

When we get backstage, Richey is wrapped up in a big, white fluffy towel cuddling a huge Snoopy; one of the many presents given to the Manics they end up ditching before they get to the airport (they're all "stuffed with heroin", anyway, according to Nicky). The band make their way down to the van. At one of the lifts, there's a mass of fans who discard their normally demure demeanour to indulge in an orgy of clothes-rending and high-octane shrieking that only abates when the lift-door closes. When the van moves off, the same fans appear, rushing out of a side door. The poor lambs have run down six flights of stairs just to watch the van's tail-lights disappear round the corner. Well, at least it keeps them fit.

On arriving back at the hotel, we embark on another night of hell-raising, starting with a full pack of Manics (watching football on satellite TV in a Brit-bar), and then carelessly losing them one by one until finally only James remains. We've arrived, via a sordidly circuitous route, at a grisly late-night drinking toilet. I use the word toilet advisedly. You have to wade – ankle-deep in used

condoms, beer bottles and macabrely-hued pools of urine –
through a genuine toilet to get to the bar. That should give you
some idea of the kind of sty it is.

Stringer, recoiling in terror from a moustachioed Dutchman who
appears to have taken a fancy to him, says in awestruck tones,
"Christ! It's just like the bar-room scene in *Star Wars*," and he's
right. May the force be with us.

James puts my hat on his head and lolls back in his chair necking
beer, curiously at home with the situation. In fact, throughout the
entire trip he's been looking curiously at home with any situation
that involves alcohol, lads-talk and 80 Marlboros. Whereas previously it was Richey and Nicky who were the decadent Glamour
Twins of the Manics – Sean and James exuding a more serious,
high-minded charisma – now James is the first to admit that the
balance within the band has changed.

"Nicky and Sean are still true to the way we were, true to the
spirit of the Manics, whereas Richey and I are tending to lose
the plot a bit."

In lots of ways, James is the most prickly, hard-to-know Manic.
Mulishly stubborn on all manner of ridiculous subjects (Londoners
are the Devil's Children apparently. They don't "even watch telly
properly"), he is a bristling jumble of barbed silences, self-igniting
fuses and lippy put-downs.

James is a Guy's Guy, a Marlboro Man, a pumper of weights and
the only person I know who's ever used a hotel pool for swimming
in instead of lounging beside with a beer. A devout anti-bullshitter,
his inveterate rudeness actually masks a certain shy charm. He
even opens doors for women, which I, for one, dart through swiftly,
just in case he comes over all Marlon Brando and decides to push
me over and beat me up. He's got that kind of vibe about him.

What does he think of Bangkok?

"Enjoying it. I've never been on an 18–30s holiday before … I just
feel like a complete lad."

How is this manifesting itself?

"Drink, and slight irreverence to women I suppose. I don't feel any need to be accepted by women whatsoever which is the way I've always felt, so it's reassuring to be me for once."

(Thank you, Monsieur Misogyny.)

Have you learnt anything?

"Only that there's no point in being a willing passenger and then trying to draw the line. It's such a classic middle-class thing to have a good time and then look in the mirror and you don't recognise yourself. Well, I'm sorry but I didn't look in the mirror and there wasn't a time I didn't recognise myself. I just got pissed."

Stringer is becoming hysterical. The moustachioed Dutchman wants him to take some heroin through customs in his bum. It's time to leave. James hurls my hat back – now stretched into a strange oblong shape (cheers) – and we make our way home.

———

OUR SECOND to last day in Thailand is spent mooching amidst the glittering golden magnificence that is Bangkok's Grand Palace. I'd considered myself quite decorously dressed in a knee-length Natalie Merchant floral number, but the guards don't agree. I am pronounced a harlot and made to go to a small, stinking room and don a skirt so long and voluminous it almost has a train.

For all its opulent curves and gem-encrusted passages, the Grand Palace doesn't particularly impress the Manics. Sean, the master of the stark put-down, later likens it to a "gaudy Essex nightclub".

That night, the Manics party posse once more takes to the go-go bars of Pat-Pong. This is our last chance to feel guilt, pity (anything) for the poor young girls clomping miserably about the stage. We blow it badly.

Not only do two of the males in our party accept a young girl's offer to let them squeeze her breasts for the equivalent of 40p (complaining loudly afterwards: "They haven't got much, have they?"), James bets Gillian the press officer 40 quid that she won't get up onstage and dance with the swimming costume brigade. She accepts the challenge, but then refuses to collect her winnings. In a fit of decadent, lordly pique, James rips up the money, admitting later:

"I was a complete lad the whole time we were in Bangkok. I took everything at face value like a complete brainless idiot. It wasn't even a matter of make sure you have safe sex because I didn't have any sex in Thailand..."

No, of course he didn't have any sex. No one did. Except Richey.

———————

BEFORE THE *NME* arrived in Bangkok, Richey travelled away from the cosy built-up region of the hotel into a side of Bangkok even seedier than Pat-Pong, whereupon he bought himself a hand-job from a prostitute in a brothel.

Before and after this little fact tumbled out, Richey and I were able to enjoy many spirited, inebriated discussions on all manner of topics. There's Richey's horror of PC-ness (which led to the writing of the apocalyptic "PCP"); his intolerance of all forms of censorship ("... shutting down the BNP could lead to so much. If you give any government the power to silence a political party, however dodgy, they will end up abusing that power"); his child-like side ("I agree that I do have a very child-like rage and a very child-like loneliness"); his non-child-like side (he's the only Manic who drives and he tends to organise everybody when manager Martin isn't around); and, of course, sex, because like Richey says:

"Coming over here, if nobody talked about sex and Pat-Pong it would be like ignoring it, pretending it didn't exist."

We're at the dank and stinking airport waiting for the plane to arrive and carry us home. Nicky has a wet flannel draped inelegantly over his head; James and Sean are stretched out on the floor; Richey and I sit a little away and discuss ... Richey.

Richey has a fear of relationships ("I've seen so many people get hurt or left. It looks terrifying") he even gets ratty with groupies who hang around waiting for a kiss after the sex ("There's no passion involved for me so it would be immoral to pretend there was").

With attitudes like these, and make no mistake Richey is crushingly, dangerously honest about them, it shouldn't really surprise any of us that he ended up in the arms of a prostitute. It might even be the best place for him.

Did you enjoy it?

"It was alright."

Was your hooker really young?

"Not especially."

What would you have done if you'd been presented with a 12-year-old?

"What do you think I'd have done?"

You tell me.

"I would never have even remotely considered it."

Richey sighs, exasperated.

"It's all done on such a business level the last thing they're going to do is stick a 12-year-old girl on you as soon as you walk through the door. A lot of people would just turn around and say 'Fuck this!' Some people might get turned on by it but a lot would find it too heavy. They wouldn't want to stay. I know I wouldn't have."

So, what was the point you wanted to make about your sexuality?

"I don't know really. Perhaps, just that I don't regard paying for sex as being that different to sleeping with a groupie. It's all done on the same functional level."

People are going to think you're a sexist asshole.

"Yes," he sighs, "that's what they will think."

Just another dumb Westerner going in and exploiting these people.

"They probably might, I know that, too."

We both stare straight ahead, too shocked to speak for a while. My head is reeling with images: the drink, the laughter, the bedlam, the shame. If Richey has spent a portion of his time in Bangkok in some sort of morality coma, he certainly wasn't the only one. Grabbing our bags, we run for the plane and home.

Rising Sons

■ Daniela Soave

GQ January 1995

Daniela Soave has cooked for many a band in her kitchen at four in the morning after a London gig, Oasis being no exception. She first met Noel Gallagher before his band were signed, and discovered they shared a passion for Neil Young. When she spent a week with Oasis in Japan, she managed to out-drink all of them, night after night, and has kept in touch with them ever since. On reading this feature of their Tokyo trip, Liam Gallagher gave Daniela a great big bear hug and declared, "You told it like it was."

It's 6pm on a September evening in Tokyo and already the sky is pitch black. As the Oasis tour bus noses its way out of traffic into a neon-lit side street, an ear-splitting shriek, louder than a wail of feedback, rips through the air. Hundreds of girls hurtle towards the vehicle, pounding on its windows, rocking it from side to side.

"I told you it would be like this," says singer Liam Gallagher, his eyes sparkling with anticipation.

"Here we go!" exclaims drummer Tony McCarroll. "Fucking hoorah."

There's little to equal the exhilaration of sharing a tour bus with the future of rock 'n' roll. Oasis, hailed as the most significant British band of the Nineties, have kicked off their seven-month world tour here, a move that has provoked mass hysteria in the normally restrained Japanese fans. As the tour bus crawls towards the tiny Club Quattro – where, in less than an hour, 500 people will find out why this five-piece from south Manchester inspires such a fevered response – the atmosphere is taut with excitement.

When the band step out into the night air, they are sucked into a vortex of arms, pulling them deep into the swell. Lavish gifts are thrust at them and luscious teenage girls leap forward to fasten their lips onto their idols. "Gi's a kiss, then," cajoles Liam, as a particularly stunning girl thanks him for an autograph. Her friends squeal with excitement, surging forward in the hope he will repeat the request with them.

I could be witnessing the second coming. And the irony is not lost upon the band for, more than any other, the success of The Beatles is what Oasis aspire to repeat. ("If you don't want to be as big as The Beatles," they are fond of saying, "then it's just a hobby.") In a country where John, Paul, George and Ringo are still revered beyond belief, Oasis are Japan's Fab Five. Hyperbole is their shadow, following in their raucous, rock 'n' roll wake.

Since the release of their debut single, "Supersonic" last spring, Oasis – Liam Gallagher, his older brother, guitarist and songwriter Noel, Tony McCarroll, bassist Paul "Guigs" McGuigan and rhythm guitarist Paul "Bonehead" Arthurs – have been the subject of more superlatives than any band in recent history. They make the hoo-ha attached to Suede two years ago pale into insignificance. Such praise is usually the kiss of death: how many times has a band been showered with accolades, only to sink into oblivion barely twelve months later? But with Oasis the fuss seems almost justified. Here, at last, is a rock group whose songs might just stand the test of time in the same way that the Stones or Stooges classics sound as vibrant today as when they first came out.

"Every now and then," confirmed *The Face*, "a band comes hurtling out of nowhere that stops you in your tracks and makes you re-evaluate everything." "Gigantic, roaring and life-affirming; these are the anthems for the next pop generation," proclaimed *Vox* in a live review. "Noel Gallagher is a pop craftsman in the classic tradition and a master of his trade," trumpeted the *NME* in a review of their August-released album "Definitely Maybe", the fastest-selling debut of all time.

"Noel has an intense, arrogant pride in his songwriting that I really like," says *Guardian* critic Adam Sweeting. "Rock 'n' Roll Star' is one of the finest songs of the last ten years: they really do make the best rock and roll din since The Clash. It's very nice to have a group we can wave in the face of the Americans and say 'fuck you'."

The critics have not been alone in their praise. The Lemonheads' Evan Dando, who followed Oasis round Britain like a star-struck groupie during their autumn tour, cites them as being the most important band of the moment. Neil Young's band, Crazy Horse, impressed by the calibre of Noel Gallagher's compositions, invited him onstage to play with them in London last June. John Peel, upon watching Oasis deliver a blistering rendition of "I Am The Walrus" at the Glastonbury Festival, told them that John Lennon would have approved.

With healthy record sales and an astonishing collection of unrecorded new material, Oasis could well be the first super-group of the Nineties. Yet Noel Gallagher remains sceptical about the fuss, saying it detracts from the music. "I don't think the kids who come to our gigs are arsed about how important we are, and I don't want them to be," he says in Club Quattro's cramped dressing room, moments before he is due onstage. "It's entertainment you know, just like turning on the telly. Nobody should worry about whether it's important or not. Bollocks, man. You shouldn't even think about it. If it makes you feel good, if it makes you jump up and down, if it makes you cry, just do it. Don't worry about it."

WHEN OASIS stroll onstage and Noel's lead guitar slams straight into "Rock 'n' Roll Star", it's evident, despite Noel's protestations, that the audience agree with the god-like status conferred upon them. Japanese audiences are renowned for being the most reserved in the world, but here they roar with approval and start corkscrewing en masse.

As a front-man, Liam Gallagher is still discovering his power. He spits out Noel's lyrics with the panache of his two heroes – Lydon and Lennon – over a wall of sound provided by Bonehead, Guigs and McCarroll. For the most part, he is oblivious to the audience. His microphone is placed so that he has to crane his neck to meet it, eyes squeezed shut. He swaggers about insolently, carelessly shaking his crescent-shaped tambourine, or sings with his hands clasped behind his back, occasionally catching somebody's eye in the audience. Then he waves artlessly and the entire crowd melts.

By the time the band hurl into their pulsating version of "I Am The Walrus", the audience is ecstatic. Layers of guitar and Liam's sneering vocals swirl around the auditorium for what seems like an age, yet at ten past eight the show is over. The audience look wrung out. It feels like the early hours of the morning.

Backstage, in the dressing room, even more presents and cards – mostly Beatles memorabilia – have been delivered. "What am I going to do with all these?" asks Liam, as he regards the pile of expensive books, rare discs and posters. "I've got a whole fuck-ing room full already."

OASIS CAME together in its present form three years ago when Noel – then working as a guitar roadie for indie band The Inspiral

Carpets – came back to Manchester and hijacked his brother's group. Their songs, he proclaimed, were diabolical, but if they agreed to him calling the shots and writing all the material, they were guaranteed to go far.

Having signed to Creation Records in autumn 1993, whispers of The Next Big Thing began to reach London where seasoned industry insiders took the news with a liberal pinch of salt. A one-sided white-label demo of their song "Columbia", circulated at the end of the year, proved exactly why Oasis were special: bursting with an insolent groove and sinister overtones, it rocked right off the turntable. Live reviews further confirmed they had barrel-loads of attitude and the songs to match. By the time Oasis played their first London gig at the end of January 1994, more than 200 people had to be turned away from the 300-capacity venue.

Underlying the media furore was the quality of Gallagher's compositions, which draw from a musical vocabulary that includes a reverence for John Lennon, Neil Young, the Faces, the Stones, T Rex (as heard in their single "Cigarettes And Alcohol"), the Stooges and even the New Seekers. Yet for all Gallagher's influences, which he blatantly wears on his sleeve, there is something refreshingly original in his work. He takes hints of favourite songs and pays homage to them by turning them into something new.

"I think that's what music lacks," he says. "A lot of bands are too inward-looking. They're all trying to create something original, but the guitar went as far as it could go 30 years ago. I think people love our songs because they connect with them right away. The best thing John Lennon ever said was how he always went for the most obvious melody he could get, no matter how naff it sounded. And I agree. The best songs are the most obvious because the listener becomes part of the record and knows the chord change before it happens. It's like when I first heard 'Hey Jude' I immediately picked up the guitar and played it. And I was only twelve at the time."

The influence of The Beatles has never really faded in Japan, as each new generation has grown up with the songs of Lennon and McCartney. Consequently, although there is a homegrown music scene, Japanese fans reserve their passion for British and American bands, subscribing to foreign rock weeklies and monthlies, from which they voraciously devour all new information about their idols. It was in these pages that they first noted Oasis. When tickets for the Japanese concerts went on sale months in advance, they sold out within two days even though, at the time, Oasis had yet to release a record there. Now it's almost as if this generation of Japanese music lovers has decided to adopt them as their very own Beatles, Nineties style.

That much is evident when the band turn up, after their last gig in Tokyo, at The Cavern Club, one of Japan's numerous Beatles clubs, where a four-piece called The Parrots are doing justice to a Beatles repertoire. There is a noticeable frisson as we walk into the club. We are followed by a trail of fans who have shadowed us from the venue.

"Fucking tops, I'm going to live here," spouts Liam as the hits keep coming. The Parrots' singer launches into an indecipherable spiel, in which we recognise the word Oasis. He's asking Noel to do a song with them. Liam's lower lip sticks out like a shelf. He's sulking. When asked why he doesn't join his brother onstage, he erupts: "'Cos I'm not the fucking star!"

The kohl-eyed boy is still coming to terms with being a popstar. Having just turned 22, Liam is an unpredictable, volcanic source of pent-up emotions, often at odds with himself and, sometimes, with his older brother: a situation that has been known to descend into fisticuffs and silent, simmering, weeklong feuds. Gallagher senior, at 27, is less vocal but more focused. His confidence in his band and his talent seems to be so unquestionable that it borders upon insolence.

Still, the bedlam surrounding their tour has astonished Noel, who experienced Japanese audiences when he was a roadie.

"I said to this lot, don't expect too much because the crowds are a bit reserved. Then we walked on stage the first night and the crowds were going wild and stage diving. We've had girls hanging round hotel foyers until seven in the morning, we've been mobbed wherever we go, and we've been given the most incredible presents." Most extravagant so far: a Jean Paul Gaultier jacket.

Oasis certainly embrace the rock 'n' roll lifestyle with gusto. Their reputation as hotel-trashing, drug-loving, alcohol-swilling shag-monsters goes before them. There are tales of them being thrown out of hotels and even deported – from Holland after causing a riot on a cross-channel ferry, and from Sweden after going on the rampage with Primal Scream. In a recent incident, a table was hurled out of a window at London's infamously laid-back rock hotel, the Columbia, resulting in them being banned – it landed on the windscreen of the manager's Mercedes. And, allegedly, Bonehead has sometimes had to play an entire tour for nothing because his wages have gone on hotel repair bills.

The trashing of hotels and taking of illegal substances are not on the agenda in Japan, yet Oasis have lived up to their party image. Although they have had only one night off and there is a fair amount of travel between gigs, nobody has seen their bed before breakfast. Every night after the show, the group trail off to some club or other, where free drinks flow and beautiful girls cluster around the band. And then it's back to the hotel for duty-free alcohol swigged from tooth mugs, games of football in the corridor and scores of giggling, drunken girls singing down the telephone line to Creation Records' MD in London.

Everyone has existed on a diet of cigarettes and Jack Daniels and as the tour progresses, it begins to take its toll. Guigs' eyes are almost black and blue from over-partying; Liam's voice is shot to bits by too many cigarettes; and Bonehead, after one particularly heavy session, is almost too ill to make it through the penultimate gig.

Missing from the action is the almost customary punch-up be-tween the two Gallaghers. Instead, in typical drummer fashion, Tony McCarroll appears to be chief whipping boy. One night, while claim-ing my hotel key from reception, I chance upon Guigs and Liam, who make no attempt to hide a full-flung argument with him.

"You've got three weeks to prove yourself or you're out," Liam snarls, jabbing his finger dangerously close to Tony's eye. "You've rubbished my brother and the reason we're all here is because of him."

———————

THE JAPANESE tour is drawing towards a close and, in Nagoya, I watch the final gig from the side of the stage to see what the band have been looking out on. Girls cram tight against the barrier, arms outstretched, looks of pure adoration painted across their faces; boys sport Manchester City football shirts in honour of the band's favourite team. The crowd jump up and down as one; you can see the steam rising as they get wet-ter. They're crowd surfing! This is unheard of in Japan. They haven't quite got the hang of it and the surfers keep sinking back down into the crowd, as if a black hole has swallowed them up.

Liam is getting emotional. "You're the best fans in the world," he tells the crowd. "I mean it."

When "I Am The Walrus" shudders to a halt the band are reluctant to leave the stage. "Thank you very much," says Liam. "Thank you for all your letters and presents." He throws his tambourine into the crowd. There is much shaking of hands. Tony throws all his drumsticks into the air.

But the crowd isn't having any of that. They stomp their feet, clap and chant for a full quarter of an hour. The promoter looks amazed: normally, Japanese fans clap politely for a few minutes before filing obediently out of the venue. And then Oasis march back on stage for a rare encore. "Can we have our drumsticks back please?" asks Liam. Reluctantly two people give up their prize. The band bursts into "Rock 'n' Roll Star" as if its words have new meaning.

Back at the hotel the lobby is packed with chattering girls waiting to thrust presents and cards upon the group. As they wander up the corridor, one of the band calls out: "Lads! These two lesbians are offering to put on a live sex show in one of our rooms!" Sounds of guffawing and whooping ensue.

"I can't stand these groups who whine on and on about how tough life is on the road," says a raddled-looking Guigs. "If they don't like it, they shouldn't do it. We love it and we go for it. There's no other way to do it."

The party continues in Liam's room. There are girls all over the place. Noel is listening to the tape of tonight's show with a cluster of admirers at his feet. Over in the far corner, one girl is lurching around precariously, rather the worse for wear. "Here!" snaps Liam, shoving the waste paper basket under her nose. "Don't you be sick on my bed. If you're going to throw up, do it in this, you hear?"

I become aware of someone stroking my thigh. It is one of the girls sitting next to me. "Did you know you are a really sexy woman?" she says. "I would really like to make love to you."

"How lovely of you to say so," I reply politely. Luckily her attention is diverted by the very drunk girl keeling over. I decide to make my exit – it's well past five and we have to check out at 10.30.

LESS THAN four hours after I bade him good night, I'm sitting in the hotel restaurant pouring tea and facing an equally bleary-eyed Noel Gallagher. He didn't get much sleep either.

"See after you left?" he says through a mouthful of toast, "I went back to me own room and fell asleep. I half heard the door opening, someone undressing, and then felt my bed covers being peeled back. It was that drunken girl. I was going, 'Could you get out of my bed please?' And she was just mumbling incoherently and then she passed out. I was sitting on the edge of the bed, scratching my head and wondering what to do, when Mark (Coyle, co-producer and sound engineer) walked in. So we just carried on drinking instead."

On the journey to Narita Airport, there's an air of sadness as the band realise this is the end of the Japanese tour. The next day Oasis begin their first major tour of America. For the next five weeks, home will be a twelve-berth bus with no shower and only limited toilet facilities.

The younger members of the band, particularly Liam and Guigs, are eagerly anticipating the experience, while old hands such as Margaret, the tour manager, and Noel take a more sanguine approach. Liam makes no bones about how he thinks his twat older brother is going soft.

Listening to a tape of last night's gig on the tour bus stereo, some of the band and crew start singing along to "Digsy's Dinner". Liam is smouldering. "Look, just shut the fuck up and listen, will youse?" he yells. There is an embarrassed silence. The song plays on. "These could be the best years of your life," echoes Liam's voice through the speakers.

The Vanishing of Richey Manic

■ **Gina Morris**
Select May 1995

ichey Edwards of the Manic Street Preachers disappeared from London's Embassy Hotel on February 1st, 1995. He has never been found. Many people believe he is still alive – apparently before he vanished he was investigating the perfect disappearance, and, as journalist Simon Price once said, if anyone could do this, Richey could. He was easily intelligent enough. But no one knows for sure what has happened to him. His unfinished tale has become one of rock culture's biggest mysteries.

While Gina Morris was researching this piece for *Select*, she received no co-operation from the band, their management or their press office because Richey had only been gone a few months and those who had been close to him were still very hurt. Consequently this was the most difficult piece Gina has written because although she never wanted to adopt the methods of a tabloid reporter, she was uncomfortably aware of coming close to feeling intrusive and insensitive.

RICHEY EDWARDS is 22, and he weighs just under six stone.

In his third year studying Political History at the University of Wales in Cardiff, he's diligently revising for his finals, but he's having difficulty sleeping. It's important to rest properly, but there's

so much noise at night that he just lies in bed waiting for uncon-sciousness. So he starts drinking vodka, just to get to sleep at the right time, to be in control. Progressively, he begins to drink a lot and eat very little. But when the exams start, alcohol no longer provides enough control for him.

One day, poring over his revision, he reaches across the desk for a compass. He digs the point into his arm and draws it slowly across the flesh in a series of straight cuts. A lot of other people at university have cut themselves like this. But it's to be the first time Richey's friend James Dean Bradfield has ever seen him wil-fully injure himself.

─────────

IN THE last four years, the Manic Street Preachers have burned themselves into the popular imagination in a way that once, no one would have thought possible. When they arrived in kohl, blouses and a welter of contradictory sloganeering, they were laughed at, widely detested and, frankly, not very good. Now, after three scabrously brilliant LPs and a decade's worth of trauma, they're held in genuine affection and respect, and their following is as fanatical as The Smiths' ever was.

The Manics' achievement has been to take the boiling stew of rage, hatred and alienation that we usually suppress and dismiss as adolescent angst, and make it as relevant to an older audience as it is to a teenager. Listen to "Motorcycle Emptiness" or the later, more sophisticated songs like "Faster", and you'll feel that resentment rising again. Other bands allude to modern cul-ture's bankruptcy and corruption: the Manics confront it squarely, time and again, and their moral revulsion has never faltered.

Much of this is down to the ideological wing of the band, Nicky Wire and, ever more dominantly, Richey James. Being an angry pop band is not all that difficult – all you need is a guitar and a sneer – but there's little mileage in *"Fuck you, I won't do what you tell me."* What the Manics managed, in their transition from the comical soundbite Rude Kids of "Suicide Alley" to the sophisticated nihilists of "The Holy Bible", was to stay intellectually angry without lapsing into pretentiousness or sermonising.

Richey was once lampooned as a kind of blouse-wearing Bez. But by the time of "The Holy Bible" he was unquestionably the band's lynchpin, and James Dean Bradfield once said that "If it ever comes to the point where Richey's not coming back, we won't continue". His words became less song lyrics than fight-them-to-the-last-paragraph ideological battles, both at odds with Sean and James' anthems, and exactly what made the Manic Street Preachers so important.

But Richey's ever desperate struggle with the world outside involved him in an internal arms race that, even with his arsenal of literary weaponry, it seems he could never win. On February 1 this year, on the eve of a promotional American tour, Richey disappeared without trace.

RICHARD JAMES Edwards was born on December 22, 1966 in Gwent, South Wales. He had a happy childhood no different from that of thousands of other kids all over the country. He was brought up by his grandmother and his parents – in the bungalow at the foot of a steep cul-de-sac in Blackwood where they still live. They treated him well. He had a dog he christened Snoopy. He went to school, came home and played football in the fields. He went to chapel on Sundays. "A lot of people," he said later, "had terrible childhoods, but up to the age of 13 I was ecstatically happy."

Even so, from an early age Richey believed that everything that happened to him was part of a wider pattern. Maybe he thought about things too much ... even at infants school, if something happened to him he'd be convinced everyone was against him. And as he grew older, he became a shy, private youth with very low self-esteem. He kept himself to himself. He didn't feel he had the right to intrude on anyone else, and didn't think anyone should necessarily want to listen to him. By the time he started attending Oakdale Comprehensive at the age of eleven, the blissfully content child was already withdrawing.

As Richey approached adolescence, he became an insatiable learner with a huge appetite for knowledge, particularly of history and politics. At 14, he was fascinated with the IRA hunger strikers in Northern Ireland's Maze Prison, who refused to eat as they protested for political status. Later, he said that he felt Bobby Sands, who finally starved to death on May 5, 1981, made "a better statement than anything else that was going on at the t ime, because it was against himself".

BLACKWOOD IS one of those small towns you could easily drive all the way through from one side to the other without really noticing it. Richey, James, Nicky Jones and Sean Moore, who had all met at primary school, were in their early teens as the once-thriving pit town went into terminal decline along with the rest of the mining industry. The locals found work on three-month contracts at the Aiwa and Pot Noodle factories, and filled their leisure time with a brutalising regime of lager and after-hours brawls.

Alienated by the dead-end culture around them, the four boys became ever closer friends. Yearning for the excitement and inspiration of the world outside, they became a gang who would hang out in James' bedroom, obsessing about pop music. While other kids spent their nights in pubs, the foursome spent all their time together, drinking tea, reading William Burroughs and Hunter

Thompson, watching telly, devouring the music press and writing to almost everyone associated with the music business.

No one making records at the time could sum up how they felt about life. No one could articulate the bitterness and rage Richey felt. He wanted a band that sang about politics, that sang about a culture that said nothing, a culture that made him feel like a no-body, treated him like shit. Inspired by the ten years of punk celebrations of 1986, James, Nicky and Sean formed a band of their own, including one Flicker in their line-up. In the meantime, Richey had begun his University course in Cardiff. He had started drinking and had become increasingly burdened by his lack of self-worth and feelings of isolation and paranoia. He'd got three As in his A-levels, but he didn't think they were as good as other people's As; other people would look at him as if their As were better. He'd always set himself ridiculously impossible targets, expecting to fail.

He left University in 1988 with a 2:1 in Political History. Convinced that his decision to cut himself and not eat very much had paid off.

"I found that I was really good during the day. I slept, felt good about myself, I could do all my exams. I got a 2:1 so I wasn't a 100 per cent success, but I got through it. I did it."

In 1989, Richey replaced Flicker – because he was good-looking and had a smart guitar – as rhythm guitarist in the Manic Street Preachers.

———

IN AUGUST 1989, the band had pooled their giros and put out 100 7-inch singles of "Suicide Alley". They sold some through classified ads and sent the rest to bands, journalists, promoters, agents and record companies. At a gig in the small backroom of The Horse & Groom pub in central London in 1990, playing to about 30 people, they met Ian Ballard – the one-man operation

known as Damaged Goods Records – and agreed to record a
one-off single, "New Art Riot".

Ballard was surprised at how informed Richey was: "He must
have read books from day one while the rest of us were watching telly. He's very intelligent, I think he finds it difficult talking
to people who aren't similarly educated. He'd sit there quoting
things and I'd be nodding, thinking, I don't know what you're
talking about."

It wasn't until 1991 that the Manics really came to public
attention, releasing the singles "Motown Junk" and "You Love Us"
on Heavenly Records. At this time they were befriended by Philip
Hall, a devoted London PR who then became the band's manager.
Not only did Hall understand what they were trying to do, but he
believed in them enough to virtually finance them before they got
a deal, lending them £45,000. He invited them all to stay in his
home. Along with Philip's wife Terri, the six of them lived together
for almost a year. Every day, while Philip was out at work, they set
about cleaning his house. At six o'clock every evening, the Manics
would gather in the kitchen to prepare his tea. As scary, destructive
and rock 'n' roll as they appeared in public – with their protestations
about hating Slowdive more than Hitler and spraypainting sense-
less Situationist slogans on their clothes – in private they were im-
mensely charming and polite. Philip liked to say they were sweet.

In May, the band signed to Sony. They had their first music
paper cover, and with their make-up and slogans, quickly became a deeply contentious prospect. Misunderstood by people
who refused to accept that their ideas were genuine, they were
seen as a cartoon Clash espousing early learning punk rhetoric.
This both hurt and deeply affected Richey.

"The difference between me and Richey," Nicky Wire said last
year, "is he always wanted to be understood and I prefer to be misunderstood. I don't feel the need for people to love and respect
me. Richey really did. He couldn't take strength from the fact that
people didn't like him."

RICHEY HAD now taken to cutting himself frequently. In the evenings as they sat around Philip and Terri's living room watching TV, he would distractedly carve away at his arms. Often, someone would cough and nod at him to stop and he'd apologise. But it had become a habit. He subconsciously drew blood in the same way others would chew their nails.

But it was four days after the band signed their major label deal – on May 15, 1991, backstage at a gig in Norwich Arts Centre – that Richey's tendency towards self-mutilation became graphically public. An interview with Steve Lamacq, then of the *NME*, developed into a passionate argument. Lamacq expressed concern that the Manics' cartoon image would drag them down. He concluded by saying that "some people might regard you as just not for real."

After the interview, Richey asked Steve if he had a minute and they stood talking at the side of the stage. During their conversation Richey picked up a razor blade and, as he talked, began, slowly and deliberately, to carve something into his arm. Lamacq was dumbfounded. He couldn't believe what he was seeing: the words 4 REAL appearing in striated red slashes across Richey's skin. Lamacq was so shocked that the idea of trying to stop Richey didn't even occur to him.

"He was so calm, absolutely calm, and didn't look in any pain whatsoever. One of the things that was so strange and frightening about it was that he was so calm. You didn't even feel like he was making a point. He could almost have been writing it in biro."

Afterwards, in the casualty department of Norwich General Hospital, Richey insisted that all the patients with accidental injuries be seen before him, anxious not to waste National Health time on a self-inflicted wound.

The following morning, Richey rang up Steve to apologise for any distress he may have caused him.

"It never occurred to me he may be fucked up," says Richard Lowe, who interviewed Richey for *Select* shortly after the incident. "He seemed really level-headed. But running through the Manics was this 'life is futile, life is crap' idea. He really believes that. Everything for him is sad, he's not a happy-go-lucky person. He takes everything seriously, not just music. That's his problem. He feels personally burdened by everything horrible in the world. It upsets him and hurts him. That's the sort of person he is."

———————

THE 4 REAL incident was a clear demonstration of just how much the Manics in general and Richey in particular, meant what they said. Other bands would have just punched a journalist they disagreed with; Richey had a more effective means of emphasis. In the same way that he felt cutting himself had helped him through his degree, 17 stitches had proved his point. In his already unstable mindset, negative actions had positive effects. He felt vindicated.

"I never shout at anybody," he said later. "So if I cut myself or stub a cigarette out on my arm, to me it's a release.

"If somebody pushes me or punches me when I'm out in Cardiff, that hurts me more than having a couple of stitches in my arm. That's someone taking their frustration out on me, if I have a fair deal of contempt for humanity it's because it's never honest with itself. I'm weak.

"All my life I've felt weak compared to other people. If they want to crush me then they can. But I know I can do things that other people can't."

———————

THE RECORDING of the Manics' first and according to their original manifesto, supposedly last album "Generation Terrorists" was enormously stressful. In the studio Richey indulged in every kind of abuse. He cried a lot. And although he seemed able to sort himself out again quite easily, James was more worried about him than he had ever been before. It became common knowledge around this time that Richey had told James that if the band ever split up, he would have nothing left. The band continued. The LP was released in February 1992. Richey was rumoured not to have played a single note on it. The rest of the year they spent touring, including their first American dates. By December they were back in Britain in time for Nicky Wire's bizarre comments about Michael Stipe, onstage at their show at Kilburn National.

When they returned at the start of 1993, they began recording "Gold Against The Soul": some of it in a £2,000 a day studio in Surrey, complete with snooker tables and a swimming pool, the rest in the red light district of Cardiff. It was then that James, Nicky and Sean first realised Richey was having real problems. He was drinking increasingly more and his moods were at a constant low.

Andrew Collins (then *Select* features editor) who met Richey in the studio says: "Drink was his only recourse. It probably would have done him some good to have taken drugs. He never wanted to take E, hated the idea of it, he never wanted to take a drug that made him happy. He couldn't imagine anything worse than a drug that made everybody happy – he didn't think there was anything good in everybody being happy and thinking every-thing was OK. He preferred the traditional route of drinking to dull the pain."

Not being the kind of person you could tell to just stop drinking, the band sent him to a health farm. Twice. They practically forced him both times. He came out recuperated. But, once separated from daily routine, he soon deteriorated.

In December Philip Hall died of cancer. The band were shat-tered. The death of their manager, mentor and friend seemed to signify the start of their worst year ever. It made them realise, James said, that "things were coming to a head".

IN 1994, RICHEY Edwards finally moved out of his parents' home. He was 27. He saw a flat, liked it and bought it the next day. For the first few months of the year, Richey was smoking 40 cigarettes and drinking a bottle and a half of vodka a day. Everything he already ever was, felt and feared had massively intensified. The problems he experienced getting to sleep at university had escalated, he was now actually scared to go to sleep, things got into his head he didn't like. He'd tried sleeping pills but didn't like them either, and so he achieved what he described as a "blank sleep" from turning once again to alcohol.

In April they toured Bangkok, where Richey's second public display of self-mutilation occurred. He had been given a set of knives by a fan at a gig, who asked him to look at her when he cut himself. Horrified, he told her: "I'm not going to be anyone's circus sideshow freak." Even so, he took the knives backstage and proceeded to slash a series of lines across his torso, before walking out onstage.

He spent the night walking around the seediest parts of the city, alone. He went to a massage parlour and paid for a hand-job. "I'm not a very sexual person," he said later. "I don't need the physical closeness of a relationship and I'm afraid of the pain that goes with it, to be honest. Sleeping with someone, for me, is a change from wanking."

Richey had never been in a relationship. His idea of a sexual act was cutting himself. He's admitted to having sex with groupies, but insisted he'd only felt dirty afterwards. But his lack of interest in a relationship went much deeper than merely not enjoying physical closeness. "Some can divide themselves and give something of themselves to another person. I've never been able to do that because I've never trusted another person enough to do it. I don't feel strong enough to cope with the rejection if they left me."

——————————

BY AUGUST "The Holy Bible" was about to hit the shops. Their third album, it was unmistakeably Richey's. Sweeping away the shiny big rock sound of "Gold Against The Soul" in a squalling punk howl, it was a terrifying black hole of shrieking misery, a vision of the world almost too bleak to bear: anorexia, the Holocaust, totalitarianism; songs like "Die In The Summertime" and "She Is Suffering". Since the band started, Richey had been writing more and more of the lyrics, and for the seething horrors of "The Holy Bible" he'd written three-quarters of the words.

In the weeks immediately before the LP's release, he told his management he needed psychiatric help. He was suffering from nervous exhaustion and clinical depression. He was intensely irritable. After the previous health farm attempts, James admitted he never really thought it would go this far, that it all just went off, very unexpectedly. "There's a trigger in him that he can't control. He has a mental illness. It's not schizophrenia or anything like that, he's mentally ill. Manic depression."

The decision to seek help was Richey's. He knew his mind wasn't functioning very well and that his mind was stronger than his body: he was subjecting his mind to things his body couldn't cope with. He knew he was ill. Before, he had always felt he could handle his own problems. Now, for the first time, he was scared.

On the verge of anorexia, he went to a Cardiff hospital. There he was drugged on Prozac to the point where he couldn't even talk. This was no good. After eight days, Martin Hall, who took over management of the band after his brother Philip's death, discharged Richey and took him to a private clinic, The Priory, in Roehampton.

In the following months, the Manics played Glasgow's T In The Park festival and Reading without Richey. Tracing his friend's life over the preceding four years, Nicky Wire concluded that he'd been "walking the artistic abyss and he just fell in". Anorexia, he thought, was the ultimate act of self-control, a kind of suicide where you don't have to die. He had faith enough in Richey's sense of humour and humility to suggest that when he re-emerged he'd probably quip "I'd rather be mad than a moron". When Richey did re-emerge three months later, looking relatively healthy, he was apparently functioning normally: or, at least, as normally as he ever had.

He'd been prescribed Prozac to combat his long-term depression. He agreed to do interviews and spoke candidly about his experiences in an institution, on a 12-Step Recovery Plan. He talked positively about the upcoming dates in France with Therapy?, knowing he could use them to ease himself back into the band and playing live.

He'd been out of the clinic one week and seemed to be making good progress. Only Step Three had been causing problems: "Reconcile yourself to a god of your understanding." Richey regarded other people's choice of icon – friends, relatives, cats, dogs – as nonsensical. Surely their gods would one day die, something gods just aren't supposed to do. Nature seemed a good idea for a while, until he remembered how cruel nature can be. Never mind. He had no other obvious choices, but he'd figure it out sooner or later.

At the time, Richey called himself a melodramatic drama queen. He couldn't help the way he acted. In anything literary he'd always identified with the victim. Although he talked like someone fresh from a programme, he did his best to think positively. But when he took off his parka, there along his arms with the mottling of scar tissue from old cigarette burns, gashes and deep cuts, there were other, redder marks. They were the new ones.

RICHEY EDWARDS disappeared at 7am on February 1 from The Embassy Hotel, West London, on the same day he and James Bradfield were due to leave for America on a promotional tour. In the wake of the success of their three albums, along with current British successes Radiohead and Blur, the trip almost certainly would have broken them in the States, making them one of the biggest rock bands in the world. Bradfield's stadium power chords, with Richey's poetic lyrics of despair and self-loathing, would have reached an entirely new and considerably wider group of people. Part of the baffling tragedy of his sudden disappearance was that it happened on the verge of his band becoming just what he'd always wanted; a band who could articulate his bitterness and rage to a huge audience.

Early in January Richey shaved off all his hair after Snoopy, his dog of 17 years, died. A severe reaction for someone who made "all is vanity" his favourite epithet, lied about his age and periodically stopped eating in an attempt not to look fat or blotchy from alcohol abuse. At the same time as he shaved his head, he threw 80 per cent of his notebooks – filled with his lyrics in scribbled note form – into the river outside his house. Those which he deemed good enough to keep, he bundled up and handed to Nicky. A few days later, he disappeared.

THE STORY of Richey James Edwards is much more than the tale of another tragic rock star. Richey is not a rock 'n' roll burnout, someone who fried themselves on a cocktail of drugs, publicity and international travel. His is a darker story of something that has perhaps been waiting to happen to him for years. The grim possibility is that what made him such a brilliant artist, and the

Manics' records so unique, is precisely the same thing that
drove him over the edge.

Even the rest of the band, his closest friends for most of his life,
seem not to know. At the end of 1994, on the European leg of the
Manics/Suede tour, the normally taciturn Sean Moore sat at the
bar in an Amsterdam night club. Appalled at how people regarded
Richey's illness, he offered his own opinion. "No one knows anything about Richey, perhaps not even us. No one knows anything
about what's happened with him this year – it was serious total
depression. And you don't know anything about that until it happens in your own head, do you?"

The Year Skunk Broke

■ **Lucy O'Brien**
Vox September 1995

In Los Angeles with Skunk Anansie, Lucy O'Brien experienced one of her most enjoyable trips as a journalist. Not only did she find Skin a truly inspiring person to hang out with, but any artificial divide between journalist and band was completely broken down, thanks to the genuine attitude of everyone she met. In her resultant piece, Lucy managed to find out why Skin hates being labelled as the angry, bald, black lesbian, and exactly what has fuelled the volatile vision of her colleagues.

Less than a year ago, terror rockers Skunk Anansie were confined to London's indie hot spots like the Camden Monarch and King's Cross Splash Club. Having made an immediate impact in Britain on the strength of a couple of militant EPs, they are due to appear in a Hollywood film, *Strange Days*, with key members of the glitterati, Ralph Fiennes and Juliette Lewis. This is the band's big moment – such exposure means that they will be catapulted overnight from One Little indie cult status to American rock superstardom without having to do the interminable coast-to-coast US tour of duty. Or that's the plan. What follows is a diary of what really happened.

Thursday 12.30pm

"Shall I say: 'Excuse me, I think we're on the guest list?'" says Ace, the guitarist. We are at Gate Five, Heathrow, waiting to board the midday flight to Los Angeles. Only it's late, and there's an enormous queue, which grows longer by the minute. We are glumly watching the monitors when Louie, Skunk's new drummer, a long-haired lad from the Medway towns, comes rushing up to Ace. "Quick, quick!" he says. "Tony Iommi's downstairs."

"You're joking! My riff god hero!" says Ace, dashing off in search of the Black Sabbath guitarist. Later he explains the reason for his fan worship. "I grew up with Black Sabbath, I was obsessed with them as a kid. They were my favourite band. The two biggest riff merchants were Jimmy Page and Tony Iommi. Tony was the under-dog cos Page had the suave cool and big flares with a dragon up the side. He was a bit more art school. Whereas Iommi was a Birmingham dirty city lad who started in '60s blues bands and wrote classic riffs. It's the *Beavis and Butt-head* syndrome – it's Tony Iommi riffs they sing. We have the same accessible, straight-ahead riffs."

Words like "accessible" and "straightahead" don't immediately come to mind when listening to Skunk Anansie. Hardcore, maybe; challenging, yes. Within their cult vibe, though, is a mega-rock band aching to burst through. It was this quality that convinced Kathryn Bigelow, one of Hollywood's few female big-time direc-tors, with films like *Point Break* and *Blue Steel* to her name, that she needed them for her end-of-millenium movie, *Strange Days*. "When we sent a demo of 'Selling Jesus' to Kathryn she respond-ed so strongly to the song that they decided to re-shoot a seg-ment of the movie to fit in with the band," says Dave Massey, head of A&R at Epic, the group's label in America. Hence our four-day trip to downtown LA.

Friday, 10am

We're having breakfast in the hotel, an unassuming establish-ment on a leafy drive in West Hollywood. Surprisingly bright-eyed after the long flight, Skunk talk about the Rage Against The Machine gig they went to last night in a poor Hispanic section of LA. "Everyone was just standing around and then, when the gig

started, it all went off," says Skin, the band's striking, bald front-
woman. The moshing pit had become a free-for-all, with fists flying and bouncers going in for the kill. The band, however, were
no wimps. When a belligerent fan behind (bassist) Cass said,
referring to his dreadlocks: "Move that shit out my face, man."
Cass replied: "If you think it's shit, you move it." The guy stood
for a while in contemplation, decided the better of it and quietly
moved off.

Friday, 11.30pm

Friday night is Viper Room night, Johnny Depp's haunt on Sunset
Boulevard that since River Phoenix's death has been filled every
weekend with rubber-neckers, musicians and English tourists. A
relatively small place, it has a velvet and chintzy wallpapered
lounge bar, with a separate room for the dancefloor and tiny stage.

Naturally the place is rammed, even though the musical entertainment is a spangly trio playing disco covers rather than Depp's
own grunge outfit, P. Skunk amuse themselves trying to guess
the next song: "Boogie Nights"?, "Born To Be Alive"? No, it's
Chic's "Le Freak". Skin leads me down the front and sashays.
"Couldn't you just close your eyes and run your hand down his
torso?" she says of the lead singer, a guy with an improbable
Afro and a chest that looks like plastic.

Later we bump into the club manager on the stairs. "Would you
like to come to the office?" he asks Skin magnanimously. She
shrugs: "Yes, OK."

It may look like a regular office with a desk, several chairs and
monitors to spy on bar staff, but it is in fact the Innner Sanctum.
The room is full of Hollywood's alternative great and good, from
Julien Temple to producer George Drakoulias to Johnny himself,
who pops his head round the door, almost unrecognisable in his
thrift-store gear. Temple, who looks remarkably like Malcolm
McClaren, tells me about his new film, another urban end-of-
millenium affair starring (you guessed it) Johnny Depp. "It's a

projection into the '90s of what the world would be like if the '60s ideal had really happened," he says, laconically drawing in a cigarette.

Downstairs, Cass is hiding out in the bar, foregoing his opportunity to hobnob with Hollywood. The manager had introduced him to Depp earlier, saying: "Cass, this is Johnny. You know Johnny, don't you?"

"No."

"Johnny, you know, Johnny."

"No, I don't."

It was only later the penny dropped. "Never mind," says Cass philosophically.

By 2am, it's chucking out time and everyone, as Ace would say, is bladdered. Back at the hotel, Ace, Louie and Skin pile into the vodka, a garden chair is totalled, window box plants get thrown into the street, Ace collapses into a drunken heap, while Louie and Cass fall asleep. Skin surveys the boys snoring amid the wreckage. "Lightweights," she says. "Lightweights."

Saturday, 1pm

"Clit rock is slippery, wet, swollen and full on," says Skin, describing the Skunk Anansie sound. It's lunchtime and we are sitting by the pool with Ace, the sun hot on our backs. Skin acknowledges she is giving new meaning to the term "female-fronted band". "I'm not up there trying to be a babe. I'm sexual but not in a girly, wimpy way. Our music has attitude, it's in yer face, so I have my own parameters. Some women who front bands are very interested in pleasing males, they've got to be attractive to men, whereas I don't give a fuck." She says that it has less to do with her lesbianism than "a personal perspective on life".

Skin has had acres of press coverage – she's even done a photo session for *Elle*. Much is made of her penchant for face painting, her supermodel looks and the way she dives fearlessly off stage. She has been compared to every black female singer from Aretha Franklin to Grace Jones, yet in terms of delivery, she has more in common with Robert Plant. She is perplexed that because she sings very loudly and makes faces, people find her frightening.

"I may seem scary on stage but I don't walk around being scary 24-hours a day, I'm not that one-dimensional. I know I'm aggressive and in people's faces, but what's scary is you have someone like me doing that. If it was just a white guy no one would be scared. It's the old black lesbian thing – she's got a bald head, she's hard. It's almost taking away my femininity."

As the interview unfolds, it becomes clear what gives Skunk that vital cohesion as a band: each member is motivated by a personal sense of rage that is channelled into their music, from the declarative tones of their first single "Selling Jesus" to the more MTV-friendly yet sincerely perverse "I Can Dream". "We're all quite desperate, frustrated characters," says Skin. "We've always been fighting." Though affable and engaging off stage, there is gripping intensity in their grooves. "The band might seem really chilled," says Ace. "But if someone fucked with our thing, we'd kill them."

"I grew up in Brixton. You know the people you fuck with and those you don't," continues Skin. "People who walk around boasting are the pussycats. The hardest are those who sit and smile, yet if you cross them they go BAM! You know it yourself, if someone fucks with you, you'll deal with them. So we don't walk round trying to be Big Man Rock Star."

Skin and her three elder brothers were brought up almost single-handedly by her mother, a former nurse who went to nightschool and worked her way up to head the Environmental Department at Lambeth Council. In the same way that her mother fought for her vision, Skin gave up a good job as an interior designer ("I was the archetypal Buppie") to write songs. For years she did nothing but go to gigs and play in bands, honing her style until she, Cass and Ace connected through the North London Splash Club scene and launched Skunk Anansie.

Ace, meanwhile, comes from a "poorish, urban" background in Gloucestershire. His parents have always encouraged him to do what he wants, even if they don't quite understand it. His mother once said to him: "Why don't you play with The Brand New Heavies? They make records. They're nice." Part of a three-piece grebo band who lived it up around Gloucester for several years, Ace made money, partied and went out with all the girls before he realised that he had to fight to make something out of his music.

"You can spend the rest of your life in a small town and fill all the pubs out. I'd got to 24-years-old and I was going nowhere." He crashed and burned, destroying what he'd created through a "drink /drugs scenario" before moving to London. "I knew no one, had no money, nothing. But it was the best thing I ever did – it straightened me back out again. Now I'm happy in this band I don't need to go on benders. Adrian Sherwood once said to me: 'You gotta surround yourself with people you like and spend time with them. You build your little society of people and everyone else can fuck off.'"

We drive to Venice beach for a photo session amid the palm trees, muscle men and *Baywatch*-lookalikes on roller blades. Cass smiles for the camera, but on the way back becomes reflective as he tells me his story. Formerly a "violent nutcase" from a troubled family background in Ladbroke Grove, he grew up fighting. "Some of my friends are dead. Some are in prison, Some are still on the streets."

As part of his rehabilitation, Cass worked for Chiswick Women's Aid, stopping violent fathers from snatching their children. The founder Erin Pizzey took him under her wing, and he went with her family to New Mexico. For a year he built adobe huts in the desert, hung out with Indians and began to seriously play music. Until then he had only tinkered on the guitar of his best friend Mikey, the bassist who went on to huge success in Culture Club. "I'm a bit of a spiritual warrior," he explains. "Now I direct my aggression into music."

Louie, too, has found escape through music. A former session drummer for The Cure, he was a fan of Skunk Anansie before they asked him to audition. "They're real rock, none of this new wave retroshite." He talks dryly of his Cypriot father who, after his business folded, "fucked off to Cyprus and never came back". When I mention the strong female influence in the band, Cass says "I'm a firm believer in a matriarchal society. I've seen what a patriarchal society does, and it doesn't work for me. Sexism, racism, it's all the same thing. With men, testosterone fucks up thought patterns. All of a sudden your chest goes out, the ego comes out – d'you know what I'm saying?"

Saturday, 7pm

It's a warm summer night and Los Angeles Street in downtown LA has been cordoned off with military precision. At one end, cranes hover over a futuristic stage set and a giant video screen, while at the other, 150 extras put finishing touches to their make-up. An end-of-millenium rag-tag mixture of *Blade Runner* binliner punks, transvestites and thrift-store freaks form the moshing crowd at a mad 1999 New Year's Eve street party, and Skunk Anansie are the band.

The stars are not present tonight, but this is to be a key scene in a film that has been shrouded in secrecy. On set, a few details emerge: it features special glasses that video violent thoughts, Ralph Fiennes plays a virtual reality drug dealer, Juliette Lewis is a babe in a silver dress and Angela Bassett gets to beat up a policeman. "That's my kind of babe," says Skin. "A black woman who beats up a policeman!" The former partner of James-*Terminator 2*-Cameron, it's not surprising that Bigelow's *Strange Days* will be a dark, metallic, futuristic epic. Tall and slender with long hair, white jeans and a black leather jacket, she keeps a cool, tight rein on the proceedings.

By 8pm, Skin is in a trailer having a large white cross painted on her face. An extra in a bandanna and camouflage suit pokes his face round the door and says to the make-up artist: "Can you check my teeth alignment?"

The woman looks at him. "Are you serious?"

"Yeah. I had my teeth done recently and I wanna check the alignment."

She doesn't even bother to answer.

Just after sunset, the crew begin filming the party scene. "Selling Jesus" thunders out from the playback, while Skunk mime rock 'n' roll abandon, swathed in dry ice and 14 hand-picked moshers engage in imaginative stage-dives. The band play magnificently, the crowd are suitably chaotic, but that's just the first take. Filming is due to go on until six in the morning.

Just as shooting is about to start again, a killer possum invades the set. Possums look bug-eyed and sweet on TV – in real life they are absolutely revolting. This one looks like an enormous mutant rat with sharp teeth, and sends the extras screaming. The producer, who has "SLEEP IS FOR SISSIES" emblazoned on the back of his T-shirt, yells at everyone to keep quiet, while a security guard chases the creature back into the sewer.

By 4.30am, it's a race against the dawn. Can we shoot with the jumbo camera before it gets light? There have been roughly 25 takes. "I'm flagging," says an exhausted Cass. "And I've got a sore ass. One of the bouncers accidentally kicked me." The producer calls for one last shot, importuning everyone to give it all they've got. As the by-now familiar chorus begins ("They're selling Jesus again/They're selling Jesus again"), the extras sing along, looking bedraggled, including two transvestites wearily stomping their two-foot high platforms.

When it's finally time to wrap, Ace says: "It was like doing an eight-hour gig," before collapsing in the trailer. As the sun rises over LA, Skunk's first US appearance is captured forever on celluloid. What seemed like an easy option became the gig from hell but, for Ace, the experience was much more than a US marketing strategy.

"Just think: we started at the Splash Club, and now we're flying to LA, sipping drinks by the pool, and we're in a film. I'd never have believed it could happen like this."

Too Drunk to Fake

■ **Barbara Ellen**
NME September 30 1995

T he following piece was written at the height of the Oasis/Blur wars, in reaction to the *NME*'s pro-Blur stance. Barbara Ellen, believing Oasis to be the more exciting band, sat through two interviews with Blur's bassist, Alex James, once when he had a hangover and was incapable of rising to her bait, and once when he was vivacious enough to bandy back at her. Her final impressions of Alex? He's bright, evil, a great raspberry blower when things turn too pompous, and she wishes him all the best in his bid to become a "Soho alcoholic".

The week that Blur go to Number One with "Country House", bass player Alex James saunters into his local wine bar, Mars, already discreetly pissed.

Louche, raffish, silly, Alex is my favourite member of Blur. The "social diary" he kept for *NME* recently made me smile: all that haunting of Soho hotspots (here, Freuds, Grouchos) the shameless name-dropping, the petty intrigues, the veritable *smorgasbord* of hangovers. Whatever your opinion of Blur (and mine happens to be pretty low), no one can deny that Alex James is a conscientious celebrity. Come rain or shine, he's out there, knocking them back, sliding down walls, acting, as he himself would put it, "contemptibly".

Furthermore, Britpop's answer to Jeffrey Bernard ("I aspire to be a Soho alcoholic") has his dark side. A tummy-baring pussycat by nature, he turns into a vicious, giggling hyena when provoked.

Above all, though, Alex is a "tart". Within minutes of his arrival, he has instructed the barmaid to be bereft of underwear next time they meet. Then, turning his attention to me, he drawls:

"You have no respect for me. That's why you're here. But none of that matters because I *know* you fancy me."

This is our second meeting. The time before, Alex was on one of his "dry" days (a weekly ritual which he believes counteracts the other six days of relentless boozing). On that occasion, Alex was not "quite himself" and agreed that it would be wise to meet again. Now, as he heads upstairs to a dusty attic room, somehow managing not to spill his beers and flavoured vodkas, he looks on form, ready for action; even his fringe is swaggering.

"I love booze," he confides unnecessarily. "It's a good thing for purveyors of pop art to drink. I can drink five pints of lager and go up to Stephen Fry and say "Hello, I'm Alex from Blur". If I had a cup of tea I wouldn't do that, and if I had heroin I probably wouldn't do that … drugs are just boring. And drug bores are the worst bores, possibly only beaten by drum bores and travel bores. You can have a lot more fun with booze because it's legal."

Have you ever come close to alcoholism?

"I probably drink too much but I can handle it. I can suck corporate cock when I'm sober and I can do it when I'm pissed… I can do *The Times* crossword when I'm pissed! But having one day a week off is good because you shouldn't get too used to doing everything drunk.

"Anyway," he sighs languidly, "let's change the subject. I didn't come here just to talk about alcohol."

True. In the week that Blur got to Number One and Oasis didn't, there are much better things to talk about. Victors of one of the most hyped chart duels ever, Blur must be feeling pretty smug and vindicated. However, in public at least, they are opting to exude an aura of serene, diplomatic calm. Alex even wore an Oasis T shirt on Blur's triumphant *Top Of The Pops* appearance.

"It was a magnanimous gesture," he explains. "I think that they're a great band and that this is the defining Britpop moment.

"It's not Blur versus Oasis," he adds emphatically. "It's Blur and Oasis against the world."

I'm not so sure. Blur versus Oasis ... Oasis versus Blur ... whichever way you cut it, something doesn't quite ring true about this most copyworthy of stand-offs. It could be that too much emphasis is being put on their superficial differences (geography, class, genre). Perhaps it's time to calm down and realise that what sets Blur and Oasis apart has nothing to do with accents, table manners or musical talent. Judged on this level, a brute truth emerges: Oasis are a good band, a 4-Real band who have the potential to be a great band. Blur on the other hand ... are not.

Indeed, in their efforts to be Magnanimity Made Flesh concerning the recent chart stand-off, Blur have hit upon a salient truth. It's actually significant that the rivalry between them is purely of a commercial nature. It could even be the case that Blur simply aren't capable of competing on more important levels.

Whatever you think of Oasis, the fact remains that they deserve better than to be lumbered with such embarrassingly lightweight rivals. The key heads-to-heads of the past weren't like this. They featured very different but evenly matched, *mutually respectful* adversaries. Bands with some kind of spiritual empathy. The Beatles had the Stones, The Sex Pistols had The Clash, the Roses had the Mondays. Oasis have ... Blur. You can't help but feel gutted for them.

What does Alex think about this thing with Oasis? Is it really just a North/South, working class/middle class, rock/pop thing?

"It's definitely *Coronation Street* versus *Eastenders*."

Or, given Blur's nature, *Coronation Street* v *The Late Show*?

"Yeah, well ... triangles versus squares, apples versus oranges ... who cares? Basically, there hasn't been any football for a while and the tabloids want to make everything a football match."

One suggestion is that you did Oasis a favour, giving your "slow-witted" northern rivals a free ride into the limelight on your coat-tails. But Blur got far more out of it than Oasis. Not least in terms of reflected credibility.

Alex smiles. "When we want credibility we'll suck our cheeks and tummies in."

How does it feel to be dismissed as soft Southern streaks of shite?

He laughs. "Flattered! But it's dead true isn't it? People think that we're not real and Oasis are, just because Oasis swear and are horrible to people. But we prefer to rise above it all. At the end of the day, it's easy for us to be magnanimous because we sell more records than they do. We're Number One and they're Number Two. That says more than saying "Come on you cunts!'"

A lot of people think that you keep quiet because you don't have a creative leg to stand on.

"Well, a lot of people think that they've got no manners."

Manners?

"Yeah, Liam shouldn't call his mum a cunt and he shouldn't call Japanese people cunts, and he shouldn't say he takes drugs, and he definitely shouldn't call us cunts! It's bad manners. *Intolerable!* But, you know,"Alex shrugs, smiling indulgently, "maybe that's why we love him."

You've made it clear that you respect Oasis, but do they respect you?

"We drink together."

That doesn't answer my question.

Alex smiles stiffly. "The thing that most people don't understand when they read the papers is that this rivalry is all made up. I know that when I want to hear a good song I can write one and when I want to go for a drink, I can call up Liam. There's few people I'd rather drink with than Oasis."

And with that, Alex James leans over the tape recorder and howls,

"GIVE US A KISS LIAM!"

———

IT WOULD be childish to deny Blur full credit for their achievements. A lot of people out there enjoy their tinny, brittle pop: The sub-Kinks/Small Faces/Madness/Fun Boy Three rip-offs; Albarn's tortuously self-conscious Martin Amis (s-the-point) lyrical style; the jingoistic cod-Britishness; the class tourism; the "eerie" shuddering fairground vibe; the Ray Davies-esque character sketches; the fluctuating accents; the cold-blooded gimmickry; the emotional bankruptcy; the blatant theft; the knowing winks ... Yeah, a lot of people enjoy that kind of thing.

In fact, the odd slivers of material ("End Of The Century", "This Is A Low", "The Universal", and "Yuko And Hiro") make you wonder what Blur might be capable of if they ditched the irony altogether.

My beef with Blur is that, while they're not a bad little pop band, they *are* ridiculously overrated.

Alex shivers into life. He wants to share something important. "I don't like arguing. I aspire to agree with everybody. That way I don't get beaten up ... it's Damon who likes arguing."

Tell me more about Damon.

"Damon?" he purrs carefully, "What can I say? He's a confrontational ... objectional ... big-headed ... arrogant ... *beauty*."

Despite Alex's game protestations that Blur is his band (he's the
archetypal frustrated frontman), it's obvious to everybody else
that Albarn *is* Blur. Indeed the way Alex talks you'd think that
Albarn was Suede as well.

"Brett Anderson got his impetus from Damon coming along and
nicking his bird. Suddenly he had an axe to grind. Ask Freud,
that's all you need to make your art."

Codswallop. What Albarn definitely is, is the songwriter, the
frontman, the face, the ego, the driving force, the spermatozoa
and ovum of Blur. In fact, depending on how you look at it, Blur
are Albarn's fault/triumph and it's him we must despise/thank
for their current success.

Looking at it negatively, you can see Albarn's prints on everything that continues to be just that little bit suspect about Blur:
the homogenised, pretty-wrap nihilism; those dreadful kink(s)y
characters; and, most gratingly, the unsettling aural resem-
blance to any musical starring Tommy Steele – the brash yet
curiously frigid showmanship of it all. Perhaps there are some
out there who would happily trade Liam Gallagher's obstinate
stillness for Albarn's hyperactive caprice. But not me. No way.
Not even for half a sixpence, mate.

That said, people get it wrong when they harp on about Albarn
being an ex-drama student. The fact is, there's nothing "ex"
about Albarn's drama studentness. He is reputed to have left
drama college because he thought he couldn't act. How wrong
he was! Albarn is this country's most hard-working method
actor, devoting his life to his role of choice: Mercurial Genius
In Pop Band. One could even say that Albarn is wasted on pop –
we've all seen him ham, might his *Hamlet* be even better?

Alex smiles politely, refusing to rise to the bait.

"I suppose it is a bit funny that Damon went to drama school.
I wouldn't have. But he's a good performer isn't he? That's
important."

Would all musicians benefit from a background in the dramatic arts?

"Not necessarily – but if people thought that all people who went
to drama school were idiots they wouldn't watch the telly, would
they?"

Television is where actors belong. The question is: do we want
them in bands?

Alex laughs again. "We'll stay home if you like, pick our noses,
take five years to make an album!"

But acting is all about pretence, which is the main criticism of
Blur. That you're willing to pretend to be something you're not
in order to fit in with what sells.

He looks annoyed. "In *what* way do we pretend to be something
we're not?"

First puppets, then losers, then Kings Of The World, Blur have
always had a strong instinct for survival which, at times, has
strayed into the realms of overt opportunism. No one minded when
they jumped on the Madchester bandwagon (why shouldn't they
when everyone else did?) or re-invented themselves as mods (Blur
showed guts then. A defiant refusal to die.) It was the quasi-Essex
yobbisms of "Parklife" that stuck in the craw. What were a group of
middle-class boys doing betting on greyhounds, with Woodbines
behind their ears? Criticised for "playing with working-class
imagery", Albarn quickly invented the term "ultra-normality".
Unfortunately, nobody knew what he was talking about. Not
even his band.

Alex. "Ultra-normality? ... Hmmm, I don't know really ... maybe it
was to do with ... oh bollocks, who cares? ... do you want a shag?"

He yawns, exasperated. Haven't I seen the sleeve art for "The Great
Escape"? Blur are wearing braces now, posing with '8os computers.

"All that class stuff is irrelevant now," he chides. "The imagery on 'Parklife' is almost exclusively working-class but this album isn't. We've moved the goalposts and we'll move them again. We'll move the goalposts as much as we fucking want. It's our ball."

We descend into an unseemly squabble concerning what makes a band fake or genuine.

"I'M A FAKE!" he shouts grandly, at one point. "There! What could be more genuine than me saying 'I'm a fake?' "

Inevitably, wires get crossed. Alex seems to think that by "genuine" I mean po-faced U2/Alarm types straining and yearning over their guitar licks. He says that if I had my way pop bands wouldn't be allowed to be playful with images. He even accuses me of being against bands changing altogether. This is ridiculous. All decent bands, be they rock or pop, change all the time. It's called development. But Blur don't change so much as fumigate and start again: out with The Kinks, in with The Specials; out with the greyhounds, in with the computers. The problem being that you can only do this so many times before it all starts to look a bit desperate.

Alex disagrees. "There's nothing suspect about us changing. The more things change, the more they stay the same, as they say in France. That's important because every time you change, you hint at the essence of who you are."

That's one way of seeing it. But isn't Oasis' strength the fact that, regardless of trends, they will always be Oasis. Whereas Blur are prepared to be anything the public wants them to be?

He shakes his head. "Being able to change is a good thing to have up your sleeve. There's nothing noble about not changing. "

I disagree. I think that there's a certain romance, a gravitas, to bands who have a very clear vision of who they are.

"Blur have ultimately one vision too. It's just that the means of achieving it have changed."

So why are Blur widely perceived as fakes?

"Because we're good at it."

Alex stares me out then says, very coolly, "What do you want us to do – sing about going to grammar school?"

Why not? At least then you'd know what you were on about.

He groans. "If you only sang about things you know about or have done, it would be very dull, wouldn't it? We're dreamers of our dreams, mate. Music is a fantastic arena for dreamers and romantics. If you're dreaming about something, that's a much more emotional state than talking about something you know. You can be quite cold about things when you know about them but if you're imagining something you can get very subtle emotions.

"People always go on about us using characters, but you can see Damon in all our songs. He's singing about himself really. The fact that he uses other names and characters is probably something to do with his Ray Davies obsession. But he's met Ray now, he knows him, so he can't really… "

Rip him off any more?

"No. He can't continue to be obsessed with him."

Alex lights a cigarette, grinning wryly. "That's how it should be kids! Go and get drunk with your heroes, snog them and then tell them to FUCK OFF!"

The main reason, clearly, why he adores being a celebrity is that it brings him into contact with other celebrities.

"It all gets a bit odd. You read the papers and you suddenly real-ise that you know everybody. But it makes sense really. Plumbers drink with plumbers, Oasis drink with Ash, famous people drink with famous people. They've got more to talk about."

Alex announces that Blur's next goal is to become even more famous ("The biggest band in the world by 1999"). To achieve this they will have to crack America. I'm startled. This from the Little Englanders who used to burst into "nationalistic" tears every time they saw a McDonalds. Do they seriously think that America will want them?

Alex blows a raspberry at me. "We know that we can be big in America on our own terms. Anybody can buy a Les Paul and a Marshall stack and sell American culture back to the Americans. Trust me, that's easy! Our mission is to sell British pop culture to the world. And don't tell me that that's not fucking genuine. All we can basically represent is British pop culture."

Are you referring to Britpop? People say that you invented that, but I'm confused. Which of those bands are actually Blur-inspired?

"It would be big-headed and indiscreet to answer that. Ask Damon, he thinks we're responsible for everything."

Menswear are the obvious ones, but then you wouldn't want them to be your fault, would you?

"Oh, I don't know. They're nice boys really."

Would it be fair to say that, because of the kind of band you are, the only people you're likely to "inspire" are chancers and opportunists. People who specialise in schmoozing, networking, cutting corners ... A little bit of this, a little bit of that.

Alex grins, eyes flashing. "Well, who wants to go to fucking music college and learn how to do it properly? Who wants to 'feel it, man!'? That's the whole point of pop music, it's a con. People don't care if things are frauds!"

That's a very cynical viewpoint.

"The world is run by cynical maniacs!"

ALEX CALLS a halt and ambles off downstairs to fetch us both a drink.

When he comes back, he toys with the idea of terminating the interview.

"*NME* readers are such pompous cunts aren't they? They think that what they think about music is so important but there's no point in deconstructing anything. At the end of the day, talking about music is like wanking about rain.

"The truth is, there's nothing unusual about what we do. I hate all that, 'He's a genius, he was just born with it' crap. Playing a guitar is about as mysterious as using a typewriter. It's the same thing only you have the hands the other way up."

You don't believe in talent?

Alex blows a deafening raspberry. "Talent, genius, BOLLOCKS! There's no such thing as genius. Some people just *want* it more, which is twice as important as being good at it. That's what Damon's got – DRIVE! And Oasis. Noel really fucking wants to be the daddio and you won't ever be that unless you really want to be.

"Musicians just like to over-complicate what they do. When we're in the studio, I can't see anything mysterious going on. We don't waste time worrying about *vibes*. We're all good players so we talk about what we want, work out the quickest way to do it and then fucking get on with it."

You make it sound like a manufacturing process.

"It is!"

Could this attitude explain why the bulk of Blur's work lacks emotion?

Alex gapes at me. "You can't say that we're unemotional! Emotion is inherent in everything we do. Emotion isn't about standing on mountains going, 'I'VE GOT A BROKEN HEART!'

If you're going to sing about your heart, you might as well rhyme it with fart as far as I'm concerned. That's the only way you can get away with singing about your heart in the '90s."

He laughs scornfully. "That's the thing about rock music. It has a set of rules, doesn't it? It's easy to be a rock star – you get leather trousers and long hair and sing about the way you FEEL! And it's easy to be in an indie band: you ge ... whatever they get ... and sing about the way you FEEL! And it's easy to be ..."

A pop star?

"Well, it is for me, darling."

Doesn't pop have it's own set of rules?

"Yeah, but only to break them. The point of pop music is to keep redefining itself. Pop is the art of compromise and being too precious about things is just as bad as being too flippant. You really want to make this precious thing that's perfect but then everybody's got to like it as well. But that doesn't mean that we don't feel passionately about what we do ... are you listening to me?"

I'm listening very carefully.

"Because I've been thinking about this and I'm really upset about the way you say we're not genuine, that there's something ungenuine about us... What does fucking genuine mean anyway?

"You could just as easily argue that *everything's* genuine. It's like that old art bullshit about straight lines not existing in nature. Everything fucking exists in nature."

OK, how far would you go to convince people you're genuine?

Alex explodes with laughter. "I wouldn't fucking walk to Freuds, mate."

I had a hunch that you weren't the type to carve "4-Real" on your arm.

"How theatrical a gesture was *that*?"

I was speaking metaphorically. The point is – what was behind the gesture?

"A fucking suicide!"

That's pure speculation. We don't know that.

"*I think we do*. He's had his week of mourning, thank you very much. Let the music carry on. There's no point killing yourself to prove that you mean it. You can mean it and still enjoy yourself. You don't have to paint yourself into a corner. Start with the corners and end up in the middle, that's what I say.

"I hate *any* bands who take themselves too seriously," he continues, bristling now. "Be serious about what you do by all means but don't bore me with your fucking righteousness. This is the '90s. Who needs visceral geniuses who just 'feel it, man!' "

"Don't believe it," he snaps. "They're just as contrived as us."

———

THE THING that makes Alex's attitude sad rather than admirably pretentious is the selectivity of his cynicism. One minute he's enthusing about his art-buddy Damien Hirst ("He's inspiring! A *serious* artist... but he can still get into the tabloids!") The next, he's telling me that neither genius or talent exists in his own field, trying to convince me that all musicians are like Blur: workaholics who got lucky simply because they put the required amount of hours in.

But he's right about one thing. This "real" thing isn't something that you can argue about. It's something that bands have either got or they haven't. Hard to define but impossible to fake, it's the X factor that makes people love bands, stick by them. Sometimes, it even makes them want to form "real" bands themselves. What's "precious" or "righteous" about that?

For their part, the thoroughly modern and cynical Blur may discover that they are the type of band who are doomed to spend the rest of their careers surfing a zeitgeist they once defined, risking being drowned with each new wave.

Alex demurs. "It all gets very convoluted because if you can get hold of the zeitgeist you can change things."

Would your fans wait for you for five years?

"That's a good question," he says, but fails to answer it.

"I'm not that keen on obsessive fans. I'm not being dismissive or anything, but I really don't want to appeal to people who need that kind of thing in their lives. I just want to give everybody a little kiss ...

"I know what you're saying ... Bands have always been about far more than music. But we're not judgmental about stuff like that. I don't want to tell people how to live their lives. I did to start with, but people don't want a revolution, people don't want to lay down their tools and stop working ... They just want something to whistle in the dark."

———————

HE'S RIGHT and wrong, of course: some people want a lot more than that – some may even want less. What the Blur/ Oasis sack-race proved was that, at present, Blur have a vast army of the latter type (floating voters/children/mobile disco DJs) supplementing their fanbase. No one's sneering (all bands want to cross over), but what happens when the chips are down and Blur discover that even their diehard fans have died pretty easily? How magnanimous will they feel when bands like Oasis recover from the lost battle and go on to win the war?

Indeed, perhaps the most important, if not the only yardstick by which to judge the essentially spurious Blur/Oasis conundrum is that of motivation. Blur would settle for being "the biggest band in the world". Oasis won't rest until they're the best.

Straight to Hell... Yeah!

■ **Gina Morris**
Select November 1995

After splitting Happy Mondays, Shaun Ryder went on to form Black Grape, who have since gained a notoriety similar to that of his previous band. Loud, lairy and renowned for "larging it", Ryder has never been the easiest of interviewees, and Gina Morris's experience with Black Grape in Paris did nothing to disprove this. Following an aborted trip to Amsterdam, where the band disappeared altogether, she eventually managed to pin them down in France, an hour before she was due to return to England. Although she says they were nice boys, she also admits this is an interview she'd rather forget about. Nevertheless, her vivid depiction of Manchester's maddest-for-it captures the best of the worst, and clearly shows why men shouldn't monopolise the lads when it comes to reporting.

Salford Primary School 1966. The lesson is drawing to a close. Standing at the head of the class, the teacher casts a prudent eye over the group of infants. It's reward time, for well-behaved children. Picking out three pupils, she motions them to the front and produces a large tin of brightly wrapped sweets from her desk. Eagerly, they each take one. The bell rings for lunchtime and one four-year-old kid, always sat at the back, who never, ever, gets chosen, shrugs and saunters out, grinning mischievously.

Ten minutes later he's back, crawling into the dim and abandoned classroom through a slightly open window. He's been doing this for weeks now, stifling his giggles, he creeps over to the teachers desk, gently slides open the bottom drawer, reaches in and begins stuffing his mouth with toffees.

Suddenly the lights snap on. It's an ambush. Caught red-handed, surrounded by angry adults, with his mouth almost bursting and sugary saliva dribbling from his lips, he attempts a sheepish smile.

"Shaun Ryder," says his teacher in a low, stern voice. "You really are a bad boy."

—————————

SHAUN WILLIAM Ryder is, without doubt, one of the most impor-tant British artists of the past 20 years. If he'd died five years ago, he would now be widely regarded as a cultural icon. Ryder the working-class Salford kid, largely accountable for the inauguration of "baggy" and its popular side-kick Ecstasy; initiates a musical movement as significant to kids in the late '80s as punk was in the '70s. Worth a statue at least. But, as it goes, Shaun Ryder didn't die. And today, August 23, 1995, he's in Paris celebrating his 33rd birthday with some people he's never met before.

It's 9pm, and seated at a large round table in a swish French rest-aurant called Bofinger there's Shaun, his girlfriend-soon-to-be-wife Oriel (who flew in especially this morning), Bez, Kermit and their manager Nick. Then there's *Select*, the press officer and six del-egates from their European record company. Shaun is behaving like your dad. Hunched over a menu, pronouncing dishes badly and joking about how snails taste like phlegm ... or sperm (apparently).

Although in good spirits he seems slightly embarrassed by it all, not used to such fuss. The biz people have a surprise for him later, too, a huge birthday cake with candles on it, to be presented to him during a resounding chorus of Happy Birthday. He'll love it.

His best friend Bez hasn't got him anything, never has. Not even a card. "We've not given him any grief today," he says, and

Kermit agrees. "That's his fucking birthday present from us."

Oriel (referred to as O), however, has bought him a thick gold chain, which he flaunts, proudly, over his sweatshirt, in between squeezing her thigh under the table. The waiter appears and they order duck paté to share, followed by a couple of medium rare steaks ... and more drinks.

"I asked for a large vodka and orange juice at the hotel last night," says Shaun (nickname X), "and they brought me this fucking massive ... jug, glass thing."

A pitcher?

"Sorry, no," he grins, "I didn't take one."

As the starter plates are cleared away, the atmosphere changes. Shaun is growing visibly edgy. It's obvious this really isn't his scene. He wants to go to Pigalle, to celebrate in the city's notorious sex'n'sin district. More drinks are ordered and the main courses arrive. The table is becoming increasingly rowdy. The ceaselessly hyperactive Kermit is threatening to get his arse out again, like he did last night, to prove some point or other to the label women sat either side of him. A real charmer.

Suddenly, Shaun stands up. "I'm going, O, are you ready?" He hasn't touched his food. "C'mon, I'll wait outside."

He strides out of the restaurant. Calmly Oriel eats a few mouthfuls, knocks back a double Jack Daniels and Coke, slips on her coat and follows him. The label people exchange bemused and flustered glances. "Qu'esque le gateau anniversaire?" they whisper.

"X, hold on," shouts Kermit, jumping up. "I'm coming with you."

Within two minutes there's four empty chairs.

———————

IT's NOW midnight. We're sat two feet away from a tiny raised stage watching a "sex" show. At least, we paid 300 francs (£25) to see two haggard dolly-birds take their kit off. Shaun likes it, he has a thing for older women. "They're not doing anything to themselves," he moans. "Let's go."

Outside there's a conflict of interests. Oriel wants to go back to the hotel, skin up and drink champagne, but Shaun wants to walk around some more. He's bought some "charlie" off a man selling roses and he's not ready to go home yet. Shaun walks on ahead, Kermit is lolloping behind him and O saunters some way back.

After a while they stop in the middle of a crowded street and a massive row breaks out. Everyone's screaming at everyone else. Kermit's shouting that he's leaving the band because no one respects him; Oriel says she's had enough of Shaun; and Shaun keeps punching the air and yelling "It's my fucking birthday!"

Eventually, Oriel jumps in a cab, Kermit disappears down an alley and Shaun is left alone. He shakes his head and skulks off down the street.

IN SEPTEMBER 1992, Shaun Ryder appeared on the cover of *Select* above the words "Crack Heroin Gangrene?". It was the full, unexpurgated account of the Happy Mondays recording of "Yes Please" in Barbados: the car crashes, broken limbs, fights, burglaries, destroyed apartments and Shaun's newly-acquired 50-rocks-of-crack-cocaine-a-day habit. It wasn't the entire story.

The saga in the Caribbean actually reached its gruesome nadir the day Shaun stormed into the studios, picked up the phone and dialled Factory Records. Gripping the receiver between his chin and his shoulder, he glared at the contents of his violently trembling hands. He was holding the near-completed master-tapes of their new album.

"I'll fucking destroy them," he yelled down the line. "I'll fuck you all ... and I don't fucking care. Just you see if I'm fucking bothered."

Shaun was after money. £10,000. To buy more crack. Factory told him they didn't have it. In a semi-deranged, drug-craving fury, he viciously shook the precious tapes, desperate and crazy enough not only to threaten Factory's future but also his own. He was serious, he'd do it, and within the hour the money was wired to a small bank on the island.

"Actually," spits Anthony H Wilson, crossing his legs and gazing briefly round the hotel bar in Manchester, "it was £30,000. And the great Chris Smith, our finance director, put his own credit down for that. And you know what's interesting is, after he put his card down, his house was in jeopardy for the next three years."

Interesting? No. It was arguably a completely pointless submission with devastating after-effects. In February 1993, both Factory Records and Happy Mondays were buried. Dead.

"Everybody warned me to stay away from Shaun Ryder," frowns Nick Nichols, who, along with his wife Gloria, has managed Black Grape from day one. "Everybody I met told me, "He's a lunatic" and "You're a fucking idiot for getting involved" or "He's totally fucked on drugs ... he's over". But he's fucking talented and so important – I don't think he knows how important he is. But we had faith in him. We even re-mortgaged our house."

"He's a genius in the real sense of a genius," admits Tony Wilson. "When you're touched by that thing but have no idea how – that's Shaun, he has no fucking idea where it comes from."

In 1993 it seemed Shaun Ryder had no idea where it went either. Furthermore if the "thing" started touching him again, would it matter? Ryder, conceivably, had no more chances left. He had, in some way or another, managed to alienate just about everyone.

"At the end, he was surrounded by liggers and vultures and sycophants who just indulged him while they scavenged for leftovers," says Jayne Houghton, ex-Mondays press officer and Shaun's trouble-buddy (she still represents Paul Ryder).

"He had such a lot of genuine friends there too, but he was in such a state, I'm not sure he could tell the difference."

Ryder was a shambling mindless wreck, and he didn't care who knew it. So intent on self-destruction he'd begun chasing the dragon onstage, poorly hidden behind the drum riser, and even smoking it in the dressing room right under the noses of journalists.

After the Happy Mondays split, Shaun appeared on *The Word* and revealed he was going to form another band with a Manchester rapper called Kermit. And then he stumbled off to dance with Zippy and Bungle...

Yesterday afternoon, Nick dashed into the hotel foyer with some news from England. "No one believed me," he yells, waving a piece of paper. "No one fucking believed me, but look at it now. We're number fucking one! 85,000 copies sold in under two weeks. What do I want to say to the disbelievers? Only one thing... " He wrinkles up his face and crudely raises his middle-finger high in the air. "Swivel!"

———————————

"WHY DO I always have shit birthdays?"

It's two in the afternoon the following day. Shaun was the only one who finally made it to the bar last night, he stayed up all night drinking, something he rarely does to excess these days. He returned at 7am to discover his room had been completely trashed.

"She broke me fucking Ray-Bans, man," he smiles, settling down in a chair in the hotel bar. "That's the sixth pair."

He rolls up the sleeve of his sweatshirt to reveal a huge bruise on his upper arm. "We were both a bit drunk," he says taking a sip of Coke, "But we made up this morning. She's a fucking top woman. Yeah, we're still getting married."

———————————

SHAUN "X" Ryder was born in Salford on August 23, 1962. The eldest son of a postman and a nurse, both strict Catholics, he grew up on a rough council estate in Swinton. Having discovered both "crime" and girls at the early age of four, it wasn't long before he'd moved on to burglary.

At seven he was stealing from shops, people, homes ... anyone who looked like they had more than him. Even at that age he was developing a thirst for money. He hung out with his brother Paul, who was 18 months younger, in a group of about ten kids, including his cousins Mat and Pat (later of Central Station design). They lived for the chase, getting their willies out to shopkeepers or throwing bricks through windows, just for sport. It was like being in a film, everything felt so unreal.

"We literally hid our crimes from our parents," explains Paul Ryder, sipping a glass of water in his ex-tour manager's office in Manchester. "We had this dressing table in our bedroom with a big gap under the bottom drawer and that was our hiding place for years. Shaun's was on the left, mine was on the right and we had everything in there – money, starting pistols ... I remember Shaun had four pairs of patchpocket flares and a pair of shoes that he could never have afforded on his spends. He had to hide them there and sneak 'em on when mam went out."

When the two of them were eleven they broke into some Carlsberg wagons and stole crates of lager, selling them to the drunks at the local pub. This was the only crime their father praised years later, impressed by their entertaining scam. Usually, though, bad deeds meant a good slapping. One time, Shaun tried to escape punishment by running off but was completely humiliated in front of all his tough mates when his dad chased after him down the street wearing only a pair of big white Y-fronts.

When Shaun started at Ambrose High School he was in all the top sets, within a year he'd slipped down to the remedial class. Now if he bothered to turn up at all, he was immediately given rubbish duty. "I didn't mind doing that," Shaun laughs. "It meant I could walk around the playground smoking fags."

But for the most part, Shaun never bothered attending, he felt he had nobody to answer to but himself. His mother's attitude was, "Shaun is not going to be clever, so it doesn't matter if he's in school or not."

At 13 he lost his virginity. He also had his first acid trip with his new friend Bez; they'd drop a few tabs and go wandering about the Arndale Centre. It was about this time he saw his first syringe. He was on a fairground ride with his girlfriend and she suddenly started shoving them into her knickers having spied the police below. He thought she "was mad". At 14 Shaun got his first job. It was on a council estate, he got £30 a house to strip the wallpaper and remove the window frames. It was easier, he found, if he just knocked down the walls completely. He was fired.

On the days he didn't turn up for school he was to be found on the nearby estate, shagging all the lonely thirtysomething housewives and loving every minute. Sex, he thought, was ace. At a meeting with the school's career officer he said he wanted to make porno films in Amsterdam, they replied, "OK Shaun, whatever."

Having spent some time in and out of detention centres, he finally left school at 15 and got a job as messenger boy at the post office. For kicks he began stealing cars, he drove a brand new Granada through an old couple's new extension.

In 1979 Shaun made the headlines of the national press for the first time. He and his mates had succeeded in exploding 3,000 pigeons in Manchester by feeding them "tampered" bread which swelled in their stomachs. They were branded the "sick face of Great Britain".

By now Shaun had formed a band and got married. He was 18, had his own house and had "made" a bit of money, it seemed the thing to do. He spent his wedding day tripping on acid. The marriage lasted 18 months.

At 19 Shaun picked up the nickname X. "You know, from *The Exterminator*," explains Muzzer, the Mondays and now Black Grape's tour manager and Shaun's best friend for over ten years. "He was always getting girls pregnant – one a week."

Now separated, Shaun moved in with Bez, Muzzer and another friend in a big and fairly nice house. "Me and my mate used to buy all the bog rolls and milk and stuff," laughs Muzzer. "The two of them didn't know what shopping was, they lived to party."

Following a trip to Ibiza, Shaun discovered Ecstasy and Es became his staple diet; one for breakfast, one for lunch, one for tea and two in the evening. He'd do that for three days at a time, then crash out for two days, then start again.

"Living with them," Muzzer recalls, shaking his head, "was like experiencing all the maddest things in the world."

"GOT ANY money, X?"

Bez, very sensibly, did not come out last night. He stayed at the restaurant, eating good food and enjoying himself. Consequently, he's the only member of Black Grape who looks relatively alive this afternoon. Shaun hands him a handful of notes and Bez happily strolls off.

Would you marry Bez if he was a girl?

Shaun almost chokes on his fag. "No fucking way!"

Bez and Shaun have been mates for over 15 years. They were introduced by mutual friends who thought they'd get on really well. They didn't.

"Everyone kept saying, Oh you've gotta meet Bez, you've fucking gotta meet Bez. So when I did it was like, Oh, you're Bez then."

They ended up smoking hash and talking all night and haven't been apart since. They stay at each other's houses when bad things happen, always there for each other. They're a partnership.

"I don't really know the alphabet," mumbles Shaun. "Trish taught it me when I was 28 but I can only sing it." Illustrating the point he starts singing "A B C D" in true *Sesame Street* style, pausing for breath before spitting out "X Y Z". He looks pleased with himself. "Bez knows the alphabet but he doesn't know the months of the year. He goes January, February, May, July, September... I know me months, so it's alright."

Is there anything Bez could possibly do that would threaten your friendship?

"Anything he could do?" Shaun looks aghast. "He's done it. Don't kid yourself, he's fucking done it all."

Twenty minutes later, Bez swaggers back into the bar, walks over to Shaun and hands him a large bag.

"What's this?" he asks puzzled. "You got me a birthday present?" He opens the bag and pulls out a brand new dark blue Lacoste shirt. "Fucking hell. Cheers B. I needed a new top." He holds it up against his chest. "It's alright innit?" His smile abruptly drops. "Hold on," he says, looking at Bez slyly. "You just bought this with my money."

———————————

MARK "BEZ" Berry was born in Liverpool on April 18, 1964. The son of a strict CID officer, he moved to Manchester soon after. As a kid he enjoyed all kinds of sports; when he was four he got a Manchester United strip for his birthday, the best present he ever got. He was showing a lot of promise as a young footballer, playing for Prestwich Heyes, who were in the Northern Premier league. But sports, well, they didn't pay very well...

Unlike Shaun, Bez had little interest in clothes, he wore what-ever his mother told him to wear – shorts, T-shirts, trainers. He also had a skinhead crop – jokingly, he says he looked very much as he does now, only littler. Early on, Bez developed a craving for excitement fraught with danger, much like Shaun's desire for the chase, he became a problem child. Bez was a "delinquent". He rode around his estate on a self constructed bike, a nick-it-yourself kit. He didn't go to school (something he hugely regrets now) and started stealing. And as he grew bigger, so too did his crimes.

The first drug Bez ever did was speed. Then dope. By 15 he'd tried acid, smack and cocaine. "I must've taken every drug going."

Bez also frequently bunked school, mostly to hang out at the Arndale Centre with Shaun. Then he left to get a job. It was to be the only job he ever had, loading wagons and humping boxes and containers in a warehouse. It lasted five months until he was eventually sacked, for consistently failing to turn up. He began dealing drugs instead. At 19 he was in Strangeways.

"He was like the daddy of the prison," Shaun jokes, "he was hard but he never bullied anyone." The day of his release, Bez went home, packed a bag, got on a "Magic Bus" and went travelling. He was gone for 12 months.

"Bez is one of the nicest, politest people imaginable," muses Phil Saxe, the Mondays first manager. "Most people don't realise it. He was never a problem, always well-behaved. I know it sounds crap but it's true. Bez is a really nice lad."

——————

KERMIT, SHAUN and Bez are holed up in a room at the American Hotel in Amsterdam, being quizzed by a German fanzine writer. They arrived in from Paris a few days ago, on their press tour of Europe, and are due to stay here for four days. It's late afternoon and the band have been in interviews since midday, on a continual rotation of foreign journalists. The air along the corridor is dense with the stench of smouldering leaf. The door opens and the fanzine writer skips out smiling. Five minutes later Bez staggers out, his usual bug-eyed eyeballs barely visible beneath the lids. He nods a greeting and falls into the lift. Kermit hobbles out next, also unbelievably stoned, he can barely speak.

"What ... have ya been up to?" he mumbles painfully before he slumps, exhausted, into a chair and closes his eyes. There's no sign of Shaun, this is the last chance we have to interview the band. Something needs to be done. Kermit suggests he acquire something that might help accelerate the Black Grape frontman. "Come on, let's go to the square."

Half an hour later I find myself in the back of some guy's speeding car cutting up cyclists and trams, on the way to this apartment, house music blaring, windows down.

The dude is at least 50. Moments later we're at the top of several flights of stairs at his front door. He motions for us to go in. The lounge is the last word in '70s pimp den sophistication: two faded and worn brown leather sofas, a bong on the coffee table, a cocktail bar with four high chrome and black plastic bar-stools at one end and pictures of Isaac Hayes all over the walls. He hands Kermit the wrap. And then throws us out.

Back at the hotel, Shaun is mooching about, frowning. He's not happy. Wants to know where we've been. What we've been doing. The now bubblingly enthusiastic Kermit bounds out of the lift and hands him the package, by way of explanation. "That's alright then," Shaun grins.

PAUL "KERMIT" Leveridge was born on November 10, 1969 in "another galaxy". As a small boy, living with his parents in Moss Side, he danced in front of his bedroom mirror, loving the idea of performance. Music was his passion, and although his parents really wanted him to become a lawyer or a doctor they encouraged him musically. Thrilled at the interest he took in the violin, they bought him one for his sixth birthday.

At that age, Kermit was a "proper kid". He had a Chopper, played marbles, used his jumpers for goal-posts. He even had a paper round. But two years later everything, he says, "went a bit fucking mad". He started questioning things, like, So God created us, well who created God? and his mind spun...

Kermit had started writing songs when he was ten, although he dismisses these as "shitty schoolboy shit". After that, having become a huge fan of the Sex Pistols and The Specials, he started rebelling, abusing the fact that he was a lot smarter than his age. He lost his virginity at 12 and went girl crazy, spending most of his teenage years obsessed with sex, drinking and experimenting with drugs. At 16 he was dealing. Secretive about certain aspects of his life, he refuses to elaborate. "I've done questionable things."

In his late teens, now a fully-trained classical violinist and at Manchester Polytechnic studying a Psychology degree, Kermit was dabbling in harder drugs. Heroin. As intelligent as he was, it wasn't enough to outwit his inquisitive nature; he knew where the end of the line was, and in a few months had reached it. He was now using daily.

Kermit had already met and befriended a kid called Bez, a mad character who just seemed to be everywhere. Not long after, he got talking to this guy Shaun Ryder, who was usually always there at some dealer's house or other. Bonding on an unsociable habit, they became smack buddies.

When Kermit was in his late teens, he was arrested for selling narcotics and put on remand. Further charges against him failed, and within a couple of months Kermit was free.

———————

"I DIDN'T want to be in this band." Bez is huddled over a cappuccino, sat at a table outside a Dutch coffee bar, watching the cars go past. "I thought I'd done it. To me it was a one-time thing, not to be repeated but Shaun convinced me. He said that no matter what I've done or what happens in the future I'm Bez. And I'll always be known as Bez out of the Happy Mondays. So I might as well carry on 'cos that's who I am. Bez. It makes no difference what I do. "

But you're glad now?

He laughs, "I don't know yet."

Almost everyone involved with the Happy Mondays (bar its other members and their families) agree on one thing, that, if forced to compare, Black Grape are the better band. Now if only they can keep it together long enough for it to count ...

Is Kermit serious about leaving the band?

"Oh he's always going on about that," dismisses Bez. "He just likes a good sulk. You've got to coax him out of it."

———————

IT WAS less than a week after the Mondays split that Shaun got together with Kermit and started writing songs. That was the easy part, convincing record labels to take a chance on them was much harder. It took over two years to get out of remaining contracts and find a new label. Few people wanted to know – as far as they were concerned, Shaun Ryder was a fat smackhead, has-been lunatic.

"He *is* a fucking lunatic!" wails Kermit, striding around his hotel room later that evening, now fully restored to his usual animated self.

"He's a proper psycho-bastard, that's what I like about him. Me and Shaun have had some seriously deep conversations, to the point where neither of us wants to leave the room in case we fall into the void."

Black Grape are undoubtedly the best surprise of '95 – both on the strength of their debut album, "It's Great When You're Straight ... Yeah!", and the fact that Ryder seems to have pulled himself back from beyond the brink of destruction.

Shaun Ryder is the core and drive of Black Grape – without him, Bez would be Bez without a job, Kermit would be dimly remembered as that guy who used to be in Ruthless Rap Assassins ... who could sell you some drugs. The future rests on Shaun, because the unpredictability that made him, the Happy Mondays and now Black Grape such a success, could just as easily destroy it all. Again.

"His lifestyle's been glamorised too much," reckons Jayne Houghton. "And the truth is, nobody would want him if he was really straight. It's all part of the appeal, but he can't draw the line between his public persona – letting people think he's this mad, fucked-up creative genius – and letting it spill over into real life where he actually starts over-indulging.

"I don't think he knows where the line is... I hope to God he's found it."

Living in Oblivion

■ **Sylvia Patterson**

Sky December 1995

T im Burgess, singer with The Charlatans, is one of the most likeable rock stars in action. His passion for music is inexhaustible, he dances constantly to his own inner tune, clicking his fingers, grinning till you think his face will split, extolling the joys of music and most other things in life. I once danced with him in his own living room to his own record after a deliriously drunken night out, and left at eight in the morning, glad to find a rock singer who didn't care two monkeys for cool.

Here Sylvia Patterson takes him out for lunch, watches him get heroically drunk, graciously accepts his gift of a watch, and tries to deposit him home despite his not having a clue where he lives.

"Mam? Your friend. He has fallen down the stairs."

The barman is concerned. He has the look on his face of someone who is considering calling an ambulance. Tim Burgess is not concerned. He has the look on his face of blithe oblivion because he, unlike the barman, is the happiest man in the world.

He is also the drunkest man in the world. And, in the last two hours, he has not only fallen all the way down the pub stairs and gained a profound limp, but proved himself a spectacularly bizarre, bona fide nutter of pop rivalled only by the king of errant lunacy himself, ie Bez from Black Grape.

Firstly, Tim was "jet-lagged out of me head" so there was only one thing for it: four bottles of wine with the Italian meal. The Italian meal of broccoli pasta which he half ate and then enquired four times as to whether we'd eaten yet or not. He didn't remember drinking his beer either. Waited for the return of his credit card when it was sitting in front of him inside the leather recipt book for half an hour. Gave me his watch, a fake $35 Rolex affair with special countdown effects on for deep-sea divers, for no reason whatsoever howling "Cheers! Nice one! This year's been the day of the presents!" Attacked the ivories of the restaurant piano player on the way out the door. Couldn't find the pub he's been drinking in for years. Started cuddling everyone; great big huge bear-hug embraces to knock the wind out of a typhoon. Showed everyone his new tattoo of a sleeping cartoon tiger on his back. Ended up with his head in the lap of your reporter's chum after giving her his plastic Beatles bag and all its worldly contents. Sang Oasis's "Champagne Supernova" from the bonnet of a car. Couldn't even remember he lived in London. Was told by a homeless person in a doorway that if he didn't get up off the Soho pavement he wouldn't get a taxi to take him anywhere. So he steadied himself on a wall.

"You live in Chalk Farm, Tim," said my chum who was the only person not on the pavement in Soho, to which he replied "That's it! Ace! I'm going home!" So, finally, he went home, unconscious in a taxi. Or woke up in hospital, or in the wrong continent, whichever came first. For a man whose behaviour borders on the suicidal, Timothy Burgess, the people's friend, is what you'd call a life enthusiast.

He is also mad. It's a much abused word, mad, attributed to anyone with a semblance of personality, but he really is proper coo-ee-clouds pan-dimensional *mad* mad. He doesn't sit, he grooves in his seat, shoulders undulating to some constant inner rhythm, fingers clicking, his arm shooting into the air every three seconds with mad-for-it delight. He does this in front of the waiter and the startled fellow flinches as if the Northern loon was about to sock him in the jaw for not pouring the wine fast enough.

He speaks to you on the end of your nose in a low Northern slur of pronounced inarticulacy, ending a theory with "You know what I mean, though ... or whatever ... " veering into a polar opposite subject and/or emotion until you haven't a bloody clue what he's on about any more. He means everything he says. And then he'll say "Fuck it!" or "I can't be arsed!" and break out in uncontrollable cackles. He is a seven-year-old boy tumbling around in the deceptively big-boned body of a 27-year-old man. And a top geezer, a real-deal pop persona and the happiest man in the entire world in the zenith of a personal vindication because up until this year, he and his band were universally presumed to be, as Tim would have it, "a gonner."

In the triumphant pop year of 1995, The Charlatans' triumph shone the brightest because everyone thought they were dead. From the bench on the side of Britpop pitch hysteria, they quietly brought us their fourth LP, "The Charlatans" and from oblivion, it went straight into the charts at number one; a huge, sumptuous, celebratory album of power-pop excellence hailed as the second LP the Stone Roses took five years not to come up with.

For the second time in their six-year history, The Charlatans were number one LP titans of pop; it happened before with their debut "Some Friendly" in 1990: The Year of Baggy. Their year of *Smash Hits* superstardom, of being lost in American deserts, of psychedelic rock 'n' roll jubilation. And then The Curse began. Madchester was stoned to death in the grunge avalanche. Their new tunes were panned. Martin (Blunt – bass) went down with clinical depression. Jon (Baker, guitar) left. Mark (Collins – guitar) joined and became an alcoholic within six months. On 3 December 1992 Rob Collins (keyboards) drove the getaway car in an armed off-licence robbery. The band carried on, didn't really think he'd go to jail for you know, *real)*. Rob's case came to trial in September 1993; he was sentenced to eight months in Shrewsbury prison. Now, two years later The Charlatans are enjoying a return to "Flavour of the moment" status with, it has to be said, unfeasible gusto.

So. What went right?

"All right," says Tim, downing at least half a pint of wine in approximately four seconds, "it was the realisation, when Rob went to prison, of everything that we could lose. So me and Mark started to write tunes."

It was the first time they'd written together, just the two of them. They wrote somewhere in the region of five songs every week, no matter if they were rubbish or not. They weren't and it saved their lives. And saved Tim from the demons in his inner asylum.

"I went through a real self-loathing period, me," he says, puffing on the hour's 87th cigarette. "Seriously. Honestly. I just hated everything that I did. When the second LP got trashed I really thought it was all my fault and everything that I ever did was shit. But there was something weird inside that made me want to do it even more. I never did this to start with for any other reason other than to be a great band. I didn't do it for the girls – I never had a real phobia about being an ugly git, I never had Pete Townshend syndrome, know what I'm saying? I just got addicted to doing LPs, which sounds really shit but it's true. So it wasn't a case of holding onto the reins; it was a case of setting them on fire and that's what we did, so ... cheers!"

Tim didn't visit Rob in jail once.

"No," says Tim looking suddenly forlorn, "I apologised to him at the time but I didn't approve. Of what he'd done. Because he put my life in jeopardy and I wasn't asking for it. But we survived and I love him; he's spooky but he's a good guy at the end of the day."

Do you know why he did it?

"For the buzz," says Tim plainly, "He's into danger, he's just like that (begins fiddling with watch which is even too big for his enormous wrists). I'm going to find the perfect person to give this watch to – I love giving me stuff away... "

How come you've never lost the plot like some of the others did?

"Dunno," grins Tim. "I just have a good time, me – you've just got to be yourself, haven't you? Oh God (sets his hand on fire with his fag), now I've burnt meself. I reckon I'm *The Observer* and everyone else is the *Sunday Times*, know what I'm saying?"

Frankly no.

"Rob's definitely the *Sunday Times*, he's always getting out of his mind. Rob's the kind that'll kick the door off it's fookin' hinges and sleep in the bath. Oh God, I can't be doing with all this me representing the band anymore! What's that there? Is it vodka?"

It's water. Maybe you should have a small sip?

"Where's me beer? Oh, I've drunk it."

In 1983, aged 15, Tim left school with one O-level in English and a head full of Milky Way, quite possibly.

"When I left school I was told I was never gonna get a job," he says, rolling around in his seat, "I was fookin' told it. And it wasn't a put-down; it was just the truth – there was no opportunities in this country."

From the age of 11 Tim had been a music obsessive. Went to see Killing Joke aged 11 in his school uniform. Spent nights hiding in his room listening to John Peel and making up imaginary setlists for The Fall and New Order. So, naturally, his personal pop dream began.

"No," corrects Tim breezily, "the band thing never came into me head at all. I didn't think about anything. I thought I'd just do nothing. Did not know nothing, honestly. Then I got a job at 16, which me dad put me up for at ICI (where his father worked along with the entire population of Northwich), and everyone thought it was me dad that got me the job but it wasn't. I just said the right things. Said it was a brilliant job, said it'd be top and I could do it better than anybody else, so put your faith in me."

And you were completely lying through your teeth?

"Honestly, between you and me," says Tim, because he is nuts, "I've wanted to do every single job I've ever had properly. Whether it's the mail in ICI or working in an office pressing computers – and that's the scary thing. I must be a bit of a jobsworth."

Good Lord.

"It's the truth!" he hoots. "I've fookin' made sure I've given it my all every time. I have to do things right and it's the same with singing. You're dying to laugh, aren't you? I know you are!"

Every weekend he'd take coach-trips to Manchester with his gang, hang around the station and the record shops. Went to gigs. Some mates formed a covers band, The Electric Crayon Set, with Tim singing, or rather screaming Iggy Pop and Zeppelin tunes. Madchester was inventing itself. His mate Steve Harrison from the Omega Music record-shop told him about this new band, The Charlatans, and they went to see them. They had something, principally a groove-monster Hammond-organ nutter called Rob Collins, but they needed a proper frontman. Then the rubbish one left; Tim joined. In the summer of 1989 they wrote a song called "The Only One I Know", put it out on their own Dead Dead Good label; it went straight to the top of the indie charts. The rest is hysteria/wilderness/hysteria and several billion sentences with the word "lips" in them. And right now, those lips were made for drinking.

"I think we're getting a bit of a reputation for being drinkers, aren't we?" supposes Tim, ordering another bottle.

Well, yes you are, but then so's everybody else.

"It's getting serious," notes Tim, "Gets to me that, a bit – it's better to be a thinker than a drinker."

Oh, you can be both.

"Well, yeah, you can be everything (massive grin). There's definitely something that's happened this year – everyone's just up for it! Don't know what it is. The brilliant tunes? Maybe you have to drink to do something brilliant. Which comes first?"

Tim loves his fags and his booze. He once said "I love smoking, and I love drinking because it makes me smoke more." He can open bottles of beer with his ear. The Charlatans have just returned from their latest American touring jamboree – 18 days and 10 gigs with Menswear. The two bands rapidly bonded and proceeded swiftly on to the rock 'n' roll diet of "blow and bevvy – Menswear are brilliant, it was house-on-fire stuff. We all lost our minds a bit heheh."

Before they'd even landed The Charlatans were arrested – for enjoying themselves in the company of "a tosser". The bloke in front of Tim's seat objected to the beery tomfoolery behind, put his arms around the back of his seat, hands deliberately obliterating Tim's in-built TV screen.

"So me and Mark," giggles Tim, "started tickling his fingers."

The bloke went berserk. Slammed Tim's seat, made a formal complaint to the appropriate authorities.

"So when we landed in New York," says Tim, "there was a Tannoy announcement saying the plane would be delayed while they waited for the police. They moved everyone out except us and the police came on and cuffed us all up. We got taken to the Port Authority cells. There'd been all these Chinese whispers that we were all swearing and spitting and smoking on a no-smoking flight, which was all lies. I was a bit scared, the guns and being cuffed and they're massive on planting stuff on you. They read us our rights, all this knobhead stuff. Got the FBI in. Took our passports off us and took our shoe-laces off us – don't know what that was for, I thought maybe it's just because they think we'll hang ourselves! (looks bemused) I wouldn't hang meself, I'm loving it at the moment, you can't put a downer on me!"

Three hours later the FBI pronounced the situation "ridiculous" and freedom was granted. Jail-bound or not, Tim loves the travelling, he loves America and he loves his new tattoo, taken from the *Daily Express* cartoon by Kelvin and Hobbs: "I love it because it looks like he's asleep and he can't get out of bed. Tigers are top: they're ferocious and cuddly." He also loves Chloe, his girlfriend of the last two years, the two years in which Tim's been happier than he's ever been before "but never content: there's too much to be getting on with, but happiness is cool." And so's being in love.

"Everything revolves around it," notes Tim, "everything that I do. Every day I consider Chloe's feelings. She inspires me. I think it's the best thing in the world, I really do."

It's easy for him to fend off the inevitable lure of female fandom.

"I like meeting new people," he states. "I'm into it, but I'm also loyal and that makes people sick, but loyalty's cool. I think when you're loyal you have to question why (begins to crumble for no reason whatsoever). I think too much. Honest I do; I think too much all the time and I don't even know what I'm thinking about. I always thought that Timothy Burgess was a cool but classical name but Martin Blunt was very sporty."

Help.

"Chloe's me stabiliser," says Tim, returning to the plot. "She's mental but she's me voice of reason, she's a Taurus, a bit of a back-bone. I've got a fully-formed backbone, but there's someone there just needs to pull it from the back, an outer-puller. Oh God."

Well, indeed.

"I'm so shit with words, me, I'm tellin' yer. No one fookin' ever understands a thing I say – now why is that?"

You're a somewhat bizarre conversationalist.

"No one gets what I mean or say," says Tim, looking perplexed. "They feel it but they don't get it. I wish I could be really... what's the word... integral and talk about proper stuff. I always imagine Jarvis Cocker to be really clever. I'm averagely statistical."

He begins shouting, becomes finger-snappy demented.

"May Jarvis never die!" he shouts, "He's one in a million! And I'm one in 10 (gales of laughter). Nah, I'm one in a million as well. I think. I don't know what I am, but I'm finding out."

I doubt there's many of you in a pound.

"Honestly, just tell me," he intones, "just tell me what I am! Because I've not got a clue! I still don't know what the fuck's going on in my head."

Have you always danced at all times, while sitting and walking, the lot?

"Yeah. It used to be with a hunch, but now I'm a bit straighter. Now why is that?"

Haven't got a clue, mate.

"I think people slouch when all they've got in the world is hatred. You straighten up when you've got something to celebrate."

And he's got much to celebrate, not least being so good-looking it's preposterous. He's got those sweepy eyelashes that form semi-circles on the cheeks. His eyes are gigantic and ink black. The thick, dark hair. The snub nose. The famed lips. The perfect teeth. Must have a profound effect on your life, being beautiful. What does it feel like?

"Feels like nuthin'," he cringes, genuinely mortified. "Dani Behr is officially classed as good-looking, but you wouldn't want to go out with her, would you? You'd hate her!"

There must be security in good-looks: after all, people have killed themselves because they're ugly.

"Yeah, but I'm really... like in some relationships I'm really not self-assured at all. Seriously. I'm not into people for looks; I'm into what people get up to, what they kick up about, people who make a fuss. Rather than just sitting there being gorgeous. I don't even think I'm good-looking (begins flattening hair down into deeply nerdy bowl-cut). I've never ever, ever fancied meself. Oh God, so what do I do? Is that weird? Do you think that's weird?"

I think everything's weird.

"I like records. I like records more than I like people! Hyickick!"

I go to the bathroom and leave Tim with the tape-recorder on in case he feels like telling a story. He does. And it goes like this:

"Hello. This is Tim. I'm going to tell a little wee story about the time we went to Sweden. It was top, right – we were playing on a little boat in Sweden sailing down the river and we got to the end of it and it was unbelievable right, our sound geezer he got taken off the boat and he got slammed into prison and no one knows what the story is because it was kept really quiet and he's only just got out. The only problem with telling this story is that everyone in The Charlatans seems to have been in prison and that really worries me. Because I really want to be taken seriously for our music and I get scared sometimes that people don't take us that seriously. And it's probably one of the hardest things in the whole world to get. But I think we're getting there. And all the devils inside me are beginning to turn into angels."

Tim is a "big-time insomniac" who often wakes up at 3am with the urge to wash all his clothes and have them ready for 6am, whereupon he will hang them over the doors. He gets lost every-where he goes; never been able to find his way back to the same place twice, "not ever". He reckons it's because he can't drive and he's used to being dropped off all the time. I reckon it's because taking responsibility for yourself is boring and there are more important things to think about.

"You're right," he nods, "but I'm too scared to admit it."

He has two astonishingly distinct handwriting styles and whisks his Filofax out to prove it: one a beautifully neat, boxy, level set of capitals, the other a swirling extravagance – the work of two completely different souls.

Which one is the real you?

(Becoming incapable of speech) "The real me ish the capicals."

Tim was told by a woman he spoke to in San Francisco he was "ultra Gemini. She told me I was Geminied out me mind." It seems we have the evidence. And now an alarm's gone off in his head. There's something he's not said and he must say it imme-diately. He switches the tape recorder back on.

"The Charlatans," announces Tim, "are at the forefront rather than the backfront of anything musical in the last fookin' 20 years. Everyone always thought of us as part of this baggy scene and I always thought it was something different; you can drop

out, do drugs and take over the world, that's what I thought
it was, but everyone else thought it was baggy trousers. We're
doing something that'll last for ever. I just want to be great,
that's all. And now I've lost me credit card!"

You're an absolute nutter, Tim Burgess, you really are.

"I'm shorry! I really am shorry!"

Within three hours Tim will find himself comatose on his living-
room carpet. For my part, I will awake with a dodgy eye from a
close-range arm-shooting incident, a limp to match his own and
a lovely new watch for deep-sea diving with, several sizes too
big. You don't just have a drink with Tim Burgess: you have a
surreal and life-threatening experience. Meanwhile, he's too
late for wishing he'll be great one day because he already is.
And the new-born angels inside him know it.

Delivery

■ **Sharon O'Connell**

Melody Maker December 2 1995

If ever there was a band for the nineties, Garbage is it. Fusing the power and sex of rock's aching tradition with industrial beats, string sections, and all kinds of deliciously imaginative, deep, dark and sensual detail, Garbage subvert the equation with Shirley Manson, their sassy and sussed vocalist. Unafraid of her own sexuality, in control of how she projects herself, Shirley is an inspiration for other women who enjoy feeling sexy without feeling compromised.

Sharon O'Connell spent three days on tour with Garbage in America, and despite initially feeling like a glorified snoop (something which crosses any sensitive journalist's mind when sent to effectively spy on strangers), she ended up feeling as if she'd made four new friends. Her conversations with Shirley shatter any theories concerning the irrelevance of gender and sexuality in today's rock culture, while the overall tone of her piece is warm and perceptive.

"We just got lucky," shrugs Shirley Manson, "like any band that enjoys success. There's a million bands out there who are brilliant and a million bands who will never see the light of day. OK, I think we made a cool record, but it was absolutely simple, blessed luck."

Shirley has, with the kind of genuine who-me? modesty so totally characteristic of the whole band, omitted to mention the fact that Garbage did a little more than just make a cool record and have fate give them the nod. There are maybe a couple of hundred cool records let loose every year and, if you know where to look, you can treat your soul to a squillion, short-lived jump-starts that make any shit life might throw at you that much easier to swallow.

But when it comes to hanging around longer than the moment, when a record doesn't just quicken the pulse but seems to measure the very temper of the time, to define the indefinable (obviously a different thing for every one of us) and pour it down over you in the neatest form imaginable, well, it seems like a lamentably long time between drinks.

Garbage's debut album is a potential contender for me in what is a depressingly short list of Zeitgeist-busting records. 'The Psychedelic Furs" is in there, as are "London Calling", "In The City","Unknown Pleasures", "Heroes" and "Nevermind". Plenty of other records may have done more divine damage along the way, scraped across my psyche far more savagely or just thrown a much wilder party, but in terms of putting a finger on ... *something* – and disturbing it – the list of successful records is a short one. Maybe one day I'll add "Garbage" to that list. I don't know. Only time will tell.

———————

IT COULD have gone either way with Garbage, that's the first thing. Take Shirley Manson, a singer with a no-shit, powerhouse personality, an unarguable sexual magnetism and, by her own admission, a rather less than credible past (in dodgy Scots rockers Goodbye Mr Mackenzie) and Butch Vig, one of *the* big cheese producers currently working (Nirvana, Smashing Pumpkins, Sonic Youth); put them together with a couple of other musicians/producers (Steve Marker and Duke Erikson, who've worked with Nine Inch Nails, Paw, L7 and U2 among others) and you've got either the wettest dream a marketing man ever had or the most shameless vanity unit to have ever seen the light of day.

Right?

"In the UK I did think there was an enormous possibility for us being dissed," admits Shirley "It would have been so easy for people to say this is a female-fronted, producer band and this is a load of shit."

"I know that if I heard that some producer was putting an album out," says Butch, "I would look at it cynically and think he was just a fucking egomaniac. But it's *not* my album, and we're a totally collaborative, psychotic, dysfunctional unit, like any band is."

The Garbage story, though, with its almost accidental inclusion of the nastily tarred and seductively feather boa-ed 'Vow' on a *Volume* CD compilation and ensuing feverish reception, has already pretty much become the stuff of rock legend. But it hasn't all been easy. For most of its life, Garbage was Butch, Steve and Duke, and they're the first to admit that for a long time they had no idea what the hell they were doing. They needed a woman (hah!) – specifically, Shirley – to help them find that out.

"The boys," as she fondly calls them, first saw Shirley on MTV performing "Suffocate Me" in a band called Angel Fish. They were at the time, Duke explains, "totally chaotic and really looking for someone who could focus the songs. And it wasn't a matter of just finding a singer that might have worked; we needed a kindred spirit."

So, what was it you all saw in Shirley that made you know she'd be so right for Garbage?

"It was the way I stroked my breasts and thighs!" she cackles.

"It was her voice, obviously," says Butch, as quietly spoken as Shirley is voluble. "I liked it that she sang with understatement – low and subtle instead of screaming in your face."

So, the invitation went out and Shirley flew from her home in Edinburgh to Steve's basement studio in Madison, Wisconsin. That first audition was, according to Shirley, "hideous".

There was no isolation booth, so she was set in front of a mic upstairs with Steve's two cats glaring at her, while downstairs the boys drank beer and listened.

"I remember thinking I was cheap and disgusting," recalls Shirley with a shudder, "because it felt like an audition and I'm not a session singer, even though when I first met them in London and we hung out, I loved them all as people. It was a visceral thing and I knew absolutely in my body that I would like to work with them. But the audition was an absolute disaster."

Fate, though, wanted things her way. Shirley had another bash and somehow or other, a connection was forged. It was apparently when she ad libbed "Joan Of Arc coming back for more" (from "Vow") that she clinched it.

"I thought, "this is cool, there's something going on here,'" remembers Butch. "That was the line that really connected with me. I can't imagine having made this record without Shirley. We didn't know what we wanted to do, but after she joined us, we became a band."

"And Duke connected with 'I'm gonna suck your cock, big boy!'" laughs Shirley, speaking from her personal, ever-expanding universe.

"Right," sighs Duke, who's obviously used to this stuff. "Actually," he deadpans, "I didn't like any of it. Butch had to talk me into it."

———

RIGHT NOW Shirley, Butch, Duke and Steve are on the road for the first time as Garbage, joined by bass player Daniel Shulman, an easy-going, six foot something Californian who played on the

Warren G album. They're finding out if they can do this live, whether they can survive without the props of double-tracked vocals, multi-stacked guitar parts and the endless layering of looped noises that recording can provide, whether it's smart to try and prove their pudding anywhere else other than in the studio.

This is where your gallivanting journalist comes in, having joined the band between Philadelphia and Atlanta on their first American tour for three dates – Washington DC, Cleveland and Nashville.

When I hit DC it's half closed, due to the budget-balancing ruckus that currently has Bill Clinton and Newt Gingrich locking horns, so even if I did have time to visit The Smithsonian Insititute, the Cenotaph, The American Holocaust Museum and anywhere else remotely interesting – which I don't – I'd find them shut down as "inessential services". Luckily this lock-out doesn't apply to essential soul-succouring services like the playing of gigs, so at The Black Cat on a freezing Thursday night in a run-down neigh-bourhood, I see Garbage.

———

REMEMBER THAT scene in *Spinal Tap* where there's an in-store organised and nobody turns up? That's a particularly American phenomenon known as the 'meet 'n' greet'. It's where the people who actually work your record – record com-pany employees, record store staff etc – come to shake your hand and say hi/express their genuine admiration/kiss your ass. There's one organised for Garbage before tonight's show.

There are plenty of fans here shyly asking for autographed posters, the odd fanzine wanting a few words with Butch, who happily complies, a fair few old scenesters and a gaggle of local record-store types at one table who whoop and holler and stamp their feet when Garbage come in.

"Dook! Dook! It's the Dook!" they bellow. Duke has the kind of low-key, ironic humour that allows him to take this in his stride and he bows with good-natured extravagance. Shirley and Butch don't mind it either, but poor old Steve, a polite but intensely private person, looks like he's about to turn tail and run.

Shirley gleefully points out to me the fabulous irony of the fact that in Scotland, to "greet" means to cry.

Don't you find all this stuff pretty intolerable?

"Meet 'n' greets are a strange beast," she admits, "because these are people who have worked incredibly hard on your record, and it's really easy to think as a band that the buck stops at you, which it doesn't. There are so many people who truly believe in the record and want it to do well and they work their arses off. Sometimes, when you're tired or depressed or you've fallen out with your boyfriend over the phone, it's a drag, and I'd be a liar to say otherwise, but these are the people who literally get our records out to the public so ... "

But presumably you'd draw the line at some of the tricks that the rock 'n' roll circus might one day ask you to perform?

"If I felt I was being asked to do something beyond my own desires, I would not do it," Shirley says emphatically. "But I don't see what the big deal is with going out there and thanking the people from Sam Goodys who are selling our record. I see it as payback, and I think it's only fair."

The place is rammed tonight and after a hesitant start, Garbage light the touch paper and are suddenly ablaze. Shirley, every inch a star in leopard print T-shirt, short, black suede skirt and knee boots, gets so carried away bouncing up and down to the bumpy rhythm of "Stupid Girl" that she falls arse over tit straight across Dan's monitor. She's barely fazed. And Daniel starts dancing madly across the stage, finally raising one arm aloft for a triumphant two-finger salute. Shirley gives his wrists a friendly but firm slap afterwards in the dressing room. Well, the power of the moment and all that.

Next stop, Cleveland.

—————

"CLEVELAND You @?**±!! Rock", trumpet the impressively tasteless sweatshirts on sale at the bar a few doors down from Peabody's Down Under, where Garbage play tonight. Despite these claims and the recent opening here of the massive Rock Hall Of Fame, I doubt it. I mean, the place feels like one giant Hackney, and you try and name one band that comes from this city, *apart* from Pere Ubu. Remember the ludicrous "Hello Cleveland!" scenario in *Spinal Tap*? There's a good reason why the scriptwriters picked Cleveland.

When I arrive, I'm greeted by bitter cold and horizontal sleet, but outside the venue, hours before soundcheck, a lone fan is already waiting. He wants an autograph from each of Garbage. That's cool. Then the guy wants to know if they'll put him on the guest list. This is not so cool. It's a bloody cheek, in fact. And when Garbage's manager, Shirley and I head out to grab some food, the guy follows. That's plain creepy.

You must get a fair bit of that from lust stricken/weird/sad guys, Shirley.

"No, honestly, I don't," she smiles, looking fabulous, as ever. "After a show, fans always cluster around the boys and I'll be standing there in the corner, literally twiddling my thumbs."

That seems incredible, frankly.

"I think maybe it's because I've got red hair. It's been the bane of my life, honestly! Men find it repulsive and women find it intimidating! That's why I thank God Acetone are supporting on this tour, because they speak to me and they play me songs in the dressing room and they let me paint their nails."

(An aside: the nail-painting thing has gotten a real hold on this tour. Butch, Duke and Steve all sport the same blue/black Chanel polish as Shirley. "Call me cheap," she grins, "but I think nail polish on a guy is really erotic."

_____

"I HAVE a very complicated past in bands," Shirley sighs as we settle into our plane seats, earlier that day with takeaway bagels and coffee, "and it's all intertwined with all kinds of weirdness. I was initially asked to join a band when I was 15 or 16, by a boy who just wanted to hang out with me. Well, he wanted to fuck me basically, and I wanted to sleep with him too, so it was a happy bargaining!"

The band was Goodbye Mr Mackenzie, but even after the relationship broke up, Shirley knew being in a band was what she wanted to do for ever. Just not that particular band.

"I really do love music," she enthuses, "and even now I realise that I'm awakening still. With meeting the three boys I'm now working with, I find I've been almost resensitised. One of the reasons is they encouraged me to write and be involved in the whole creative process, which I'd been deliberately obstructed from doing in previous bands. In Goodbye Mr Mackenzie, the singer and the drummer wrote practically everything and they really liked it that way. And I understand _why_, but you lose enthusiasm for what you're doing if you're not involved in creating.

"When I first met Steve and Butch and Duke, they said they wanted me to bring in ideas, and that regenerated my enthusiasm for music. I finally feel as if I've moved on as an artist. I'd always been really musically retarded, because I didn't get to express myself in any way at all. I feel like I've taken this huge creative leap since I met the boys. It binds me to them in a really strange way, because they freed me of an awful lot of baggage."

_____

AT THE top of Shirley's list of heroines are Siouxsie Sioux and Chrissie Hynde. The Banshees was the first gig she ever saw and it made a big impression.

"She was *amazing*," Shirley tells me. "It must have been during the 'Kaleidoscope' tour, because Siouxsie had a camera and was taking Polaroid shots of the crowd. I just thought she was *the* coolest creature ever. I can't really put into words why I connected with her – it was something I felt in my gut. She just thrilled me and made me feel that things were possible when I was at an age where I thought I would be in the mud forever."

And Chrissie Hynde?

"The way she played her guitar I think was the coolest thing. Certainly she was one of the boys, but I wanted to be like her because I didn't want to be a girly girl and connect with whoever was out there at the time. Who was there? Hayzee Fantayzee?" Shirley pulls a face. "The Thompson Twins?

"I wanted to be cool, and the great thing about Chrissie Hynde was she retained her femininity about her. Even though she was in jeans and she played her guitar down low on her hips, she was still a woman. And her voice was so vulnerable and yet so strong. To me she has the most perfect voice in the history of modern rock music."

I can understand why you shrank from the idea of having to connect with girly girls. On the role-model scale, they notch up a fairly fat zero.

"Oh, I like girly girls too," Shirley says quickly, "I mean, I am a woman and I like being a woman, but there are still areas in life that, as a woman, we're not supposed to be interested in or to embrace. We're not allowed to be aggressive, we're not supposed to be vicious and we're not supposed to be sexually upfront or even have desires."

It must be pretty strange being the only woman on a tour where both bands and the entire crew is male. It's a bit of an energy imbalance, isn't it?

Shirley nods. "Albeit that they're all truly wonderful, non-misogynistic, brilliant people without exception, it's still hard. You sometimes just feel like an outsider, even if you're not.

"Occasionally I'll forget and I'll say something that, when you're around a lot of men, isn't a sensible thing to say. Like, you could be sitting there and say, Oh, God, I feel so horny tonight! And then you think, hang on, I'm in a van with 16 poor men who have been away from their wives and girlfriends and I don't for a minute want them to think I'm trying to come on to them. And they would never think that, but at the same time, it makes me feel a bit uncomfortable. Sometimes I forget that I'm not one of the boys."

Would you say you felt more male than female, or vice versa?

"I'm not ghettoised by my sexuality at all," says Shirley. "I'm not a man's woman and I'm not a woman's woman. I love both parts of me for different reasons."

OK then if you could swap gender for a week, would you do it?

"Definitely!" she says excitedly. "I would love to have sex with a cock! Sorry, but I would *love* to do it; I'd do it happily for a year!" She laughs her fabulously infectious, filthy laugh. The air hostess looks at us both very strangely indeed.

(An aside: I ask Butch and Duke the same question later. They both say yes, they'd love to have sex as a woman. Shirley is clearly delighted. "I *knew* you wouldn't let me down, boys" she says, beaming at them.)

———————

FACT; ANY woman who looks as drop-dead gorgeous as Shirley, who is as sussed and savvy and who projects a powerful sexuality over which she obviously has full control, is going to end up fuelling fantasies from a thousand bedroom walls.

Does that ever bother you? I mean, those posters you were signing in DC are going to be used for something other than scrap paper, aren't they?

Big deal, reckons Shirley.

"Even if I was in the background in every single photo," she reasons, "someone, somewhere would pick me out and masturbate over me. If I was completely covered so you couldn't see any of my features, someone would find *that* sexually thrilling. You can't avoid people finding you attractive and I have no problem with masturbation. I know it probably goes on and there's nothing I can do to stop it, so I'm not going to worry myself about it. At least nobody's catching any horrible diseases or hurting anybody. And they might have a good time. I am an entertainer, after all!" she laughs.

"But seriously, I've never done anything I've felt uncomfortable with in regard to my own sexuality. If I wear a short skirt, it's because I want to wear a short skirt because I think it looks good, not because I want to turn someone on in the front row. But there are things I deliberately will not do, because I know it's not doing women any good. If someone wanted to take a photograph of me nude, I'd like doing it, but I'm not going to because I don't think that's how I should be portraying myself as a woman."

You mean you feel a certain social responsibility?

"I don't let other people dictate to me how I present myself or what I choose to do, but it's in my mind all the time that there are women who are not as able to articulate themselves and their desires as I am. We have a long way to go in society before the mass of women feel comfortable with themselves.

"Already I've had accusations of being a toy, of being sexual, and I just say if you can't stomach it, that's tough. If someone *does* find me sexy, what can I fucking do about it?"

IT's SATURDAY and the Garbage tour has just hit Nashville. It's cool. At least, it's not Cleveland and the sun is shining. The legendary Music Row is a massive disappointment – a huddle of shabby stores selling phenomenal amounts of absolute shite. But it *is* the setting of Dylan's "Nashville Skyline" and it's a great place to pick up absolute essentials like a snakeskin cowboy belt, nail clippers in the shape of a guitar and a bunch of magnetised Elvis postcards. And tonight Garbage play at Exit/In, the bar featured heavily in Altman's *Nashville*.

"Garbage" is very much a record of the Nineties. If it does glance back at all, it's to the early Eighties and English bands like The Psychedelic Furs and Roxy Music (of whom Butch, Steve and Duke are all massive fans), who share that same viscous, slicked-down darkness, who, like Garbage combine the gently melancholic with the downright malevolent, who love hooky, groovacious tunes as much as they like a heavy rock riff. It makes for a pretty claustrophobic, self-obsessive album, despite the impressive pop clout of songs like "Only Happy When It Rains", "Vow" and "Queer".

"Yeah," admits Steve over a bowl of pre-gig soup, having successfully avoided all previous attempts to engage him in conversation. "We dug down pretty far when we were writing those songs, so it's fair to call them self-obsessive. It was a chance to get a lot of stuff out, and it's almost like there's a fifth member of the band – this weird, psychotic, paranoid, mutant ... thing."

In the cab last night, Butch and Duke and Shirley joked that you were a band fuelled almost entirely by self loathing. How serious were you?

"I don't think any of us feels very settled or comfortable with the world, and that's where that comes from," offers Shirley, who's whipped out a mirror at the table and is starting on her make-up.

"That's part of the mystery of life though. You don't ever feel like you've arrived or that you've got everything in order and I really don't think anyone in the band is particularly enamoured of themselves. I think if you could say that you were really comfortable with yourself, you'd have to be criminally insane!"

Butch: "It's much more difficult to deal with living in Western civilisation than it was, say, 20 years ago. Then it was easier to get ahead and make money and fit in with your peers and accept whatever dream was passed down from your parents. Now everybody's fucked up in some way; some people deal with that, some people don't.

"I know sometimes I beat myself up psychologically, and I need to obsess about a record and lose myself in it in order to feel that it makes sense. It's not a very healthy thing, because I give up my personal life to some extent – not only on the Garbage record, but on everything I've worked on over the last five or six years. You'd think I'd be able to separate it and walk away at the end of the day, but I can't, and we were all that way making this music. It permeated everything we did."

_____

OK, A flippant question. Quickly, while the waitress brings that last round of drinks with the bill.

If you could time travel, where would you choose to go?

Shirley: "I'd go to Paris in the late 1920's , because it's one of the most beautiful cities in the world and there was so much going on there. I love the music of that time and I love the clothes."

"Possibly New York post-World War Two," Butch decides. "It seemed like there were so many opportunities and it has such a glamorous look in photographs. I don't know if I'd want to visit the future, as enticing as it is. It's kind of scary."

Steve would, though.

"I would definitely go forward, because I'd like to know if there can still be humans. I'm pretty pessimistic," he smiles.

"It would be safer to go back, but then I already know what happened."

And Duke?

He laughs. "I'd go back to when I was 12 years old and try and fix everything that I fucked up along the way. I'd be a new and improved me."

Duke, there's really no need. Believe me.

White Heat, White Noise, White Out

■ **Lisa Verrico**
Blah Blah Blah April 1996

s a rule, The Prodigy don't like the press. Basically a bunch of lads from Essex, they're a tightly knit, self-contained unit who approach life like it was a Boys' Own Adventure, and they rarely give interviews, preferring to hang out with each other rather than members of the music industry. But when Lisa Verrico flew to Switzerland to interview the band for the first issue of *Blah Blah Blah*, she arrived to find "demented dancer" Keith Flint in slippers and jogging pants, cuddling a cat. After such an unexpected introduction, Lisa proceeded to break through the band's barriers, and returned home with a potential cover story. In the end, Blur were *Blah Blah Blah*'s cover stars, although The Prodigy went on to shake up rock culture with their number one hit single, "Firestarter", proving that Lisa's judgment had been right.

Halfway up a snow-covered mountain in a picturesque, Swiss ski resort not far from Lake Geneva, The Prodigy are playing house. Keith Flint greets guests at their luxury, three-storey wooden chalet fresh from a stint in the sauna. Dressed casually in jogging bottoms and jumper, his multi-coloured spikes of hair drooping lamely, he looks nothing like the demented dancer who fronts the band's live show, or rolls around the stage in a transparent, plastic ball. Cuddling the chalet's resident pet, a white Persian cat called Figaro, Keith slumps down on a sofa and raises his legs to show off some designer slippers.

"*Air Perrys*, if you don't mind," he demurs, in a very well-mannered voice. "*Everyone* on the slopes is wearing them this season."

The Prodigy have come to the tourist town of Leysin to feature in the second series of Channel 4's snowboarding show, *Board-stupid*. Other artists invited to spend a similar four days here include Goldie, who arrives tomorrow, The Chemical Brothers, Jamiroquai and Gabrielle. That The Prodigy are first is a mark of their well-publicised interest in the sport. The whole band took up snowboarding two years ago, after songwriter Liam Howlett bought his first board.

"I went round Liam's house one day," says Keith, "and I caught him carpet-surfing. He was in the lounge, standing on what I thought was his nan's ironing board. I told him to sit down, breathe deeply and I'd make him a nice cup of tea. Then he explained what it was and showed me a couple of videos. Straightaway, I was hooked."

Since then, The Prodigy have been to France, Switzerland and Colorado in search of the perfect piste. Liam, who has been practising on dry slopes in England, is probably the best, although all admit to being pretty poor, thanks to a relentless tour schedule over the last 18 months. What The Prodigy lack in experience, however, they make up for in enthusiasm.

"On our first day," recalls Keith, "we were so keen that we started riding down the mountain before finding out the route. God knows where we went. It took us hours to get back. At one stage, when we were miles off-piste, I seriously considered abseiling.

"I enjoy the adventure of cross-country. I like being out in the wilds, reading the terrain and the chaos of trying to avoid trees. It's a lot like motorcross, which I used to be into, but without the noise and fumes."

Clearly, Keith is as mad on the slopes as he is on the stage. The other members' snowboarding styles also reflect their personalities. Liam, who grew up on BMXs and skateboards, prefers the technical aspect of learning to do tricks and jumps. Maxim Reality, the band's MC, is into the adrenaline rush of fast, downhill speeds. Leeroy, Keith's 6'4" dance partner, enjoys the challenge and sense of achievement. All share the same pet hates – "fashionable", fluorescent gear (none will wear the designer label clothes they get sent for free), show-off snowboarders and, worst of all, skiers.

"We don't get involved in the rivalry with skiers," claims Keith, unconvincingly. "At least, we don't hit them on purpose, it's only 'cos we're crap. Although if I am going to collide with a skier, I'll make sure my elbows go out.

"I ran into one woman skier in Colorado and got lodged between her legs. I'm not sure how it happened, but I got stuck facing backwards, crouching down. We must have gone a hundred yards together. When I stood up, people were holding up cards and clapping. They thought we were the next Torvill and Dean."

The Prodigy are a band on a boys-own adventure. Tight-knit and self-sufficient, they never seem to tire of each other's company. On tour, they travel, hang out and explore foreign cities together. On evenings off, they go out to clubs or concerts with one another. All still live in their hometown of Braintree in Essex, while Keith and Liam's last holiday was spent snowboarding in Colorado.

The band's line-up has remained unchanged since the summer of 1991, when The Prodigy scored a Top Three hit with their second release, the Public Service advertisement-sampling, rave record "Charly". A manic, E-infested, parent-scaring single, "Charly" spawned a string of cash-in copies. Worse still, it became a focus for the exploitation of rave culture and 19-year-old Liam Howlett was accused of selling out the very scene that had inspired him.

Little over a year later, The Prodigy's debut album, "Experience", a complex mix of samples and breakbeats, was proof that the band had moved on, although still the rave tag stuck. Moreover, their music remained slightly out of step with fashion. It was too mainstream for the techno purists, too hardcore for the pop lot. Despite continued commercial success, The Prodigy stayed industry outsiders. But if the press didn't want to write about them and the radio wouldn't play their records, the band could keep in touch with their fans through their shows. At a time when most dance acts thought that playing live meant miming to an E'd-up crowd on a tiny stage, the size of The Prodigy's audience allowed them to take the rock route. They played large capacity venues favoured by guitar bands and, instead of relying solely on a light show and computer-generated graphics, put on a proper performance.

So *Boardstupid* thought they'd have no problem performing at a 500-capacity club in Leysin. However, since all of their equipment is in Australia (where the band recently took part in the Big Day Out, the Antipodean equivalent of Lollapalooza) the programme's producers tried to come up with an alternative, suggesting that The Prodigy should record an acoustic session inside the chalet.

"Someone obviously forgot to mention that we're not too impressive unplugged," laughs Liam. "Had they warned us in advance, Leeroy would have brought along his tap shoes. That's about as good as it gets."

Unfortunately, getting out of their TV interview, scheduled for tomorrow morning, is not quite as easy. At one end of the chalet's spacious sitting-room, the finishing touches are being put to a makeshift studio set. False walls have been filled with insulating foam, burnt to give a "cratered" effect, then painted a lurid mix of scarlet, lime green, bright blue and acid pink.

"If you could turn this set into fabric," notes Keith wryly, crossing the purple carpet and slumping down on a brightly-coloured sofa, "you'd probably make the top ski outfit of all time."

The Prodigy finally shed the last of their rave roots in 1993 when they began working on their second album, "Music For The Jilted Generation".

"I stopped writing all that hands-in-the-air bollocks," explains Liam. "The spirit of the rave scene stayed in that it was still good-time music you could dance to, but the songs had a new attitude and energy and hardness. It wasn't a conscious decision to change. I just wasn't listening to much dance music anymore and most techno bored me. Rock became a bigger influence. I liked its energy. I think the Smashing Pumpkins are wicked and I was really into the Chilli Peppers."

In addition, Maxim had turned Liam onto Wu Tang Clen, Leeroy liked '60s soul and Keith discovered Stone Temple Pilots. Guitar samples, deep dub, jungle and hip hop were packed into a string of successful singles. "No Good (Start The Dance)", "One Love", "Voodoo People" and anti-Criminal Justice Bill anthem "Their Law", featuring Pop Will Eat Itself, all made the Top 20. Inevitably, critical plaudits followed with the band being nominated for a Mercury Award. Meanwhile, The Prodigy's live show had absorbed all the attitude and energy of the music.

"Go to a Sepultura concert," says Keith, "and it might be loud and the singer may say he wants to go out and kill children, but it's not necessarily hard. Our show kicks ass. The crowd really let off. They jump around manically for a couple of hours and they remember that night for a long time to come. You can sit around at home and listen to music for years, but it'll never drive you to leap around the lounge like that.

"The real challenge for us is to rock people who think they don't want to be rocked. Before The Prodigy, I used to hang out with a bunch of strict metalheads. We'd go to real rock venues and if I danced I was dissed. I was suppressed by my mates. You could smoke a ton of draw, drink 14 Special Brews and fall over, but if you shuffled your feet, that was the end of you. Now metalheads come to our concerts and don't notice they're not listening to traditional music.

"They start moving around without even realising. Suddenly they're like, 'Oh my God, what am I doing? I'm dancing!'

"The live act is what we're all about. We've dedicated the last five years of our lives to it, so we don't just want a polite round of applause at the end of a show. We want to stir people up so much that they have to be carried out, exhausted, on a stretcher. To watch thousands of Oasis fans trample down 500 tents to get into our field at Glastonbury was a dream come true."

The Prodigy's triumphant Glastonbury gig, easily the highlight of last year's festival, altered the band's status overnight. For the first time, they became both a mainstream act and achingly hip.

"We actually asked to play Glastonbury the previous year," says Liam, "but the organisers wouldn't let us. They said we weren't big enough and got Orbital instead. We just wanted to take part. We offered to do it for free, even pay our own expenses, but they preferred to bore the audience with some so-called 'cool' bands. That really annoyed me. If people want to see a nice light show, they can go to the Planetarium. I don't like putting other bands down, but you'd need to be on 30 mushrooms and at least a couple of Acid to have fun watching that."

It's hard to imagine Liam Howlett getting angry, in spite of a nose-ring and brightly-dyed hair that make him look almost as manic as Keith. He is polite, softly-spoken and thoughtful. He'll chat only if Keith lets him get a word in edgeways and is surprisingly content to let the others speak for him, even on the subject of his songwriting. The only business-minded member of the band, Liam insists that The Prodigy have never sought commercial success, and recently turned down a major label offer, preferring to stay on dance label XL where he has total control over the band's output. His only aim, he says, is to write songs that the whole band are happy with and, most importantly, to keep his music credible. Nevertheless, platinum sales of "Music For The Jilted Generation" have made Liam more than enough money to indulge his passions for fast cars and snowboarding. He has also installed a studio in his converted coachhouse home. It is where he is supposed to be right now, finishing The Prodigy's third album, originally due out in May, but already put back to the summer. Liam, it seems, is in no hurry.

"I'm a slow writer," he says. "I like to take my time, always have. It doesn't matter when the album comes out because I've finished four tracks already and two of them are singles. Anyway, it amuses me that we became so successful last year without releasing any new music at all. I may wait until 1997 to put out another record. If I can hold out 'til then, we should be massive."

Liam describes his new songs as similar to "Poison", the fifth and final single from "Jilted" and The Prodigy's only output last year.

"There's definitely more attitude coming through in the music," he says. "It's still hard, but there's not as many big breakdowns. I'm constantly coming across tunes that give me inspiration. That's why I'm always out and about watching bands at festivals. At the moment I'm really into the Chemical Brothers. I think that whole breakbeat with acid and hip hop scene is pretty cool. It's the little things I usually pick up on though. For example, someone put on a DJ Shadow record this afternoon and the beats were wicked. So I stole them. Shit! Can I take that back? Now DJ Shadow will be scouring our record for his beats. He'll be ringing up, demanding royalties."

Despite delaying the release of the album, Liam insists that he doesn't feel under pressure to better his own success.

"The only pressure," he says, "is to progress the music. I want to surprise people every time a Prodigy record comes out. That's what I'm thinking while I write."

The band's new single, "Firestarter", out this month, contains the first surprise for Prodigy fans. It features Keith Flint on vocals.

"To most people, Keith is just that mad bloke who has been wiggling his legs about on stage for the last five years," says Liam. "Now he's having a go at some lyrics. That came about by accident. 'Firestarter' was a good instrumental track but I knew it was missing the usual Prodigy hook that sticks in your head. Keith came into the studio, said he'd like to try singing on it and went away and wrote some words. What's a firestarter? Isn't that obvious? It's Keith – it's his personality."

"Firestarter" loops a distant "hey, hey, hey" sample from Art Of Noise's '80s pop hit "Close To The Edit", and is slightly slower paced than the bulk of "Jilted". Keith's twisted lyrics and punksy, staccato style recall Flowered Up's more animated moments.

"Who on earth are Flowered Up?" asks Keith. "We've never heard of them. Are they still around?"

You remember Flowered Up. Third wave of baggy. One great single ("Weekender") and a Bez-like attraction called Barry Mooncult who liked dressing up as a giant daisy. They self-destructed after too many drugs and the singer ended up flogging dodgy tapes down Camden Market.

"Wow, cool!" exclaims Keith. "Not that we're into drugs ourselves. Honestly. We've been a drug-free zone for a number of years now. That's why we're strong on stage, not all mashed up. I mean, we might be stoned every now and again – alright, most of the time – but weed's not a drug. It's a plant. We're on a natural trip, man."

Tonight, the only stimulant available is alcohol. After a meal in the chalet, The Prodigy head out to a club in Leysin. They are clearly unimpressed by the resort's social facilities. Yesterday evening, they spent three hours in a "shit restaurant" before going on to a hip hop club that turned out to be empty. Tonight's funk club is scarcely more exciting. The music is barely audible and no one dances all night. While the rest of the band drink beer, Liam, who has decided to rename the town Bored Stupid sinks a succession of straight tequilas.

The next day, the TV production crew wait patiently for the band to appear. They play Prodigy CDs on the chalet's stereo system and dance about their gaudy set in Arnet shades. It is 10am. An hour or so later, Keith, Leeroy and Maxim stumble downstairs.

Liam, who has been throwing up for hours, locks himself in the toilet and refuses to come out. At noon, the interview takes place without him.

"So what's happened to Liam?" asks one of the programme's two presenters.

"We could tell you," begins Keith, "that he's up in the mountains, getting in some early morning snowboarding. But we won't."

"We'll just say," continues Leeroy, "that he's upstairs, praying to the bowl."

Both presenters look bemused. "Oh okay," stammers one. "Can someone tell us a Prodigy story then?"

Immediately Keith is off.

"We were at this festival in Scotland last summer," he says, "when these two kids got arrested. It was awful. One was caught drinking acid from a car battery and the other was found breaking up fireworks and snorting the powder."

The presenters look appalled.

Conveniently, as soon as the interview is over, Liam appears, insisting that an hour up on the slopes will make him feel better before the flight back to England.

As The Prodigy get out of a cable car at the top of the mountain, a Japanese rider recognises Leeroy and points him out to a friend. Trying to explain who he is, the boy starts singing "Poison" in an Oriental accent.

"I don't believe it," cries Keith, "he really does know who Leeroy is. Yesterday, someone mistook Maxim for Coolio, and Liam got told he looks like that bloke from East 17. It's not nearly as bad as what someone said to me though."

Keith lowers his voice and checks to see who is around.

"You don't think I look like Leo Sayer, do you?"

Drumnbass

■ **Charlotte Raven**

The Observer Life April 21 1996

F or her first piece of music journalism, Charlotte Raven chose to examine the mostly male premise of drum'n'bass, originally known as jungle. She swallowed her nerves and confronted Goldie (having been a little apprehensive after his previous reactions to journalists), caught up with Alex Reece on the road, and assembled the following, highly evocative appraisal of Britain's brand new punk.

British Popular Music, if you choose to believe anything you read, is undergoing a renaissance. For many people, not least the industry itself, this has come as a bloody big relief. The period between the death of Madchester and the rise of Britpop must have been hell for someone who had neither the stomach for Ecstasy nor the nerve for Nirvana. Of course, there was always the Spindoctors, but this was not an option most were keen to take. Basically, if you didn't like clubbing and you weren't up for grunge's nails-down-the-blackboard-style despair, the great British guitar revival was just the thing to get you going on about "proper songs" again.

Unfortunately, once you'd jumped about to "Parklife", become briefly convinced that you were "Supersonic", failed to buy "The

Great Escape" and named your "Wonderwall", you had come to the end of a very short list of possible new guitar-pop experiences. Britpop was never so much a scene as a shorthand for one very good band (Oasis before Noel met Paul Weller) and one not so bad band (Blur before Damon met Damien Hirst) and a bunch of bands so truly dreadful that in normal circumstances they would never have got any further than support-slots at their local Pig In Muck. Even Pulp, widely touted as the thinking person's get-out from the unseemly Blur v Oasis "debate", had been around so long before fame struck that we might conclude it wasn't meant to be. Britpop, needing something from which to suspend itself, was happy to make all these campus bands king for a day. It wasn't so much a renaissance as an amnesty from obscurity.

Meanwhile, in a parallel universe, the true saviours of British music are going about their business unremarked. These are the boys who, in backrooms or bedrooms, will coax a mysterious magic from machines. The whole vainglorious history of rock is a millstone they've done well to discard. Along with the girls – DJs and divas with names you can't remember and voices you can't forget – they've created a culture founded on something more than ego caprice. The architects of the dance scene which has flourished in this country since 1988 are, by and large, an anonymous lot. And yet the music they created is easily the boldest retort to rock's grand canon.

And so, despite the massive success of their music, the heroes of dance are unsung. This is partly in the nature of the music itself: because its arena is the club, the dance tune enjoys an autonomy from the person who nursed it to life. (The creators of these records are like well-adjusted, sensible mothers letting their babies out to play without them.) It is also due to the mainstream's inability to understand the first thing about what it all means.

At this year's Brit awards, dance was corralled into a sub-genre, while pop – which means, we must therefore assume, music you sit down to – was permitted to strut and preen like a coked-up rooster catching his reflection in a pond. Oasis, you may recall, were named the very-best-band-in-the-history-of-the-universe-ever, while David Bowie reminded us that, Babylon Zoo notwith-standing, he is still the very-best-singer-of-songs-about-space-and-androgyny-in-this-galaxy-and-beyond.

By comparison, Michael Jackson's intro as the mere King of Pop must just have been some witless attempt to undermine the great man with faint praise. How fortunate, therefore, he had chosen tonight to reveal himself as the messiah. Look on his works, dear Bono, and despair.

Eventually, they handed out the Best Dance Act award to the beau-tifully dignified Massive Attack, who insisted that they were not, in fact, a dance band. Indeed, chucking yourself about to "Protection" would be rather like pogoing to Mozart's Requiem, but this detail mattered little to the Brits' squareheads. A dance act, to them, is simply defined as a negative – not a rock/pop act – becoming a black hole into which everything inexplicable is thrown.

Dance music is enigmatic. Its resistance to hyperbole and hype, the shy shrug with which any questions are met, has made its essence hard to pin down. Its dynamism, the speed with which it evolves different sounds, the ruthlessness with which previous forms are discarded – all this makes people nervous. Should you dare start trying to unravel it, the tangle of genres will make your head ache. You are entering geeks' paradise, a twilight world of white labels, digit audio tapes and tracks-with-no-names. Fortunately, for those of us who don't spend Saturday mornings hanging out in record shops, the music is decanted into clubs.

If rock'n'pop is about attitude – individual artist set against individual artist in the battle to make their story stick – dance is about respect, the submission of personal causes to the breath-ing of the one collective soul. You can hear it exhale weekly on the *Jungle Show* which London and Manchester-based Kiss FM broadcasts very late on Friday nights. When you listen, the first thing that happens is a low-level genre crisis. The music for-merly known as jungle now likes to be called by the less loaded term "drum and bass". "If you're looking for a term, that is it. Drum and bass," says the man called Grooverider, who is likely to know these things. His friend is called Fabio, and he runs the show on alternate fortnights. Fabio has one of the great late-night radio voices. Driving through the dark or lying in it, he will make your loneliness seem apt.

———————

WHEN JUNGLE first appeared (somewhere around 1991 or 1992), it attracted a burden of bad PR through its links with the nastier aspects of urban dismay. This was not entirely unjustified. List-ening to the music was to feel yourself being tightened – like the rubber band on a catapult being pulled back. The beat is just irresponsibly fast. The vocals have been stolen from somewhere else and then mashed to meet the demands of their new home. Speeded up, they screech and squeak like sirens whose prey has sailed on.

The overall effect is both exhilarating *and* enervating. And strangely frustrating.

The next thing you observe about the *Jungle Show*'s vibe (I hope you might permit me the term), is that this music doesn't sound very much like that. Enter, I'm afraid, another term. "Intelligent" drum and bass has been used to describe a music that has departed so far from its jungle derivation that you could happily have it on while washing up. This is not to say that the new sound is trite. If anything, its jazz-inspired rhythms and tendency to imply rather than state makes it one of the most sophisticated sounds about. Its emotions are submerged but not repressed.

What it shares with the old jungle is the capacity to suggest two contradictory sensations at once. This is partly technical. The speeded-up beat is often overlaid with singing strings – making you feel that the two, having clashed, have somehow created a space. It is, if such a thing could be imagined, a double-sided absence, because loss and possibility are meeting in this gap. "Each new hour holds new chances for new beginnings. The horizon leans forward – offering you space to place new steps of change." LTJ Bukem's sublime "Horizons", dreams, paradoxically, of space as a place. It offers a vanishing point as a point of departure. Goldie too talks about his music as an "abyss of ideals". Candidates for the great millenial soundtrack contest don't come more convincing than this.

In fact, something very real has been lost. Many of the people involved in this music used to be attached to the rave scene, which is now in terminal decline. This may seem incongruous at the very moment when the world and his girlfriend seem to be "on one" and house music is packing them in every Friday night across the country. It must indeed be some kind of snooty old so-called "vibe" which turns on its heels to take off the minute the mainstream tries to touch its coat-tails. Well, please don't ask me to defend this discourtesy, but the jury is agreed. The drugs are crap, the buzz is worse and house has come to the end of its creative loop.

As the first post-Ecstasy dance scene to have emerged, drum and bass's posse is almost monkishly ascetic. Go down to Fabio's nightclub, Speed, and you'll encounter a lot of twentysomethings saying "no more" to drugs. The atmosphere is intense rather than effusive. Grin at someone and they'll smile politely. No one is going to ask you to massage their necks. This, I must say, comes as a relief.

This music doesn't cajole you into dancing, it simply tries to make it worth your while. House music these days sounds like a wheedling ex-lover who is still pushing what he thinks are all the right buttons and unable to accept that you've moved on. You need more. Drum and bass impresses like a thunderstorm on a tepid day.

IT IS always advisable, when researching these matters, to go and see the man with the gold teeth first. I am worried about meeting Goldie, not because the idea of a shorn-headed, metal-mouthed hardman is in itself alarming, but I was told something that he'd said about some other journalist who had failed to deliver the goods. On the way up to his 18th floor flat – he lives in one of those nice council blocks with entryphones and friendly people in the (fully-functioning) lifts – I decided this story was apocryphal and smiled at my silliness.

"I'll take on anyone, mate. I've taken on critics. That geezer from *i-D*, I'm going to beat him up when I see him." The man who has been dubbed "the king of the jungle" is sitting on the floor eating toast, and I am already convinced his detractors must deserve this cool comeuppance. Goldie is one of that rare breed of men who co-opts you into his world view so completely that everything he says seems perfectly sensible and right.

He was born 30 years ago to a Scottish mother and Jamaican father and lived his early life in Wolverhampton, much of it in care. He started out as a graffiti artist and went to the US where he busied himself with all manner of urban scenes. On his return, rave culture beckoned and he hung out in a club called Rage, where he met his "family": Fabio, Doc Scott and the beautifully-named girls, now DJs, Kemistry and Storm.

Pretty soon he started to make records of his own. The 1993 track, "Terminator", was what those who know about these things might call seminal. His first album, "Timeless", which has sold more than 100,000 copies to date, justifies the opinion that he is jungle's first crossover act. And, of course, he's going out with Björk.

He is leaning out of the window when I first go into the room, breaking chunks off a hunk of bread and throwing them into the sky. I'm not sure what to make of this until I get closer and see birds swooping along intersecting paths and intercepting every single morsel as it falls. The view is breathtaking. I am enchanted. The whole thing is so much like a metaphor that I am almost embarrassed to suggest it to you, but anyway ... Listen to "Timeless" and see what you think. In many ways, Goldie is a romantic, a viewer of vistas who wants to express – well, the everythingness of everything, if that's not too constricting a brief.

So how would he describe "Timeless"? "It's a canvas isn't it? It's a canvas. It's space and time, it's a vast area. I'm an artist and I have to paint a large canvas, whether they like it or not. I can keep using the same colours and the same area, but it just doesn't turn me on. It's like fucking doing the ministry (sic) position, isn't it?"

As well as promising this karma-sutric attitude to art, our man is kept busy as the self-appointed guardian of the drum and bass collective soul. "It's not my album – it's about the people who caused that album to happen, the people who mixed the records, the punters who got behind that."

Goldie likes to look after people. His Sunday nightclub, Metal-headz, is packed with people on his guest list. When somebody calls him, during the interview, from on the "inside", he promises to send them a tape so "you can get a thing going down in there, man".

In common with many great egoists (and I don't use the word pejoratively), his attachment to giving is dependent on receiving the right response. On the phone again, he complains about some girl who, having got into the club on his personal list, couldn't be bothered to say hello. I take note, although even without this incentive Goldie would not be a chap you might be tempted to ignore. But the bottom line is the music; what it does and how it unites the people it affects. It amuses Goldie that there may yet be some bewildered by this vibe.

"A lot of people have a hard time dealing with real music. The straightest people go to the Blue Note and get really fucking square and saying; "I've gotta get home" and I say: "Go home to Mummy and Daddy. You're not ready, mate." They're like virgins getting popped left right and centre.

"I'm not the Morrissey of hardcore, man. I have to be positive. I wasn't supposed to get this far, was I? I'm an institute kid, I'm supposed to fail. If I get there, I'll prove a lot to a lot of people.

And if I can get this far, I don't give a fuck if I fall off tomorrow."

Leaving is like switching off a great film in the middle. As I head for the door, we pause, and he asks me if I'm planning to go to Metalheadz this Sunday. He can put me on the guest list if I just ring and ask.

———————

MEANWHILE IN a bedroom in Acton, the hero of "intelligent" drum and bass is very keen to talk about music. If Goldie is the scene's ideologue, Alex Reece is its enforcer – a man who is making the tunes that do the job. One such was the massive "Pulp Fiction" – a record that gets everything right. Listening to it for the first time, you feel like telling everyone who didn't create it that they've simply got hold of the wrong formula. Reece makes music make sense. The pleasure you get is like cracking a quadratic equation.

Alex himself is the kind of boy who, as a son, wouldn't give you a moment's concern. His attitude is healthy. His outlook is well balanced. He is very hardworking but not obsessed by his work. He is signed to a major label now (Island), but it isn't going to go to his head. He's been into this stuff for about two-and-a-half years. Before that, it was techno. House music used to excite him but not so much now. "Basically all the best tunes have been made and the people going down there are all your Sharon and Tracey types. There's nothing risky about the music any more."

So Alex got on board the next big thing – and then became it. Island is very pleased and many people agree that if anyone is going to fire further with this music it's him. Of course, there are options to be weighed up: "I'm going to be making this music in five years' time, so I don't want to be big now and not next year." But generally speaking, Alex is well pleased. The first LP's out in July.

———————

I HAVE never before attempted going on the road with a music artiste, the logic being much the same as when I was a child, and I would turn away from the TV if some choral music happened to come on. Listening to the records, these singers sounded like angels. I just didn't want to know that they had red hair or Ratners chains or faces that contorted when they opened their mouths. My mother told me not to be silly, but I still didn't want to see them. My desire for transcendence had been thwarted by a badly-cut fringe.

Ever since, I have tried to avoid coming too close to my idols in case they too should prove mortal. One of the great pleasures of dance music for me has been the way you get touched without needing to look. I will tend to imagine, therefore, that the sound has been forged by a divine host at play on their day off from nurturing souls. Either that, or by my desire. There was nothing objectionable about Reece and his entourage; they were simply all too human. We were planning to travel from Manchester to a late-night gig in Liverpool, where Alex was booked. Me, him and an irrelevance of A&R men. Meeting in the hotel bar at six o'clock, we commenced what was to prove our most concentrated period of hanging around all night. We drink. We eat fish and chips. A nice girl called Felicia ("I'm with Stuart") comes and goes. Several hours pass and the Future Of British Music fancies one more for the road.

Eventually, Alex Reece DJs. He plays 90 per cent of his own material, is only on for an hour-and-a-half and doesn't bother mixing, preferring to slam the records on back-to-back. Some tracks are dub plates, which have yet to be released. Many boys cluster round and try to make out the names of these tunes. I lend one of them a pen. The A&R man tells me this is the *NME* gig of the week. These are the things you learn if you hang out with the boys by the DJ booth.

But turn away from these nuts and bolts, the scuzzy old Ratners chain and everything becomes clear. The music, free of its mooring, gives you a slight shock as it starts up and the fresh air hits your face. Nothing can have prepared you for the cleanness of this beat. You want to dance, but feel concerned you might not be good enough.

Fighting my way through a forest of geeks, I find Alex standing in a corridor, *sans* A&R, with his box of records ready to go back. I ask him how he thought the whole thing went. He wrinkles his nose, shrugs just imperceptibly and tells me that the speakers were pretty crap.

Lunatic Ginge

■ **Sylvia Patterson**
NME July 20 1996

Björk is one of the most furiously individual, original and inspiring artists currently alive and kicking. Yet all too often she has been dismissed as some kind of mad little puffin-eating elf from Iceland, as if true character cannot imply anything but insanity, and a heritage other than British or American automatically marks you out as a troll. She's weathered this arrogant, imperialistic attitude remarkably well, and continues on her journey of absolute experimentalism undeterred, but it's nevertheless extremely refreshing to read a portrayal of her which doesn't resort to the lazy, condescending, "she's barking" school of journalism.

Sylvia Patterson has a knack of highlighting individuality, even eccentricity, without needing to employ patronising labels. Although she remembers the singer as being very excitable – to the point where she actually belted Sylvia in the chest a couple of times – she left the interview believing Björk made more sense than most.

Björk, she'll tell you herself, is "plastered". On a rare day off from the tortuous 1996 touring schedule, she's letting it all loose on the dance floor of a Norwegian discotheque, her hair as perpendicular as the joints of her flailing limbs. Tonight, she feels *bloody marvellous*.

Already, she's persuaded her accordion player to give it plenty, guv, on the karaoke – a particularly lusty rendition of the Jovi's "Livin' On A Prayer" classic. Björk's up for Michael Jackson's "Don't Stop 'Til You Get Enough" but she's missed the deadline for the list. Curses. Never mind, she'll just freak out anyway, it'll take more than that to ruin her night. And here it comes now in the amorphous one-brain-celled-amoeba we recognise as The Posse Of Lairy Lads, all beer and bile, dancing in front of her, taunting her about being "famous", about being a "pop star" and how "we know who you are". She ignores them. It doesn't work.

She's getting annoyed now, tells them, "It's my night off, OK?" That doesn't work either: now the loudest one's frothing non-sense like, "I should ask you for your autograph shouldn't I?" It's so boring. She's had enough. She tells him to, "Fuck off!"

And fancy that, it works. He apologises, says he's always liked her music, really, and would she sign her autograph for him, no hard feelings? Well, of course she would. He proffers a piece of paper and Björk takes it from him, smiles the smile of the angels themselves, crunches it up in one hand and throws it into her mouth. Munch! Munch! Munch! Gulp!

She reaches over, now grinning the grin of the devil himself, leers right into his face, eyeball to eyeball, snatches his pen and bites the top off. Crunch! Then the middle bit. Crunch! Crunch! And the rest. Crunch! Crunch! Crunch! Gulp!

Then she swipes the pint out of his hand – Glug! Glug! Glug! Down in one! – smacks her lips with a mighty relish, hands him back the empty glass, turns her back and marches straight back onto the dance floor. To coin her own most favoured phrase of the moment: one-nil.

"IT WAS a pen like that," chortles the tangerine-haired Björk Gudmunsdóttir, aged 30, nodding to the next table's Bic-wielder on a cafe pavement round the corner from her home in west London. "But to wash it down with his own pint, that really got to him. You should have seen him, this big guy, he just crumpled down to nothing. Hehehehehehehehehehehe."

It's a gutsy laugh, is Björk's, deep in the throat and laced with purest filth.

"Of course, the next day," she grins, clutching her stomach in memory of the resultant plastic/ink/intestinal wall/bowel move-ment scenario, "I was in total pain but it was worth it. Even just to see my friends on the floor laughing their heads off. I was on the phone to Goldie telling him and he was going, 'Go on! That's my girl!' and I was going, 'Oh God! But sometimes it's just so *hard* to be hard!'"

And she makes it look so easy. If a few months later, The Lad, like the rest of the planet, saw Björk on the telly, battering the head of a journalist, by the hair, on the floor in Bangkok airport he must have considered himself the luckiest loser alive.

Björkgate, The Bangkok Incident, saw the myth of Björk – already eulogised by *Spitting Image* as the hysterical nutter who sings to fax machines – spiral into the next dimension. A tabloid media delighted to declare, to a man, our adopted foremost pioneer of soul-quivering spook-pop as The Wild Woman Of Pop, out of con-trol, officially "Bjönkers!". To Björk, it was simple stuff; a matter of maternal instinct, someone was exploiting her son, attempting to weedle trifles of gossip out of a ten-year-old boy.

"What that woman did was against all my princips," says Björk in her musical Icelandic/Cockney/almost Celtic amalgam of accents and resulting variation on the English language. "It's probably the third time in my whole life I lost my temper. Last time it was pro-tecting my brother, you do that kind of thing for other people don't you? So I just saw red. I'm not proud but if I was back in that position and it hadn't happened before, I would do the same thing today. And it happens to me every seven years, so it's not surprising it just went "priignah!" – the elastic stretched for seven years.

"The best thing about it is the woman was offered a commercial for a hairspray thing in Asia. It was going to be 'I get battered by pop stars all the time but I use this hairspray and it keeps my hair in place!' And she said *no*! I was gonna call her and say 'Do it!' I thought that was very funny."

Obviously she didn't see the funny side of it.

"I wonder why. Hehehehehehe. The weird thing, from my position, is to tear a woman's hair off and everyone goes, 'Yey-hay!' I wasn't waiting for applause. It was a very dark moment for me, to acknowledge that violence you have inside. My crew, they'd never seen me like this and they've toured with me for years and years. Three of them were holding me back, saying, 'She's not worth it' and were gonna take me off her. When they tried I just went right down (*crouches in seat*) and got some energy from I don't know where and just went 'pfoooooof', up like that, three fully grown men couldn't stop me. I don't know where you get it from, it's some door to hell. So there's seven years 'til my next one. See you all in 2003!"

———

THERE IS nothing remotely insane about this tiny woman with the great big talent, seated today scoffing fresh fruit salad and Greek yoghurt, resplendent in fluorescent orange jumper and white shiny trews, blethering on about how last night she had restless body syndrome. To wear herself out, she ran round and round her garden wondering what was wrong with her until she looked up and saw the full moon. "Aha," she mused, "so *that's* it." Volcanic impulses, seven-year cycles, moon madness – hardly "Bjönkers!" in the 1990s when the John Powers of this world have aliens living inside their ears.

Today the dynamic embodiment of the word "gusto" is positively serene, back from Roskilde Festival, now in Difficult Third
Album preparation (number of songs pirouetting in the ether
thus far – seven), putting together an album of her "favourite
remixes" and working on collaborations with the dance gurus of
the globe – about which she remains, as ever, cagey to the point
of paranoia. Any surprises? Duets with David Hasselhoff featuring Lloyd Grossman on "vibes"?

"Not with me really," she chimes. "I couldn't really surprise you
any more, could I? The most surprising thing I could do would be
a rock album, innit? With ten harpsichords and three Australian
monkeys playing phantom sticks. Actually, that wouldn't be a
surprise at *all*."

What could have been, until now, is the Saturday night headline
appearance at Phoenix Festival for which she has enlisted the
help of someone called Kristoff, a "French pyromaniac fucking
terrorist", a fireworks expert who has created displays for the
Olympics and is organising a round-the-world, time-difference-
considered year 2000 extravaganza. Three Catherine wheels
and a flailing damp squib he is not.

"He's brilliant," booms Björk, whose enthusiasm for the original work of others outlasts her own by several billion eons. "All
fireworks I've seen so far, are like a punk song, it's all 'Let's buy
loads and PSHOOOOO! just put them all in the air NOW!' But this
guy he's quite modern, he does patterns, it's not (*sings like, er,
fireworks*), 'Peu, peu, peu, pee pchkschckkcpshh!!' – his is all kind
of ... (*waves hands around*) patterns and it might not do anything
for a few songs and then suddenly just ... shimmer. I met him in
this restaurant, he's all scars and scruffy hair and lives in a barn
with another barn full of powders and just thinks in terms of
colours and explosions and the way he describes things ...
He's a scientist! Outrageous!"

It is, insists Björk, an "accident" she became The Phenomenon
she is. When she presented her record company with the demos

of "The Anchor Song" she was told it'd sell a third less than The Sugarcubes ever did (ie, one copy).

"I never thought I'd be playing so many big places," she ponders. "I've always said no to most offers because I always looked at myself as quite private and my music as quite private – kind of for headphones, really, for inside. So the fact I'm headlining festivals is just hysterical. It's weird because it's introvert music and to make introvert music work for so many people you just have to get help with things like fireworks to still have that quite sensitive, delicate manner, but it's big – like, how can you do that? Without selling out? I just want it to be good. I want to walk away from this without shame."

Björk doesn't particularly see herself as a futurist. She is – like Goldie, The Prodigy, Underworld and the ongoing perpetrators of the dance "revolution", creating the "sound of the world today". It's her religion, what she's always described before anybody else, as "taking reality and making it into magic".

"Which is the bravest thing in the world to say," she's saying, her hands rubbing all over her face, the famed minuscule digits poking randomly up the nose, as ever. "'Oh me with my gorgeous tits riding a white horse on Saturn' – it's very easy to make that into magic. But making fucking this (*belts saucer up and down*) – these noises that most people find fucking ugly, into something pretty is just, I'm sorry, fucking heroic.

"People always think the noises they live in is ugly, and I don't find that. So if the music can make magic out of a double-decker bus, I think that's just ... one-nil. Against boredom. One-nil against death. One-nil for love. And that's just the best. And people who aren't using the noises we live with are cowards. That means it's escapism, you've gone into another culture, another climate. People say techno music is cold: fuck 'em. Crap! You're blocking out half of your life, being a coward."

That'll be Oasis and the entire spectrum of Britpop seen to, then ...

"Britpop," she baulks, "for me is middle-of-the-road; stagnation and normality. If we were talking food, it'd be something very boring I don't really like, like bread. Potatoes. No taste, but it fills you up. Then some of the good things you get with so-called dance music is ... cherries! And tequilas! The extremes. Chocolate mousse with nine thousand billion fucking calories and a bloody steak with it. That's what I like in food, very spicy, fucking Indian madras. Don't give me toast and cornflakes and potato salad and a roast dinner and greasy pub foods."

Funny that; all very British "cuisine".

"Yeah!" she guffaws, "and everybody hates British food. And that's what Britpop is to me, boring and bland and egg and steak and chips and beer. I don't understand beer, it's like drinking wood, it doesn't get you anywhere. I'd rather skip it altogether or do a fucking bottle of Cognac and go the whole way. But then again most of the people I love in my life are completely there, they want roast dinner and lager and security and things to be very basic and comfortable and I respect that. Spare me the rock 'n' roll jangle, you don't wanna dance to it, you don't wanna lose the plot there with your body and you don't wanna lose the plot with your head, it's in the middle."

People do sing it, though. Very loudly.

"I'm probably missing something," she contends. "I'd be the first to say it."

You don't hear the "spiritual" Oasis dimension – all the living forever, etc?

"Hmph, living forever in stagnation," she snorts. "Sorry! I'm getting nasty here. But then again, I love going back to my family when I've toured the world nine times and done bungee jumping, going to my gran's house for pancakes. The Icelandic telephone service added digits to all the numbers the other day, and they changed my gran's telephone number and I was furious. How dare you! And then my gran moved house and I remember my grandfather wanted to sell his car – he had the same car for 20 years since I was a child – and I was like, 'No! You have no permission to change!' But I'm gonna go out now, tour, be really wild, see all the things in the world that are really extreme. New York, Paris, fucking Tokyo, and when I come back you better have the same telephone number and live in the same house and have the same fucking car or I'm gonna be really upset.

"So that's not fair, is it? So I shouldn't really attack those Oasis lager louts because it's so good they exist. They do all the dirty work for us. It's so good that somebody *bothers*. Heheheh. So, really, I think I'm quite conservative. Take the way I dress, people think I'm the wildest person on earth but I've been wearing orange since I was three. I keep buying the same garments all over again. I've been wearing red coats down to here since I was two. So I'm very conservative really."

Why the fascination with orange? In colour psychology it's the colour of healing. What d'you think that says about you?

"Well," she grins, "obviously I'm very *ill*."

———————

UP UNTIL three years ago, Björk had "no money". Life was "two jobs, working class, single mother, hardcore". Moving to London and the supernova success of "Debut" changed her life. She'd been in bands from age embryo, of course, supplementing her "no compromise, brave music, taking risks" (and thus selling three copies) ethos with work in antique shops, fish factories and a stint as an accomplished, er, thief.

"I once nicked a swimming pool," she breezes, as one might breeze of pilfering an egg 'n' milk chew from the newsie. "It was from a supermarket, an inflatable one, 'cos we needed a bath, we didn't have one where we were renting. And I nicked a disco ball! I used to do that sometimes when I got drunk and was bored.

Reykjavik is sometimes challenging, in a town of 100,000 people you run out of new things to do, and every time you go out you want every occasion to be absolutely unique, so once I nicked a disco ball, a massive one, off the ceiling and got it out the club – got away with it! I don't know how I did it, obviously hysterically drunk, but I did it.

"But then the minute I got money I stopped nicking. Before it was me saying 'I've got no money, fuck off, society revenge, let's go to the supermarket and get what I deserve."

That sort of mentality is the scourge of society, "young lady".

"Oh I can understand why people nick," she says. "I'm not saying I agree with it but I understand it. People aren't asking for a lot, asking for a fucking meal a day. The reason people nick? There's 10,000 reasons for that and I couldn't pretend to know two of them, really."

———————

GOLDIE HAS said that he and Björk were "fated", their coming-together a "big set-up by some fucker". What does Björk think? For the first time today there's a massive pause. She's notoriously private about, well, the private. She's a double Scorpio, astrology fans (ask a hippy).

"Um," she quavers, "I'm pretty anti-fate 'cos I want to know that you've got options, it's important for me. But it is very tempting to think it is. It feels like it anyway. Which is something I would-n't admit to … a lot of things, it just really … feels like it."

Their similarities are bordering on the "Björkers!": both 30, both parents, both pioneers of spook-pop, both spiritually obsessed, both speak in complex metaphors, both "misunderstood", both possessed of one name in fame.

"I've tried to explain it to myself," she nods, "But at the end of the day, when you try to explain those really important things in life, it's just not logic, is it? It's just the force of nature. We're talking waterfalls and volcanoes, y'know?"

They'd known each other by sight and reputation for years, met each other across clubland but it was the Björk/Goldie tour of last year when they finally felt the *vibe*.

"It was quite good, the way we fell in love," she chokes, mortified to discuss the personal. "We'd been touring for a few months, which is quite intimate. He was doing his first tour and I've done touring since ... well, I know it, put it that way. It was good 'cos we ended up supporting each other, him completely emotionally because I was just crashing physically.

"I mean you can analyse it to pieces and get fucking nowhere, but it wasn't until the end of the tour that we realised we'd built something up that we couldn't live without. It's good, because he saw me doing shows at 40 degrees fever, crying my eyes out before and after the show. He saw me at the bottom, finished, and I saw him as a beginner, a very graceful beginner. So (*huge grin*), it's uphill from here innit? Heheh. Aw, now I've gone shy. Maybe I shouldn't talk about it. I'm really cautious about it. It's *important*."

Love eh? It fair does you goofy in the gills. So what does being in great big huge massive love do to your head?

"Nine thousand pros and cons," she decides unhelpfully. "To me, it's back to the instinct thing, the primal needs one has. Your body creates all these things and every morning in your sleep you've created all these things and if you don't put them somewhere you go mad.

"In my case, I have to sing. Some people have to tell stories. It's finding the road. And one of the things you wake up with every morning in your lap is very romantic love innit? So it's about finding a channel for it. And when you find someone I guess you've found someone to fax to. To phone to. You've got that ping-pong going.

"We create so much love all the time. We go to bed and wake up with 59 tons of love. Where shall I put it? And a lot of people who aren't very happy are maybe running around with 97 Safeway bags full of love and they just don't know where to put it. And I guess when you've found the right person, you've got somewhere to put it."

Is the right person the person with enough room for your 97 bags then? Or is it that the bags fit that person because they're the right shape? Or something. Otherwise, you could just give the bags to anyone and we know that doesn't work (You know when you've been Björked, etc).

"Yeah, that's the riddle innit?" she guffaws. "And it ain't solved yet. It's like going to a restaurant and wondering if they'll have what you want on the menu. Well, today I feel like three bungee jumps and having a very intimate talk with somebody I've known for 11 years."

And all they've got left is a broken catapult and the nutter at the number 29 bus stop.

"Yeah, know what I mean? And it's the same thing with the Safeway bags. It's like best friends. Why do you have best friends that you've had for ten years? I dunno. Free for all. Free jazz! Improvise!"

Ahem. Björk and Goldie won't be getting married after all (employees of *The Sun*), at least not right now while everyone's expecting it. They're contrary that way – and who can blame them?

"What happened is we fooled around it," she clarifies. "Not that we were joking completely, but it just took off and everybody started talking about it and, when you've got everybody asking you about it ten times a day, you just go off the idea. We were thinking of doing something else. Like buying a football team instead."

Goldie's a birrova Sexy Beast™, isn't he?

"Coo-*or*!" slavers Björk and then rolls around in her seat in mirthful silence. There is nothing more to be said then, except LUCKY BASTARDS.

———————

LOVE, SEX, fame, wealth, wisdom, respect, health, magnificent orange jumpers. It's enough to make you sick, or at least contract Dave Stewart's Paradise Syndrome, the one where your life is so perfect you can't believe it, so you invent drastic problems in your head to keep you 'sane'. It's the timeless "be careful what you dream of" malarkey that makes the most successful people blow their brains out.

"I had this dream," says Björk, pondering the issue, "that I had to carry this really expensive porcelain Chinese vase across a motorway. And that's what it's like, you feel like you're carrying this really precious vase, like someone just gave you the best fucking vase in the world. So you're thinking, 'Aaaaaah! I can't just drop it!'"

"I mean, I've got loads of friends that are as talented as me and they haven't got this opportunity to channel it and put it out there in the world. And, at the end of the day, what I'm trying to say throughout this whole interview, is that's what makes you happy. Like waking up with not only 97 Safeway bags of love in your lap, but all this energy and ideas and to be able to put it out is just fucking brilliant. It's great and I'm ecstatic but also there's this pressure thing. "

Like, you created it, it's yours, so you have the ability to destroy it as well?

"Yeah. In one second. And, hand on my heart, I never aimed for this position, ever, and it's probably why I'm in it. So this thing, you have it now and it's so tempting to just (*mimes pushing vase off the edge of the table*). It's some sort of monster. Hmm."

As is the sex demon within. Björk, she'll tell you herself, is "greedy" when it comes to sex. She has a "big appetite", as do all people who live in the sensual world.

"I'm very healthy and natural when it comes to sex," she states, "very earthy. Strange locations always turn me on. I think that's pretty healthy. Aeroplane toilets. I think that would turn anybody on. Freedom turns me on most of all, something like 'Let's go on holiday' and five minutes later you're standing in the airport, passport in one pocket, credit card in the other.

"A lot of people talk about power as an aphrodisiac and that doesn't turn me on at all. It turns me off. Freedom and being brave, scarey things, turn me on. I remember once I camped outside the biggest waterfall in Iceland, the biggest waterfall in Europe actually. We were on this tiny place just in front of the waterfall and the tent was completely wet. That was scarey and very healthy and we had very healthy sex!"

Do you find talent is an aphrodisiac?

"Not for me," she decides. "It's not that simple, you see. But creativity is. Sex is basically creating another person innit? So if a person's creative, it helps. It can be just a good sense of humour, it doesn't mean the guy has to make excellent paintings. It's creative attitudes towards life, to want to do 700 exciting things tomorrow, that's the source of creativity. And it's courage as well: to have the courage to stand on top of a hill and take it all in. Funnily enough, there's not that many people who have that kind of courage."

Before she met Goldie, she'd given up on boys, decided she'd had enough, didn't need it, was alright on her own. Then he came along and "ruined" everything.

"That's what was tops about me and Golds," she dithers like the besotted 15-year-old she still obviously is. "I'd just gone off it. I'd tried so hard two years before and at that point I was like, 'I've had it with boys! It's not my field! I don't know how to do it, it's just pain: fuck 'em!' So you say 'Fuck 'em!' and you say it out loud, just once, and really mean it and it's like, 'Hey! Alriiiiiiight!' It's mad, innit? It really is *mad*."

A fly has just alighted on the lip of the Icelandic sorceress. She hasn't noticed.

There's a fly on your lip!

"Oh!" she chirps and sticks her tongue out to the side, flicking it up and down.

Good God, woman, are you trying to eat it?

"Sometimes I wish I could! If I'd been brought up in Jamaica or something, I probably would do!"

SOMETIMES, WHERE you're from IS where you're at, and Björk couldn't come from anywhere but Iceland, the first country in history to declare its own independence through sheer, bloody-minded Viking passion and self-preservation. A country that embodies The Cult Of The Individual, which possesses no army because, mythology has it, people wouldn't be able to march, ie, they couldn't walk together in one rhythm.

This, then, is her "madness": this unique human being who wrote her first song aged four ("Little songs, it was my diary. Things like, '*Pete likes raisins too much, I think he should actually kiss Shirley today*'. And then the chorus would go, '*If Pete and Shirley would kiss, I would giggle. Giggle, giggle, giggle 'til I die*'"). Who was a mathematical boffin at school, student of musical theory "forever" (she's as versed in the classics as much as the entire back catalogue of Jimi Hendrix who her parents played every single day "so by age seven I was 'enough is enough' – the classic rebel"), and married aged 20 "because my boyfriend needed contact lenses" (the Icelandic government operate a personal young folk's pension scheme: high interest savings which you can claim back aged 25 or when you marry. He got his contact lenses, they divorced, they're still friends).

Who, in the same year, performed on Icelandic TV as a bare-stomached, seven months pregnant punk rocker with no eyebrows and caused a 79-year-old woman to have a heart attack in front of the telly ("She didn't die! But I was nearly sued..."). Who's been making "my own music" for 20 years ("it was only last year that I realised, my God, I'm actually a fucking professional"). Who is "obsessed with truth and integrity". Who on tour – to get over the lack of sex – drinks "27 tequilas for that physical kick", who swims two hours every day ("Not paddling – fucking swimming!") to rid herself of "the madness of boredom and sitting around and doing nothing", who, today, is a bona-fide global superstar who traverses the airwaves, dines with Michael Stipe and Anton Corbijn and Madonna and...

Robbie Williams, as we live and breathe!

"Hiya!" twitters the people's pop hero, wobbling by on a bicycle, looking distinctly crispy round the edges in a crumpled blue tracksuit with his hair standing on end.

"Did you go to Heaven last night?" snickers Björk, surveying the human carnage.

"No, but I feel like it," quips the sixth member of Oasis. "I've been in Italy – fookin' mad! I've got to go to bed, I've got to sleep... *(wobbles off into the horizon)*".

Mad for it, him, eh? I believe you once drank him into oblivion to the extent he needed a Vitamin B jab in the morning to wake him from the "dead".

"Yeah. Aheheh. It was the Berlin MTV awards about two years ago, I think we drank each other into oblivion, actually. It wasn't just us two, there were a few of us, but I got the blame from the managers.

"That was one of my favourite nights actually, all the clubs were going on and it was just terrible, so pretentious and rock 'n' roll and gross, so I found some German jungle kids and them and Naomi Campbell and Take That and some of my friends went back to the Holiday Inn disco. Naomi flirted with the DJ and got him out of the DJ booth, got the jungle kids in, and got Take That on the dance-floor. Top night out! One-nil!"

Björk is, of course, big pals with the stars but she's as excited here at sneaking in the jungle mob as she is about watching Naomi Campbell on the wheels of steel "tip".

"You meet people at dinner parties, over and over, but it doesn't mean they become your best mates," she says. "And there's nothing fake about that. You can kill yourself with paranoia and think, 'Oh my whole life is so superficial!' But then again, when I was living in Iceland there's loads of people that I'd get drunk with at the local disco and it doesn't mean they're my best mates either. Friendships are on many levels and thank God for that, you can know people for 500 different reasons. Fifty-three friends is more intimate than 497 but that doesn't mean 53 is fake.

"You know the guy in the corner shop but it doesn't mean you'll go on holiday with him and it doesn't mean when you're friendly with him you're lying. The core of my friend basis is still Icelandic and the people I work with really. And some of them will become friends forever and some of them not, end of story. It's the same for everyone."

There are some things Björk cannot deal with: her phenomenon, her money and hysterical adoration by fans: "If I think about it, I have to call the ambulance because I am insane." Her money goes "back into the music where it belongs" and her greatest achievement is living "with no compromise. I'd rather be in the bravest band in Iceland that no one knows about and do two jobs than make music to pay the rent. I won't use music as a whore."

She does a lot of "spring cleaning" and it's nothing to do with Marigold gloves: "I try to be as much in the here and now as possible, I think it's cowardice to live in the past or the future so I try to be brave and spring clean and take with me only what matters. I try to make sure that in a year's time I'll be just as lost as I am now."

She sees the immediate future of music as "chamber music mentality, spiritual and free, my new thing", writes her own string arrangements on a lap-top and, at the very mention, launches on to a gigantic verbal crusade on the europhic "revolutionary relevance" of chamber music and its historical re-emergence at the beginning and end of each century.

"It will be the opposite of your old rock 'n' roll tune," she froths, "which is traditional and conservative, like oak or something. God and the Devil, like the *Bible*, the oldest story ever told. Now if you want to go into aliens and somewhere you've never been before you end up with some kind of chamber music atmosphere, not earthbound. We don't want any of that earthbound now, do we? We wanna get lost! We wanna get fucked! Lost and fucked!"

As might this gentleman here, as it happens.

"I'm sorry to bother you..."

That'll be the universal opening gambit of your standard autograph hunter, then. This one's got a suit on, a great big drip of a city gent, tie askew in the balm of this summer's afternoon, holding a page from his Filofax aloft.

"I know that you must get people coming up and asking you all the time but I really am a big fan and..."

Björk reaches into her bag and in four seconds flat, has located a pair of gardening scissors, snipped his tie off and *eaten it*!

Except she doesn't unfortunately. She smiles the smile of angels themselves, becomes eerily quiet, writes her autograph in the tiniest swirl dead in the centre of the page and hands it back, lips tight shut. He leaves embarrassed by the silence, which was its purpose in the first place. He'll never know how lucky he was.

"One day," grins Björk, springing back to life, mouthing behind her hand while striding into the cafe to pay for luncheon for herself, "I might just eat someone's camera..."

OK, Liam is a Bit Spacey, But, More Than That, He's Dreamy. One Night We Had a Little Snog

■ **Emma Forrest**
The Independent September 21 1996

Liam Gallagher epitomises the desirable lad. Bad, beautiful and barmy, with ice blue eyes and an untameable nature, the younger Gallagher has fuelled a million fantasies around the world, although, as Emma Forrest's piece shows, not necessarily sexual ones. Here, in a playfully creative departure from standard rock journalism, she dreams of sharing her house with him while he sprouts a pair of wings.

Liam Gallagher is growing wings. He will live with me until they
are fully developed. At the moment they are just blushes beside
each shoulder blade. They are coming to the surface, slowly but
surely. It was the itching of the nascent buds that drove him mad
and made Oasis cancel the American tour. It will only be a few
weeks before the wings burst through his cagoule and unfurl
above his head.

I invited him to room with me because I have my wisdom teeth
coming through at the moment. I know what he's going through
and I thought that we could whine and complain and knock back
Ibuprofen together. Patsy will come over whenever she can to
comfort us, but at the moment she's filming in LA. She's an excellent mother and very sweet, a real girl's girl. She doesn't mind her
fiancé living with another woman. She knows that these are not
wings of desire. I don't want him to be my fella, I just want to see
his feathers.

While we wait for the wings to sprout, I've been playing him lots
of records, anything and everything but The Beatles. He complained at first, stuck his fingers in his ears and refused to listen.
Now he's mad for Blondie and really getting into the Seventies
singer-songwriters. He's going to talk it over with the rest of the
band, but it looks likely that the new record will be very Carly
Simon influenced. James Taylor and Dr John are helping us write
songs at the moment.

Still, I know he misses the Fabs. Sometimes when I come home,
I can hear "Abbey Road" floating down the stairs. I walk into
the kitchen and catch him fixing a steak sandwich to the
strains of "Polythene Pam". So we've agreed a deal whereby
he only listens to George Harrison's songs until the wings are
fully formed. Apart from that, it's all non-Beatles. I don't want
to stunt Liam's wing capacity by only feeding him one thing.
He's a good boy. He is also a naturally melancholy boy. I mean,
yes, he's a mad-head, but he also feels this incredible nostal-
gia, this yearning, for a music and a time that he never experienced in the first place. He meets all these starry A-list types,

and he gets excited, but even while he's sharing his drugs with them, he often feels very lonely.

I make sure we play a game every day. Liam has an incredible imagination and we have a lot of make-believe fantasies about being in *The Lion, The Witch And The Wardrobe*. I don't have a big wardrobe in my house, so he hides behind curtains and in the linen cupboard and I put on silvery make-up and try to scare him. I think we both click so well because we have both been accused of being space cadets when, in fact, we just have radically short attention spans. OK, Liam is a little spacey but, more than that, he's dreamy. One night we had a little snog and he was the most amazing kisser. His mouth moved so softly and simply, as if he were thinking about Lennon and The Lion and chips and Marlon Brando and nothing at all.

Everything in his head is unrelated. He knows he loves Patsy, he knows he loves the band and Noel and his Mam, but he doesn't put it all together. He loves them with all his heart, but apart from his Mam, they remain disconnected from him.

We've talked it over and Liam feels bad about the bust-up with Noel and ducking out of their concerts for the rest of the year. But he's sick of being a pop star. He has decided to concentrate his efforts on becoming a better human being. This is the re-birth, not the re-union Liam is only 23. He is not the saviour of the British music industry. He is The Saviour. I'm living with The Saviour.

When the feathers first began to peep through, I wondered if he could carry it off. They were so downy and soft, so pale. They caught all the light in the room and made his shoulders glow a soft champagne colour. I worried he would think they were too giddy. In fact, they have become very imposing and majestic. As he's calmed down, the wings have fully developed. They're beautiful. Liam has blow dried them into a mod feather cut. He's standing out on the balcony now, ready to take flight. You've never seen anything like it. He is, however, threatening to revert to type. If he flies over Damon from Blur, Damon had better not look up.

Catch Him if You Keanu!

■ **Kate Spicer**

Unedited, unpublished version of article which appeared in *Elle* October 1996

When Kate Spicer was asked to grab an interview with Keanu Reeves, she had no idea it would turn into such a fiasco. While literally chasing the actor round Britain, her role as reporter was brought into question by some of Reeves' band and roadcrew's reactions to her, and her pride suffered a few dents thanks to the haphazard methods she was forced to employ in the pursuit of Mr Elusive. Her resultant article provides illuminating insight into some of the difficulties and dilemmas most female journalists are confronted with at one time or another.

"Course," said the smug show biz correspondent of *The Daily Record* , "He'll fly in first class, be staying at a top hotel. I'm pretty wise on what these guys get up to."

Keanu Reeves arrived in Glasgow with his band late Saturday morning after 14 hours on the tour bus from Belgium. "They arrived and immediately complained about the size of their rooms," a hotel worker said. Later, after the band had left town, the obliging, slightly excited manager of the four star Forte Post House showed me the recently vacated Reeves cubbyhole. Two single beds, trouser press, the usual corrosive sachets of toiletries. Tiny. "Just a normal guy. A nice polite man," he said, "I don't know why he always acts like a space cadet in interviews."

This nice polite man has a habit of being really nice and polite to his fans. You'll hear, "He had a different line for everyone". But all the time he's being courteous you can tell he's conserving his energy for something else, something he cares about. He's no winking people pleaser; no, "Keanu Reeves invites *Hello!* to his lovely Hollywood home"; no, "If it wasn't for all those people out there watching the movies"... tears in the eye kind of guy. All very refreshing but such noble demeanour tends to go hand in hand with not talking to the press.

———————————

GO OUT and chase Keanu Reeves, get an interview. "Hey. No. problem." Two days later after desperate calls to the RCA press office it became clear an interview was not on. "We don't know what's happening, they aren't cooperating." Someone at RCA in Paris said the same thing. Apparently Dogstar were keeping themselves private, didn't mix, not even with other bands, while on the Continent. On top of that, they were only talking to four hand-picked members of the more masculine elements of the serious "music" press (why were *Loaded* there then?). This is clearly man stuff, not to be wasted on the girlies who don't know their Pearl Jam from their Rimmel Shimmer Pink. The band want to be taken seriously for the music, not for the bass player. Hmm.

I scoured sources and the Keanu clippings for any trace of another way in. "Cordial." "Evasive." "Diligent." "Sincere." "Professional." A friend found me later that day, drunk, drivelling and abusive. "Piss off, I've got problems. Interview. Keanu Reeves. Won't." "No one can get an interview with Keanu Reeves," he said. "Me. Got to. Career. Finished." I fell off my stool. "Listen, I know someone who can help you." By the next day I've got Keanu's basic movements in the UK. Drink eh, magic stuff.

There's a series of quotes Reeves gave a US interviewer in July '95 regarding his films. Their publication was hurriedly vetoed by the actor's handlers in LaLaland, but still found their way into cyberspace. I used these like worry beads.

On *Dangerous Liaisons*: "Fucking frogs. I really didn't understand what was going on the whole time, and I still can't follow that movie, but I did get a peek at Uma's titties when she was doing that scene with that guy who went bald." And on *Bill & Ted's Excellent Adventure*: "Let me tell you something, for the amount of money I got paid for this fucking movie, I get called 'Dude' way too much on the street. Can't those fucking idiots remember me from any of my other work?"

The guy isn't so damn angelic, but his beautifully honed public persona remains blemish free. Because he doesn't pander to the whims of the media, his presence in town inevitably triggers a cascade of Keanu trivia for the curious. The *Daily Record* reported not only a meal Reeves ate at a local Indian, but the fact that he had been greedy, picking at his friend's plate too. It's kind of grotesque. Most of the gossip revolves around his looks, "He's got fat, he's unshaven, he's scruffy, he's ... a disappointment," was reported everywhere from the teenie mags to the tabloids to *The Sunday Times*.

While on the Continent, Reeves and the band manager, Kenny Funk had dropped a whole rack of publicity they were scheduled to do, including big stuff like *Top of the Pops*. The record company, with three months of preparation behind them for the short European tour and the imminent single, in turn, said they weren't releasing the single here at the end of July as planned. Kind of a, "Fuck you". "No, FUCK you," thing.

One of the Chosen Four – bitter perhaps that his scheduled 45 minutes with the band on Sunday morning turned into a 10 minute monologue from the lead singer and a couple of one word answers from the man he really came to see – kindly offered me his hypothesis that Reeves is screwing the drummer

Rob Mailhouse. The band, he reckoned, was a gift of sorts
from Keanu to his love. This stuff gets said when you don't
play ball with the smelly kids in the media.

After an afternoon at T in the Park, where everyone except
me seemed to spot Reeves dancing, Reeves eating a hot dog,
Reeves playing Twister with Richard Nixon and Zsa Zsa Gabor, I
spent Saturday night chasing my tail around Glasgow while my
subject sat eating a curry with his mates. An event so boring
even *The Sun* hack left before the bill came.

Still, I got to hold my camera up along with a thousand or so
other girlies at the gig in the *NME* tent the next day. Every movement or sound sends the girls off in a volley of half screams.
Boyfriends are mere stepladders; they cling on to their girls
jealously and are delighted to tell you that the band are, "crap,
wank, rubbish". All this before the first note is played. On stage
Reeves doesn't even have a mike, he plays looking down. When
he does look up he has an embarrassed and bemused expression on his face. He dances a jig when there is no music, but during the songs he just plays intently. His leg (he's still limping
after a bike accident six weeks previous) clearly frustrates when
he wants to do one of his random hyperactive jumps.

———————

"THERE HE is." The paparazzi are out of the car in a second, I run
to the door of the coach to await the descent of, "Mr Reeves, Mr
Reeves. This way Mr Reeves," as he is to the photographers. I wait,
and look, and there is the singer. I race after him, heart pounding ...
and I call him Gregg. I call Bret Domrose the – trying not to be
completely inconspicuous in the shadow of his bass player – lead
singer of Dogstar, Gregg. Domrose doesn't even look me in the
eye, just says a sarky, "Actually my name's Dale." And he runs off
up the steps into Blakes. I turn and catch the manager, the bro' by
da name a Mister Kenny Funk, who I had imagined to be a cross

between Huggy Bear and Isaac Hayes. Funk. My funkin' ass. Mr Funky turns out to be a diminutive honky, a stressed Emilio Estevez, Michael J Fox, Huckleberry Hound hybrid. I lean over the railing and trying not to whine like a toddler say, "Would the band have a few minutes to talk to British *Elle*." "No." "Perhaps the band would like to explain why the single isn't being released then?" He scowls and implies – I think – it has something to do with the media. This conversation persists in the same vein for about five minutes before Funk just turns away. Get one man's name wrong; and rub the manager not only up the wrong way, but over a cheese grater as well. Bleurgh, this whole thing's a joke.

The paparazzi laugh at me. "Where were ya girl. Old Keanu got out the other side of the coach. Bit slow aren't ya." I shrug, only a bit annoyed really. The stakeout at the band's London hotel, the exotic Blakes, has been my most successful yet. However, the likelihood of getting any real time with the band is now thin, seeing as they've pretty much all seen me lolloping around Roland Gardens like an errant newspuppy, yet to be trained.

The autograph hunters move around the base of the steps again, they can clearly sense celebrity's imminent arrival as they start nervously jiggling their pictures for him to sign. I stand by the orna-mental bay trees and as he walks down the steps duck to his side and hold my tape recorder up. "Mr Reeves. British *Elle*. I was wondering whether you could make time for an interview."

When I manage to collar him he keeps his head down. Here is a transcript of the full exchange.

ELLE: What's been the best date so far?

Reeves: T in the Park.

ELLE: How are you looking forward to playing London?

Reeves: (totally sarcastic) Well, it's pretty exciting isn't it.

ELLE: You don't appear to be very happy, what's getting to you about this tour?

Reeves: (A growl) Uuuurgh ... long story.

ELLE: Is it the media?

Reeves: Nnn ... na (someone starts dropping the old, "No more questions now," lines). I move to shake his hand, which he takes, like he's done it a million times before but he just can't help being polite to these bimbos. Then he adds, as an after-thought, "It's nice to be playing here eventually".

We chase the coach to Shepherds Bush Empire, shooting red lights and laughing in the face of tutting women in Peugeot 205's. Here, the infamous British snappers are on priceless form. Fearlessly pushing their way towards him, flies desperate to land on the celebrity cheesecake. Gaps in the paps are stop-pered by small girls. It looks obscene: the orgiastic frenzy of lusting teenage flesh, the insane grins of the paparazzi buzzing off the thrill of the chase, the rigid scaffold of the meatheads try-ing to keep them all away from the cool indifferent core. Call me, "too smooth," as the paparazzi did, but a girl has her pride, and I wasn't going anywhere near this heaving mound of slavering indignity. Jostle, "Keanu." Bustle, "Keanu." Hurunuh-thud "Mr Reeves, look this way please." "Out the way... out the way." "KEE-ARR-NU. KEE-ARR-NU." Shuffle, rustle, bump and jolt. Grunt, groan, squeak. "No more, no more." He's gone, shut away behind the stage door. A girl who touched his arm spontaneously com-busts into confused torrents of tears.

In a recent interview Björk summed up the scene just witnessed, the whole circus of hero worship. "I think it's crap. People are humiliating themselves in front of me and that's embarrassing." What does this do to the subject of such hysteria, what does it do to your head if you've been getting this kind of treatment for a while?

I stand watching the band, feeling a sense of familiarity with the whole thing. His attempts at ordinariness are, in some ways, successful. The band are incredibly ordinary.

AN AMERICAN in a lurid shirt talks to a couple of young fans (one in a "Keanu Reeves, Yes Please" T-shirt). He has a pass dangling round his neck. It says, "Dan Thomsen. Dogstar". He's doing PR and merchandise for the band. "PR? PR? You aren't doing any press."

"Yeah well people keep trying to equal Keanu Reeves the movie star with the band. Nothing is going to be as big as a movie star. We've been getting really annoyed with promoters who put Keanu Reeves on the billboard."

Fine, but the band on their own merits are not that good – they're more kind of top-flight school band plays Bryan Adams and Nirvana. Without that name who's gonna turn up? "OK it opens doors but the press, the press, and they are the worst here. Man they shouldn't make up that shit like Keanu's gay and stuff. The guys are upset. OK." Reeves seems miserable, I venture. "Hey he's not miserable he's just drinking and having a laugh. Keanu just wants to play music loud. We've all been friends for years, we play hockey and we ride bikes fast." And like suburban barbecues, everyone brings something to the party.

Dan's the merchandise and the fan club promotion man. Then there's Greg who writes and sings. Rob drums, acts dumb and shy. There's others, helping out, joining in, keeping Other People away from their buddy Keanu. Some of them admit that they don't really know him, as in understand him.

"Interview?" "No way. Just hang out with us though, that sounds cool." As long as my journalistic tools are out of sight I can like, get to look at Keanu Reeves and pretend I don't want to know what he ate for breakfast. Come to think of it, I don't. I throw away my list of serious questions along with my intentions of getting any kind of scoop. Fuck it.

Lighting a fag, I lean against a table in the bar of the Civic Centre, Aylesbury. Any minute now, everyone who witnessed my bubble-head attempts outside the hotel yesterday will be in the room. "Hey beautiful ladies don't smoke." (Dan and the rest of the Keanu entourage are either fairly dumb, or like Reeves pretty good at affecting the mannerisms of a bubblehead when it suits.) The only stick I get is a repetitive refrain of, "Hey it's the *Elle* girl." They are friendly, boystrous, slightly naive and American. The sound check man though, he's frosty. As are Reeves' half sister and the anxious Mr Funk, who are looking at me with a disdainful "who let that in" stare. None of the men have had sex for a while apparently. I point to a bunch of girls jumping up expectantly outside the window. "What, nothing available?" "Oh but we're nice guys, we can't do that."

The last few days have left me feeling like a demented over-grown groupie. There are uncomfortable moments when the band and their cohorts look at the *Elle* girl and wonder if she might fall for their amateur rock star charms. Domrose and Mail-house sign a few promo posters for the slavishly persistent US fans, overweight older women like Big Red, who has apparently followed Dogstar across the States and beyond. Reeves' face remains autograph free, he's on the tour bus. Tired, conserving energy, resting his gammy limb.

A feeling of "on the bus" superiority perforates my journalistic pride as the hopeful girl fans hanging around look at me and the other females climbing on the tour bus, wondering enviously who we are. The bus is decorated with their thoughts, loopy teenage print in pink lipstick. "Do *Speed* 2 or else," and, "We [heart] U Keanu from Tracey, Dawn and Melissa." They look up to the smoky glass. "I'm sure I can see him, he's looking at me." A beer is offered and the comfi-deluxe bus starts rumbling Londonwards. Reeves sits on the sofa, stroking a girl's arm. She has period pains. "So she says," someone comments, wryly. I'm shown round the bunks. A gay porn mag I spotted earlier is thrown across the bus. Its owner is unclear, but a lot of laddish appropriating of ownership is thrown about. "Hey ... it's a joke. Like. A. Joke," someone says and they all laugh at me. It's good to jeer at someone else's expense for a change. Thomsen, not for the first time, nervously checks me over for signs of excessive scrutiny. I feel like a fan again. It's an unpleasant, debasing sensation.

It's unusual for Reeves to join in the conversation but he does thoughtful things like hand over a Marlboro Red, unprompted. He's a lot more relaxed and happy here than out on the street. A game of backgammon is played, somewhat drunkenly. Reeves, silent for the most part, sits watching the game. Suddenly he pipes up. "Throw the dice properly. Play the rules." Premenstrual, Keanu's "friend" is from Manchester, she's a pretty brunette, skinny, not tall, ordinary. She looks pained. Feels like Half Sister doesn't like PM. When we get off the coach she [HS] is upset, muttering something about, "My brother". Any approaches from me are given an acerbic short shrift.

Reeves goes straight up to bed with Premenstrual when we get back. "Keanu's a pretty private guy. He spends most of his time in his room alone," says Dan. The others goof around, play football in the small elegant lobby and then start peeling off to bed. Dan and Bret talk while drinking Bourbon and water. "Rob's not Keanu's boyfriend. Who told you that?" Bret likes talking, he apologises for being rude outside the hotel the day before. He's pissed off that he gets no recognition for writing all of the songs. One wonders why he bothered joining a band with a megastar bass player until he admits, "Basically I'm just glad I'm not waiting tables. It's a break man. Just look at this place," he says, pointing to the oriental lacquered opulence of Blakes' Bar.

———————

ANOTHER OF those contraband quotes on the, 'Net goes, "The chucklehead crowd loved me in this [Speed], so I don't wanna hear nothing about bad acting in a bad movie. Did I tell you I've got a real cool motorcycle? Yeh, a Norton Commando, man. Cool, huh?"

The Daily Record's Mr Smug was right in a way, with his swaggering "'Course, he'll be staying at a top hotel". In the public's eye Reeves will always be Keanu Reeves the sex god and Hollywood movie star first and foremost, the man who can afford to upgrade himself and his whole entourage from a tourist hotel off Oxford

Street to the sybaritic Blakes, the privileged type who can change the rules if he so wishes, the boy who makes the girls cry. But he's trying really hard to keep life normal, you know, do the thing as any other unknown band would by sticking to mid-range hotels like the one in Glasgow. That's him in the second part of the quote, another bloke who rides his bikes fast, who wants to be in a band, tries hard at his job, tries hard to master Shakespeare and the bass guitar, wanks, smokes, eats a burger in a grungy Aylesbury pub. The "Cool, huh?" Keanu.

It's probably unfair that he gets to tour with the pretty average Dogstar but Mother always said, "Life's not fair." After five days of fannying around, I finally got on that coach. There I found a bunch of pretty ordinary, middle class, well-behaved guys who like rock music. And one of them was Keanu Reeves.

About the
Contributors

Barbara Ellen

Barbara Ellen started her career writing for *ZigZag* in 1986, until it finally folded, at which point she moved onto the *NME* for whom she continues to contribute. She has also been a contributing editor for *Loaded*, and has written for *Options*, *She*, *Vox* and the *Mail On Sunday*. Barbara is currently a columnist, television critic and travel writer for *The Observer*.

Emma Forrest

Emma Forrest began writing at the age of 16 for *The Evening Standard*, *The Spectator* and *The Sunday Times*. She has since contributed to the *NME*, *GQ*, *Sky*, *The Face*, *Loaded*, *Cosmopolitan*, *Vanity Fair* and *The Independent*.

Sheryl Garratt

Sheryl Garratt has been a music journalist since the 1980s when she freelanced for the *NME, The Face, Collusion* and *NY Rocker*. For a time she was music listings editor for the now defunct *City Limits*, and in 1988 began working full-time for *The Face* where she went on to become editor. In 1995, Sheryl left her job to go freelance, and now writes for *The Sunday Times* and *The Face*, for whom she is a contributing editor, among other publications. She has also co-authored one of the first books to deal with gender and music, *Signed, Sealed And Delivered* (with Sue Steward) which was published in 1984.

Mary Anne Hobbs

Mary Anne Hobbs began her career as a rock reporter on *Sounds*, the now defunct weekly music paper. Following its demise, she contributed to *NME, Vox* and *Loaded*, where she was commissioning editor for the music section. She has also worked for MTV, XFM radio, and currently hosts her own show on Radio One.

Suzanne Moore

Suzanne Moore has contributed to *The New Statesman, The Observer, Marxism Today*, the *Evening Standard* and *Elle*. She has worked as a columnist for *The Guardian*, and currently writes for *The Independent*. Suzanne has also been involved in live television debates and had two collections of her work published; *Looking For Trouble* in 1991, and *Head Over Heels* in 1996.

Gina Morris

Gina Morris began writing at the age of 18 for a Manchester-based fanzine called *Bop City*. She then moved to London where she spent three and a half years contributing to the *NME*, before joining *Select* magazine as a freelancer. Gina is currently a contributing editor at *Smash Hits*, and still manages to write for *Select*, *Details* and *Neon*. She is also working on a book about PJ Harvey.

Lucy O'Brien

Lucy O'Brien spent two and a half years, from 1983, working full time as a freelancer for the *NME*, before moving on to her position as music editor at the now-defunct London listings magazine, *City Limits*. Since then she has written for *Select, Vox, Cosmopolitan, The Face, Spare Rib, The Sunday Times* and *The Guardian*, and is currently contributing to *Q* and *The Independent On Sunday*. As well as working extensively in television and radio, she is also the author of *Dusty*, a biography of Dusty Springfield, *Annie Lennox* and the award-winning history of women in rock, pop and soul, *She Bop*.

Sharon O'Connell

Sharon O'Connell has worked as a music journalist for the past 10 years. She was assistant editor of Sydney-based weekly music newspaper *On The Street* for three years, a regular contributor to *RAM*, Australia's only credible music paper, and later music editor of *City Life*, an arts and entertainment monthly. She left Sydney to live in London, where she now works as live reviews editor for *Melody Maker*.

Sylvia Patterson

Sylvia Patterson began her career in 1986 working for *Smash Hits*, where she graduated from freelancer to staff writer and reviews editor. She has contributed to *Select, NME, Details, The Face, Vox* and *Sky*. She was also once the astrologist for the official Take That fan club magazine.

Charlotte Raven

Charlotte Raven has contributed to *The Observer* and *The Guardian*.

Miranda Sawyer

Miranda Sawyer started out writing for *Smash Hits*, and has since contributed to *Select, The Guardian, Elle, Neon, Arena, The Observer* and *The Face*, for whom she is a contributing editor. She has also been a columnist for *Time Out* and has worked as a radio broadcaster and television presenter for music and arts programmes.

Sylvie Simmons

Sylvie Simmons has been a rock journalist for more than 20 years. In 1975 she began working for a teenzine, and two years later moved to Los Angeles where she was correspondent for top rock weekly, *Sounds*. Seven years in America also saw Sylvie freelancing for *Creem* magazine, writing a syndicated weekly US newspaper column, co-hosting a rock radio show, and contributing to

British rock bible, *Kerrang!*. Following a three year break in
France, Sylvie is now back in London and working for *Mojo*,
Kerrang! and the European *Rolling Stone*.

Daniela Soave

Daniela Soave has been writing about music for 19 years.
She has been the deputy editor for *Scotland On Sunday*, senior
commissioning editor at the *Sunday Telegraph*, features editor
at the *Radio Times*, and was a founding deputy editor of *Sky*
magazine. Daniela has also contributed to Radio Scotland,
Radio Wales and Radio One, worked on television documen-
taries, written for *Elle*, *GQ*, been a television critic for *The Daily
Telegraph* and the *Daily Mail* and contributed to the *Evening
Standard*. She hates celebrity journalism, enjoys painting pictures with words, has a son at boarding school, and is currently
researching a political history of the hippy movement.

Kate Spicer

Kate Spicer has contributed to the *Evening Standard, The Face,
Elle* and *The Guardian*.

Lisa Verrico

Lisa Verrico has contributed to *The Times, The Daily Express,
Blah Blah Blah,* and *Vox*. She began her career working for a
regional radio station, and moved on to Radio Five before working in television as a researcher. In 1996, Virgin Books published
her first book, a biography of The Prodigy called *Exit The
Underground*.

Of further interest...

Women, Sex and Rock 'n' Roll

In their own words

Liz Evans

Over the last five or six years, female musicians have begun to stamp out their ground more effectively than at any other point in the history of rock music. The artists interviewed in *Women, Sex and Rock 'n' Roll* are among the strongest and most talented currently challenging the stereotypes which have served to undermine the significance of female rock culture since its inception.

Rock's male dominated arena is riddled with stubborn attitudes and the media and the music industry have bundled women up into acceptable packages – fallen angels, broken victims, dizzy sex queens, killer babes – squashing the impact of female power into a novelty.

Full of exclusive, in depth and intimate interviews, this book gives women a chance to speak out against the injustices of the music business, while discussing their own, very individual experiences and perspectives.

By providing fascinating insights into some of today's most creative and confrontational minds, *Women, Sex and Rock 'n' Roll* provides a crucial platform for women who have found their own voices, and are now being heard.

The Pandora Guide to Women Composers

Britain and the United States 1629 – Present

Sophie Fuller

In this ground-breaking reference book Sophie Fuller provides accessible, original and extensive information in an A to Z of over a hundred women composers from Britain and the United States, covering the period from 1629 right up to the contemporary scene.

Each entry gives a flavour of the composer's milieu as well as her music, to provide a fascinating insight into both her life and creative works. Fuller examines the reasons why women composers have been so neglected, reassesses their work in the light of recent scholarship, both musicological and biographical, and provides a critical frame of reference in which to place both the women and their music.

The Pandora Guide to Women Composers is a unique resource of information, much of it previously unobtainable, in one easily-referenced volume. It will be invaluable to all music lovers wanting to broaden their horizons, to all those interested in neglected and suppressed aspects of women's creative culture, and also to students of music and women's studies as well as music researchers, programmers and performers.